NARROW MARGINS

NARROW MARGINS

Marie Browne

Published by Accent Press Ltd – 2009

ISBN 9781907016004

Printed in the UK by CPI Bookmarque, Croydon

Cover design by Red Dot Design

Lyrics from Jenny Greenteeth, reproduced by kind
permission, © Nicole Murray 2002,
www.cloudstreet.org

This book is for my Mum and Dad – you have done so much for us that I'll just say thanks for everything, there's no way we could have done this without you.

Acknowledgements

Thanks must go to all the friends that have, in lots of ways, supported and helped us over the years. Arwen and Carl for gritting their teeth and putting up with us being weird and anarchic, Helen and Dave for being that still, small voice of calm when things became overwhelmingly chaotic, Vikki and Neal for their incredible scavenging abilities and their general loveliness, Charley and Dion for being the best neighbours anybody could want, and of course Tanya, really just for being Tanya.
We know we don't say enough to really let you lot know how much you mean to us but we often think a lot of good thoughts toward you. Thank you.

Chapter One
Four Little Words

'ROVER HAS GONE BUST.'

It's a strange phenomenon, but there are certain times in every adult life where, for various reasons, the language you have spoken since birth becomes completely unintelligible.

Each individual word is clear but when placed within a sentence makes no sense at all and needs to be repeated again and again, the verbal equivalent of someone smacking you over the head with information taped to a hammer.

'Rover has gone bust,' Geoff muttered.

'Sorry, didn't get that,' I looked up from drying the cutlery.

'Rover – has – gone – bust,' he spoke slowly and succinctly, holding eye contact throughout the sentence.

Just four little words, but, to us, whose entire – and rather nice – lifestyle was funded by the car manufacturer, they were an absolute death knell.

My subconscious was obviously far quicker on the uptake than my conscious and I found myself carefully hanging up the tea towel and very deliberately putting the carving knife that I had been holding into the fridge. Presumably my intuition felt that all sharp objects should be well out of reach at a time like this.

I turned to face my husband who had assumed a defensive position behind the table.

'I'm sorry,' I said slowly, 'say that just one more time. I'm still having trouble here.'

I followed his gaze to the well-read and slightly grubby

letter he was holding and waited; he took a deep breath and repeated the words that, even with my subconscious now gibbering that life was just about to go horribly pear-shaped, I really hoped I'd misheard.

'What do you mean, Rover has gone bust?' Finally bullying my mind to accept his words, I breached Geoff's defences at the table and took the letter from his hand. And ... how odd, now it seemed I couldn't read either. The crisp type flowed like film credits across the page; it may as well have been Ancient Greek for all the sense it made.

Geoff sighed; he had lived with me long enough to recognise the beginnings of a long trip down 'de Nile' when he saw one. Leaning forward, he gripped the letter between thumb and forefinger and with only a slight tug managed to reclaim it. Making sure he had full eye contact he slipped into 'lecture voice' and explained.

'It means we're stuffed.'

Three hours later I was still at full rant and showing no signs of even taking a breath, let alone actually stopping.

'How can they do this to us? We have an outstanding invoice with them for over £50,000! We're at the end of our money! They were supposed to pay tomorrow, TOMORROW! For God's sake. Why now? Why us? What about the mortgage? What about the bills? What are we going to DO?'

Anybody who has been in a similar position will understand this predicament only too well. There are no easy answers. You go through the procedures of closing down your company; you apologetically fire the staff; you explore all avenues – real and imagined; you delude yourself; you shout at invisible people inside telephones; you wait for someone to tell you that it's all a joke, that huge mistakes have been made and your money's in the post.

After about a fortnight, I was exhausted and had to admit that Geoff's early assessment had been totally correct. We were royally 'stuffed'!

When you have finally faced up to what is going on in

life, you can start to think of the future, but it didn't look like we had one, at least not much of one anyway. In times of crisis my mother always used to trot out the well-worn cliché 'When life hands you lemons, make lemonade' and it is in times of severe lemonade-drought that my personality flaws start to show.

I am, without doubt, a control freak. I am also completely convinced that with positive thinking and a little bit of ingenuity you can achieve anything. It is a great source of pride to me that over the years I have come up with some bizarre and ingenious ways to get us out of 'situations'. I am also very proud of my useful ability to ignore all indications that it is usually one of my 'great' ideas that gets us into these 'situations' in the first place.

After ten years, some of my more 'creative' solutions to an impending disaster make my poor, long-suffering husband nervous – very nervous. I can't really say I blame him because as bad plans and ill-thought-out schemes go, I have come up with some corkers.

So when I plonked myself down next to him on the sofa, my face pre-set in a caricature rictus grin and uttered the immortal words, 'I have a cunning plan, Lord Blackadder', I got exactly the response I had come to expect. A soft groan, before he leant forward and gently banged his head on the nearest hard surface. I had his attention.

The banging ceased after about 20 seconds and strangled tones emitted from under the hair, 'Yes, dear?'

Ignoring the rampant sarcasm, I leant forward and grabbed one of his ears to raise him into an upright position.

'Listen,' I took a deep breath (positive thinking, gallons of lemonade and a set of lungs like a blue whale have got me a long way over the years). 'As far as I can tell, we have a couple of choices: we can find work and eventually pay off our debts and the mortgage – but this will mean both of us working full-time, which means we will have to pay childcare and travel to Birmingham every day because the last thing you're going to find in Herefordshire are big multinational companies that need project managers. Even then there is no guarantee both of us can find a job because, let's face it, neither of us have been working much over the last three years, the staff did all the work and we charged vast amounts for it.

'The other option is that we don't find work, we lose the house and end up in a scummy flat, still with huge debts, no work and general misery all round. Have I summed it all up OK?'

Geoff pursed his lips and muttered, 'I don't think it's that ba–'

Cutting him off before he could pour reality onto another of my plans, I continued, '... or we could sell the house, pay off the debts and still have enough money to buy a boat.'

'A what?' Geoff frowned.

'A house boat. You know, to live on. I've been looking on the net, and talking to Sarah and Drew – they love theirs – we could buy one, too. Just think, no neighbours, no one telling us where to go. We could move it down to Cambridge to be with Arwen and Carl and all that crowd, Sam could go to school with their kids; it would be great and just think ...' Light-headed from lack of oxygen, I took a much-needed breath and callously played my trump card '... we would own it outright, no mortgage, no rates – in fact, no debts at all!'

With the trump card played, there was nothing to do but sit back and wait out the ensuing silence. If I can just touch again, briefly, on personality traits, anyone who knows me would say being quiet isn't one of mine, and patience is on the 'B' list as well. But you don't live with someone day in, day out, and not know when to shut up.

Geoff does 'thinking in silence' so well that over the years his silences have actually become rateable; with 'one' being a short silence with raised eyebrows to portray 'Yes, dear – not a chance in hell' to a 'ten', with a complete range of facial expressions. This one broke all previous records and went to about a 'twelve', lasting about four or five minutes, which is an eternity to sit still, looking innocent.

'What about the kids?' he mused aloud. 'It's going to have to be quite a big thing to fit four and a half of us on.'

There were actually three children: Sam, master of chaos and destruction, age six; Amelia, bored, gothic, art student, eighteen, from a previous marriage; and Charlie, all gangly knees and elbows, age eleven, also my daughter from the previous marriage, but a bi-weekend visitor.

We also had Herbert ... The vet assured us that he is actually a dog. He may have also been classed as a terrier at one time but was now so old that he bore a startling resemblance to a mobile piece of dirty carpet. He has three teeth, two of which actually stick horizontally out of his mouth giving him a permanent sneer; a mad coat and ears that look like they have been chewed by a weed-whacker complete his own special little picture. I didn't really feel Herb was going to be a problem as he spent most of his time asleep. This was a major blessing as, every time he moved, he exuded his own 'interesting' aroma which could be a bit unnerving if he cornered you in an enclosed space.

As usual, Geoff had managed to highlight the major flaw in my plan. Out of desperation I tried a bizarre tack – the 'truth'. You never know, it might just work.

'Yes, it's going to be tight,' I sighed theatrically and tried to fix a look of thoughtful concern on my face, 'but Charlie is only with us every other weekend and with Amelia's tendency to use any house like a hotel and a bank, we should be OK.' I paused. 'But even if they were both with us all the time, I would still rather they live in the countryside where they might have to work at getting into trouble, than on a huge housing estate where you have to permanently battle with them picking up other people's ideals and where trouble comes to them.'

Geoff went back to thinking. Eventually, he leant

forward, and the next four fateful words dropped like small explosive charges into a moonlit pool of sleeping fish...

'Show me the website.'

We spent most of that night scouring the net, our discussions and plans becoming more surreal the closer we got to dawn. By the time the first birdsong could be heard, we had convinced ourselves that the plan was actually quite a good one, which surprised me more than anybody. All we had to do now was get the rest of the family's consent, sell the house, buy a boat, find a mooring, change all the kids' educational facilities and find a way to store or – heaven forbid – get rid of all our possessions.

At four o'clock in the morning, and after twelve cups of coffee, we were convinced that all this would be easy. We were certain the kids would be delighted and it was going to be fun. This plan would solve all of our problems.

Four hours later, I beamed happily at the bleary faces around the breakfast table. Luckily this was a 'Charlie weekend', and our plan was to tell them all together, enjoy a happy breakfast answering lots of excited questions, then go out and celebrate. We had noted down a couple of local marinas that would, we were sure, have a huge selection of suitable boats from which to choose. Having already explained to the kids all about what had happened to the company, we assumed they would be expecting some changes.

'OK, listen up, folks; we have made a decision.' I raised my voice over the bickering and poking taking place on the other side of the table. Amelia and Charlie looked up suspiciously, having overheard a fair amount of swearing, shouting, crying and screaming over the past couple of weeks; Sam continued to balance his spoon on his head.

'What sort of mad plan have you come up with this time?' Amelia sighed.

I gave her 'the look' and continued with the prepared speech, 'OK, now, please just give this idea some time to sink in before you say anything ...' I belatedly wondered if the kids were actually going to be as happy about this as Geoff and me, but it was too late now, we were just going to have to deal with the fallout. So, abandoning my prepared speech, I just spat it out in a rush, hoping that jumbling the words together in one long line would make the idea more palatable.

'We are going to sell the house and buy a boat to live on.' Silence and lots of staring eyes. Hmm ... OK that wasn't the best reaction I could have hoped for. I tried to raise some enthusiasm.

'Come on, think about the fun, out in the country, no hassle, no neighbours – what do you think?' Silence, accompanied by deepening frowns. I didn't really have anything else to add so decided to wait it out. The silence was finally broken by a stifled yelp from Charlie as Sam's spoon fell off his head and into his breakfast, effectively splattering her in cereal.

'Where's this boat going to be kept?' Amelia, for all her teenage vagueness, could see a flaw in a plan when she wanted to. She sniffed and wiped some of Sam's errant Weetabix from her sleeve, 'The river here's too shallow for boats.'

I turned to Geoff hoping for some backup. No such luck; he was studiously buttering toast, keeping his eyes firmly on his knife.

'Cambridge,' I held my breath, waiting for the inevitable explosion, 'we are going to live down by Arwen and Carl.'

Kaboom! 'CAMBRIDGE!' Amelia stood up. 'I'm not going to Cambridge. What about my course?'

Yes, OK, I should have seen that coming. Adlibbing desperately: 'You've just finished your first year, you could do your second year at another college, a better college. Good grief, it's Cambridge for pity's sake, there must be hundreds of colleges there.'

Trying to avert a screaming match, I walked around the

table toward her, and decided to make a direct appeal to her common sense.

'We don't have a choice, Milly. We can't stay here, there's no work; whatever we do, the house has got to go and we have to move. We're just trying to find the best way out from all this rubbish that's hit us.'

Surprisingly, common sense worked and, robbed of her righteous indignation, Amelia sat back down and switched tack.

'What about Huw? Don't say you want me to dump him as well.'

OK, that was one potential problem I had missed. No chance of a common-sense compromise on this issue.

'He can visit ...' I took refuge in worn-out platitudes, 'If a relationship can't stand a bit of distance, it's no relationship at all.'

'What about me?' Charlie butted in, 'won't I see you any more?'

Oh poo! This wasn't going as well as it had in my head, that was for sure.

'Of course you'll still see us,' I soothed and turned away from Amelia who was rapidly going red in the face and welling up, 'nothing will change; you will just come and see us in Cambridge, that's all.' About to explain further to Charlie, I was interrupted by Amelia leaping up again.

'I'm not coming!' She placed both hands on the table for emphasis. 'I'll go and live with Grandma if I have to but I don't want to live in Cambridge, and ...' she lifted her head and stared me straight in the eye, 'I'm 18, there's nothing you can do about it.'

Oh dear, not going well at all, and where on earth had all that backbone come from?

Tossing her long blonde hair, she turned and, grabbing helmet and leathers en route, slammed out of the house. There was complete silence in the kitchen, everybody avoiding each other's gaze.

I watched Sam constructing his Weetabix castle. It seemed to be a sad metaphor for our plan. Crumbling, soggy and unable to stand against the least bit of pressure.

Eventually, we all heard the sound of her little 'putt putt' motorbike starting up. It occurred to me, as unkind things often do at times of stress, that if she wanted to make a really impressive exit she ought to have a bike that made a much deeper, more threatening noise. Heaving a big sigh, I wandered back around the table and collapsed, exhausted, into my chair.

Geoff pushed a cup of tea under my nose and a cold piece of jammy toast into my hand and gave me a quick hug.

'What do you think, Sam?' He tapped Sam on the back of his hand to get his attention.

Surprised at being addressed during one of the many emotional hubbubs involving the girls, Sam glanced up from the brown soggy mess in his bowl. He looked completely blank. 'What about?' he asked.

Ho hum.

Chapter Two
Big Ship, Little Ship, Bathtub

TWO MONTHS LATER AND, not unexpectedly, our hastily hashed plan was being re-hashed. After a short flurry of cleaning and decorating activity, the house went up for sale and, thankfully, we immediately had a good offer.

I am most definitely not going to discuss the evil surveyor, who admitted there was nothing really wrong with the house that couldn't be put down to it being 300 years old. However, he felt that prices were too high in the area and was on a personal crusade to bring them down to a more reasonable level.

Our estate agent let slip to the buyer that we had to sell quickly. In response to this exciting piece of news, the buyer... 'in light of the "cheap kitchen" mentioned in the "poor survey"' (cheap kitchen! Since when has seven grand and a new Aga been considered cheap?), blithely 'adjusted' their offer by £20,000, knowing that we had no choice at this point but to accept. Months later I was still sore about it and it only took one comment about house sales to set me off into full and furious auto rant.

We had spent a wonderful, child-free weekend at the Crick Boat Show, wandering around in the sunshine. As happy as newlyweds searching for their first home, we were completely inspired by all the beautifully fitted-out boats and enthusiastic salespeople. We feigned knowledge we didn't really possess and spent hours discussing plans and layouts with various boat builders and playing with all the fantastic gadgets that we'd surely need to fill our new life.

At the end of a perfect day we staggered, light-hearted and laughing, back to the car, both weighed down by bags of advertising, catalogues and free samples of some very strange chemicals.

This euphoria lasted for almost the whole week that it took for us to sift through all the paper, create a 'plan', work out a budget and discover that reality really, really sucks.

We had expected to have about £100,000 to play with. This amount of capital would have given us a floating bungalow with all the extras you could wish for. However, by the time the rabid, evil surveyor and his hell-spawn minions had finished butchering our house sale and we had budgeted for some debts that we'd conveniently forgotten, our budget had been halved and our floating dream bungalow had become a garden shed.

This, quite frankly, cramped our style somewhat, or to put it in my mother's words, we were suffering from 'champagne taste and beer money' syndrome. Trying to keep our sadly depleted funds firmly in mind, we gave up on the idea of having the boat created professionally and started searching for something a little closer to our forlorn little reality. It had never been so apparent that those with money get the choice, and those without have to make do.

Weeks went by, the house sale trickled on and even though we had already accepted a low price the buyers dropped the price further with every new 'expert' that was sent around. We eventually lost over thirty-five thousand on the original asking price. At that point it didn't really matter any more, as, even if our ever-diminishing budget hadn't been enjoying a starring role in our nightmares, the selection of boats that were on offer certainly was.

Too small, too expensive, too old or, in one horribly memorable case, too mouldy, leaky and definitely way, way too smelly. That particular boat had small mushrooms growing in the angle between the walls and ceiling that were leaking a brownish, lumpy and stinking ichor that tumbled in staining trails down the walls; the smell of it stayed with me for days.

We were still undecided about what type of boat to buy. We knew that with family and smelly 'dog thing' in tow, we would have to look for something fairly large and airy so, for a short time, considered seagoing. Our budget was now so small and insignificant we would have considered ourselves lucky to get our hands on a decent rubber dinghy. Something to live on was way out of our reach and we were pretty close to despair when an advert appeared that seemed too good to be true:

Barge for sale
120ft Humber keel
Back on the market due to time-wasters and dreamers
Beautiful – live aboard with idyllic mooring in Devon
Many extras included in sale
Needs some refurbishment, but basically ready to move on to
All sensible offers considered, as owner moving abroad

The excitement was close to fever pitch – this was 'it', we knew it, she sounded like just what we were looking for and Devon was lovely. OK, it wasn't Cambridge, but we kept reminding ourselves that you had to be prepared to change plans when you were doing this sort of thing.

I contacted the owner and he informed me that the price was low because, as he had stated in the ad, he was very keen to move out of the country quickly (there may have been a hint there of things to come) and he would be very sorry to lose her because he had put in a lot of time and effort and she really was a beauty.

As we all headed down to Devon (minus Amelia, who had decided that, as she was determined not to live on a boat, she didn't even want to look at them, think about them or talk about them), we were all so full of excited expectation that even Sam came out of his normal daydream mode to join in the silly off-key singing and raucous mucking about that we all indulged in on the journey.

Three hours of travel and we'd crossed the Devon border; it then took another two hours of backtracking down remote country lanes to locate the 'small, secluded bay' in which the boat was moored. By the time we actually found what appeared to be the right place, everybody had run out of 'happy puff' and was beginning to get a bit testy.

We pulled up facing away from land. Our parking place really should have been described as facing out to sea, but, as the tide was well out, the expanse before us resembled nothing more than one of the legendary ship graveyards. Interred within a slimy field of grey-green mud, between pools of weed-filled, murky water surrounding large, slime-covered rocks, downright ancient ships leant sadly at impossible angles. We climbed out of the car in silence and stared over the mud flats, each trying to be the first to catch a glimpse of this advertised paragon of nautical beauty.

Sam, as usual, was the first to break the increasingly worried silence.

'Which one is it, Mum?'

Good question, m'boy. 'I'm not sure, Sam,' I murmured and frowned at the poor selection of rotting wrecks, mired in the slimy muck.

Geoff took the details page out of his pocket and held it up, comparing the picture to each of the boats; he finally settled on one. 'That one,' he stated in a firm tone, 'look, it's the only one with that shaped wheelhouse.' He traced the outline on the picture and then again in the air, pointing toward a particularly odious-looking hulk, slumped sullenly at a 45-degree angle and cheekily showing a fair bit of bottom.

There was a loaded silence as everybody took a long look. It is always very sad to be confronted with an item so far removed from its sales pitch that you have two options: laugh or cry. I seem to remember wanting to alternate between the two.

The 'beautiful' barge was definitely large; she would easily have fitted a family of our size aboard, but that is where any resemblance to the advert ended. For instance, there was absolutely no mention that she had obviously run into or been run into by something. A dock probably, but it could have quite easily been war wounds from a volley from long nines – she looked that old and battered! There were several huge dents along the side closest to us and all around the front.

Sam took one look at her pathetically sagging bulk and stated categorically, 'We can't live on that, we'd fall off!' Pretty astute for a six-year-old. Charlie was less garrulous, but still perfectly damning, 'Oh yuk,' was all she muttered, then rushed off to see if she could find something slimy and alive in the pools of water dotted about.

Still gamely hanging on to our dream, which was rapidly becoming as dented as the old boat in front of us, we navigated our way through the mud toward the boat. It was necessary to play an odd lurching hopscotch as we leapt from one dryish patch to another. Maybe, just maybe, the inside was beautiful – finished – and the outside was just a cleverly camouflaged smoke-screen... We pressed on.

The only access to the deck was via a very precarious-looking rope ladder that led to the wheelhouse. The owner had assured us it was safe and had given us permission to just 'poke about as much as you want to'. Quite frankly, by this time, I didn't really want to 'poke about' at all. Looking over the mud, I could see a pub in the distance; its whitewashed walls and flower-filled terrace gleamed in the sun. *That* looked like a nice place to 'poke about'.

The wheelhouse, once we were inside, pretty much set the standard for the rest of the visit. It had been added fairly recently and amateurishly either by someone with no skill in welding, or a dot-to-dot fanatic with obsessive compulsive disorder, it was hard to tell. The woodwork, what there was of it, was cheap, poorly fitted and water damaged. To get into the hold, where the living accommodation was situated, a large hole had been roughly cut into the middle of the floor and the stairs down comprised a ladder and a piece of knotted rope.

With dampening spirits, we persisted in our search for something – *anything* – that could be described as 'ready to move on to'. Maybe down in the darkness, beyond the big hole in the floor, a great surprise awaited us.

Stepping into a foot of evil-smelling, ice-cold water in the pitch black is always a bit of a surprise. Over the years, my beloved, dry-humoured husband has revealed himself to be one of those people who can turn understatement into an art form – 'I've got a bit of a problem,' means he is in danger of losing a limb. So, when this dour, taciturn man disappears into a pitch black hole and all that floats back to you is a 'splosh', followed by more expletives in one breath than I've heard in 11 years of marriage, you tend to imagine the worst.

I let go of Sam's hand, needing both of mine free to lean into the hole and assess the situation. Thirty seconds of peering into the darkness enabled me to find out that Geoff was just wet and very annoyed, up to his knees in oily, stinking water. Thirty seconds was obviously far too long.

The scream was so loud and shocking that if I hadn't been backing away from the hole at the time it erupted, I would have joined Geoff in the wet bowels of the ship. Nobody, not even a professional, can scream like an enraged six-year-old.

'I just picked it up to look at it.' Sam was covered and I mean *covered* in oil. He had picked up a bucket to look inside, then, in spectacular Sam style, had tripped on some rubbish and fallen over backwards, emptying the contents of the bucket over himself.

Geoff heaved himself, dripping, out of the hole, took one look at a wailing, equally dripping, Sam whose screams had now turned to loud complaints about the smell and just sighed. 'Fancy some lunch?'

I don't know how many people remember the television show *It's a Knockout* but descending a swaying rope ladder onto slippery mud with a wriggling child covered in oil should have been made into an international game. It is far, far more difficult than it has any right to be. After an incredibly slow and careful descent, we reached the ground relatively unscathed and, except for slightly elevated heart rates all round, all in one piece.

Bringing up the rear as we began our second game of hopscotch back toward the car, I was (very quietly) amused that I was the only one of the three of us who was still clean. As Geoff put Sam on to his shoulders to forestall any more 'incidents', the oil was transferred from Sam's legs onto Geoff's hair, face and shirt. Being more 'sure-footed' than I, they strode off to open the car and find something to clean themselves up with, leaving me to pick my way carefully along behind.

I very nearly made it; about ten feet from the steps up to the road, I took a single wrong step and my right leg disappeared up to the thigh into what could only be described as a miniature wadi. There was an unpleasant squelching sound as I tried to heave myself out, but I was stuck, well and truly stuck. Geoff had to come back and pull me out.

Charlie, more sensible than the rest of us, had been watching our progress from a clean, dry, warm vantage point up on the rocks and was now laughing so hard she could barely stand.

I suppose it could be described as a 'Kodak moment', but fortunately no one around had a camera: Geoff, soaked and muddy from the feet up, oily and sticky from the head down, Sam just plain oily and myself completely pristine except for one leg, covered from foot to thigh in thick, black mud; Charlie was almost hyperventilating, she was laughing so hard.

As our mucky group stood around the car, futilely trying to get ourselves at least part-way respectable again, an elderly gent walking his dog wandered past us. Staring unashamedly at the bustle going on, his curiosity finally got the better of him and he meandered over, smiling.

'Wot 'appened to 'ee then?'

We explained that we had been out to look around the barge and the series of events that had led us to this state. He listened quietly, nodding every now and then. When we had finished narrating our sad tale, he looked us all up and down and nodded again.

'A lot of folk coom aut tay see that barge,' he informed us, still nodding sagely.

'Do they all end up looking like this?' I quipped, grinning.

'No, lass – you lot are the first daft enough to go aboard,' he said, 'you'd better get that mud off, it smells terrible when it be drying.' He smiled and, nodding one last time, carried on up the road, dragging his dog behind him

Four hours later we arrived home, stinking, miserable, hungry, depressed and more than a little 'crispy' where the mud had dried. My niggling little doubts had started to grow like Topsy.

'Are you sure about this?' I asked Geoff after we had managed to give Sam an oil change and get him and Charlie fed and into bed. Clean and warm, we were lazing about in big fluffy bath robes, I hanging on to a glass of red wine and Geoff with his usual cup of tea. 'Every boat is just hideous; it's either falling apart or it's tiny or just plain horrible. I can't see us living on any of the rotting tubs we've seen so far. Do you really think you can take one of these things apart and put it back together again in a liveable form?'

'Actually, yes,' Geoff grinned and blew into his cup.

'OK, so we haven't found anything suitable yet but I'm sure something will come up.' He mooched across the sofa until, sitting almost in my lap, he put his arm round me and gave me a big hug. 'You wouldn't be trying to wriggle out of our 'big adventure' before it even starts now, would you?'

'You make me sound like Pooh,' I grouched, disengaging his arm. 'Of course I'm not trying to wriggle out of it. I'm just beginning to find the whole thing really scary.' I stared into my sadly empty wine glass for a moment then looked round at the big, soft sofas, our huge collection of books, the pictures and the piano, all of which would have to go into storage. Thinking back over our disastrous visit to Devon, I found myself helplessly wondering, if – when – we finally moved out, would we ever be warm and comfortable again?

Chapter Three
The 'Perfect' Boat?

ONE WEEK BEFORE THE completion date for our house and we were in a complete panic. We must have seen every stinking, dented, sinking boat in a 300-mile radius and were beginning to lose heart. Some of them probably weren't as poor as they appeared but, surely if you are trying to sell something, don't you make it look its best? Three days worth of washing-up laid out for us to examine, filthy toilets, strange smells, damp patches and other nastier faults. It became glaringly obvious that these were also the boats that were very poorly maintained.

One particularly memorable vessel had the owner's entire tool collection spread over the engine room – obviously he was in the middle of some very major and prolonged repairs. This did not bode well for the future and Geoff hustled us out as quickly as possible.

We spent hours every night poring over increasingly vague websites advertising narrow boats for sale. One particular boat, '*Happy Go Lucky*', kept coming up on various sites but had been consistently dismissed due to her slightly strange shape.

One of a retired pair of hotel boats, she had been built to house seven cabins and two bathrooms, nothing else; her sister boat contained the kitchen, the communal lounge and the open deck space. At 70 foot, she was just the right size. However, to utilise as much space as possible, Happy's entire length, including what would have been the front deck on any other boat, had been fully built-in; she really was the most cumbersome looking boat I had seen yet. From the pictures, she appeared to resemble nothing more than a steel box with windows, and every time she appeared on the computer screen, I made irritated huffing noises and resolutely moved on.

Finally, after weeks of sleepless nights, eye damage and severe neck-ache, we had nothing left to view and decided to make the trip to Daventry to have a look at *Happy Go Lucky*.

The day we travelled down to Daventry, I have to admit, was not one of my 'happy disposition', let's-look-on-the-positive-side-of-things, 'Pooh' days. It was definitely more of an 'Eeyore' day. The whole family was irascible and prone to argue at the slightest provocation. The weather wasn't helping matters, being overcast, airless and incredibly hot. The stress of the enforced move had finally gotten to Sam whose behaviour had taken a serious downward turn.

We had been expecting this sort of reaction from him and had discussed how to handle any outbreaks of bad behaviour or signs of stress that were bound to come along. We were going to go by the book: be honest, forgiving and set good boundaries. Using these techniques, we felt sure that we would get through any traumas with all our familial feelings intact.

Unfortunately when parents are also stressed, miserable, worried and under the threat of living with an in-law for the next six months, all good intentions go out of the window, along with any excellent parenting skills they may aspire to. Consequently, Sam and I had indulged in childish bickering all the way down the M5, until Geoff told us both to shut up. Still sulking, we arrived in Braunston, hot, tired, angry and certainly out of sorts with each other and life in general.

This mood was not alleviated by our first sight of Happy; she was as grey as the weather, covered in pigeon poo and listing gently to the left.

'I told you we were wasting our time,' I grumped at Geoff, 'let's not bother. Can't we just go home?' I pulled Sam off the safety railings as he tried to pitch himself into the marina basin, 'Get down, Sam, for goodness' sake, this is not a flaming playground.'

Geoff frowned and, fed up with watching his wife and son indulging in a pulling and screaming match, reasonably suggested, 'Look, we've come all this way, is it really going to kill you to just take ten minutes to get the keys and have a quick look inside?'

As there was no good answer to that without resorting to outlandish exaggeration, I ignored him and continued my attempt to heave Sam off the railings. He clung on, kicking and screaming, until with one good pull I managed to physically tear him away and set him, with a bit of a thump, back on solid ground.

We tagged along, arguing hotly about the need for safety and choosing an acceptable place to play. Geoff ignored us and amused himself by having a good look at all the other boats for sale; way out of our league of course, or all of 30 foot long. By the time we got to the office Sam had turned into a 'wailing child' who told any passer-by that mummy had tried to break his arms.

He cheered up slightly as we went into the office which was situated behind a shop, and immediately fell in love with a large, badly coloured, plastic model of the duck from the *Rosie and Jim* children's television series. Its head turned and it went 'quonk' in a slightly nasal tone.

While Geoff was sorting out the keys to Happy, Sam and I had another argument about his obsessive need for plastic rubbish, and by the time we left the shop, Sam was in full flood, telling everybody about his horrible, abusive mother, who not only tried to break his arms but never bought him ANYTHING!, EVER!!!

Happy was moored between two other boats, under cover, in an open-ended shed type affair. After a sticky two or three minutes spent trying to manhandle a miserable and unhelpful child over the adjacent narrow boat, we finally stepped onto the rear deck.

Sadly, the smell of unloved and slightly damp boat was, by now, becoming almost welcoming and, sure enough, it wafted out in an effusive greeting as we opened the back doors and fell down a tall step into the gloom. Geoff decided that he was going to start at the bow (or the 'pointy bit' as I always called it, much to his disgust) and disappeared down what appeared to be the inside of a large, round coffin lined with doors.

Sam, finally free of the clutches of his hated, criminally abusive and fiscally restrictive mother, trotted after him, and I was left to wallow in the expected yuckiness of my surroundings.

The internal decor of *Happy Go Lucky* was horrible; even if I had been in a good mood it would have been horrible. Unfortunately for the boat, I was in a foul mood and it was the most horrible thing I had ever seen in my life, but at least it seemed to be free of scary fungus.

As my eyes adjusted to the gloom, the outlines of the kitchen from hell started to appear; it was the type of kitchen that usually sported the headline: 'Misunderstood mother forced to live in purgatory'. Everything was covered in dusty old grease and had obviously been thrown together by some insane and untalented DIYer with a cheap Formica addiction.

There was a microwave, which strangely enough looked brand new, a fridge which just as obviously wasn't and a glass-topped hob. A sad collection of mismatched plates, chipped mugs depicting badly drawn, very kitsch cartoons (mostly of people falling into various locks around the country) and cheap cutlery were all stacked higgledy-piggledy on old, warped shelves that clung tenaciously at strange angles to the back wall of an open-fronted cupboard.

The greasy, beige, faded curtains, which, at one time, I

imagined, were patterned and cheerful, now hung lank and miserable from the four remaining hooks still attached to a tarnished fake brass curtain rail. Fixed at only one end, it and its resident curtains drooped sadly toward a floor resplendent with greasy, pitted, beige and brown 1970s classic lino.

Happy Go Lucky was built in 1994, so the seventies decor struck me as a little odd. The whole thing had a horrible similarity in both furnishing and smell to that in my grandma's flat just before she passed away. She had steadfastly refused to replace anything and had been living in the same surroundings for about 50 years.

I wandered through the kitchen – this took about four steps – and into a seating area furnished with more greasy curtains in the same material, a very straight and hard-looking settle upholstered in a knobbly grey material with frayed edges that allowed the grubby foam beneath to leak through. The settle could just be seen, skulking, embarrassed, behind a wobbly-looking folding wooden table.

To stop items sliding off the top, someone had fixed proud-standing strips of wood to each edge. As I couldn't imagine that *Happy Go Lucky* ever had occasion to battle manfully through huge rolling waves while travelling at four miles an hour down glass-still canals, I could only assume the proud edges of the table were either merely decoration or put there as an irritant to anybody trying to clean the wretched thing.

Trying to move the table out of the way without having to actually touch it, I lowered myself gingerly onto the settle and spent a couple of minutes studying the literature packed into the bookshelves on the opposite side of the boat.

I assumed that holidays on board had been so boring that the books were there to stop the passengers committing mutiny. There was certainly no book less than ten years old. A collection of Dickensian Classics cosied up to the *Great*

Book of Vampire Stories – this, in turn, was wedged beside a set of well-thumbed Mills and Boon love stories; a book for every taste, obviously.

These packed shelves ran down the length of the boat; tens of feet of them, filled to overflowing with either novels or small books and pamphlets covering 'Things to do on canals'. I was rather confused – as far as I was concerned, a canal holiday entailed getting on the boat; floating about a bit; getting off the boat; there couldn't be much more to it than that, surely? However, the sheer amount of literature cluttering the insides of Happy gave me a bit of an insight that I might be mistaken and that a canal holiday could be much more exciting than I had ever imagined.

Bored with looking at the books, and needing someone to pick an argument with, I went in search of Geoff and Sam. Choosing a door at random, I reached across the passageway and pushed it open to reveal a tiny bathroom.

There was a small cream-coloured and yellow-stained toilet lurking in the corner, next to it was a shower, half hidden behind a faded and mould-ridden curtain. At first glance I thought it strange that someone had decided to put a black carpet in the shower tray, but, on closer inspection, it turned out to be half an inch of stagnant water. A tiny sink attached at a slight angle on to the buckled and damp-stained wall opposite completed the 'bathroom suite'. It made a perfect picture of decay and neglect which the smell did nothing to dispel. In fact, the whole thing presented the perfect site for a cholera-breeding program.

There were six cabins, each boasting a double bed filling the space wall to wall, and a vanity unit comprising a tiny sink, some shelves and an age-spotted mirror. The only way to get on to the bed was to take a flying leap from the doorway and hope that nothing collapsed beneath you.

I wandered back to the sad little seating area and, picking up one of the pamphlets on narrow-boat holidays, I decided to find out exactly what a narrow-boat holiday entailed and plonked myself back onto the demoralised sofa. Opening the leaflet at a random page, I alternated between reading it and waving it about in the air, hoping to dispel the cloud of stinking dust that had puffed up as I sat down. I was pleased to confirm that a narrow-boat holiday wasn't exactly for the thrill-seekers among the population, unless maybe you were over 105 years old and were fairly realistic about the type of thrills that you were seeking.

Finding nothing remotely of interest in the pamphlet, I shoved it back onto the shelf with a sigh and looked up as Geoff and Sam came grinning and chattering down the boat toward me. Both were alive with excitement and discussing Sam's new bedroom, how the rest of the boat would look and what they could do with it.

'Uh-oh,' I muttered to myself, 'this looks like trouble.'

'What have you been doing?' Geoff bounced up to me with a huge grin and before I could start moaning about how awful it all was – how unhygienic, nasty and smelly – he rushed on with his thoughts.

'Isn't this great? I'm pretty sure it's bone dry and just think with all the cabins and extra walls that would have to be removed, I might never have to buy any wood at all, what a saving.' He paused for breath and looked around. 'Is this as far as you've got? What do you think?'

What I wanted to say was 'I think it's horrible, *it smells*, I'd rather wee over the side than use that toilet, it looks as though it wants to eat you, *it smells*, and if I stand in the middle with outstretched arms I can touch both sides, where are we going to put everything, how are we going to live in this, *it smells,* it's tacky and epitomises all that was bad about the seventies, how am I going to cook, I miss my house and I haven't even moved out of it yet and I miss my garden even more, where are all my clothes going to go, there isn't even enough storage space for my shoes and that includes that ridiculous excuse for a kitchen, AND IT SMELLS!!!'

My traitorous brain, however, committed mutiny on the spot and, obviously taking pity on my poor, hopeful husband re-wrote the script and forced me to say, 'Erm ... it's got potential?'

It was obviously the right thing to say, as, with a huge smile, he grabbed hold of my hand and pulled me toward the pointy end (sorry, the bow), excitedly explaining as he went along, 'We'll have Sam's room here and the galley (the what?) will have to be moved to here; this will be the saloon (the what?) but we should be able to have a fair-sized head around here (a fair-sized what?); of course she will have to be surveyed and hopefully they'll accept an offer, but as long as all that goes to plan, I think we've found our home – what do you think?'

I looked into his eager, excited face and told another huge lie. 'If you're sure you can make her lovely, sweetie, I'm with you all the way.'

Arrrgh! Noooooooooooooo! IT SMELLS!

Chapter Four
Dumping Shoes is Grounds for Divorce, You Know

TWO DAYS BEFORE OUR house completion, knowing that *Happy Go Lucky* had been on the market for some time, we put in a ridiculously low offer. Geoff lived in the hope that the offer would be accepted and I half hoped that it would be turned down. However, as moving day was rushing toward us, there wasn't really that much time to gripe about it.

As the packing ploughed on we had a few minor tiffs, especially the day that Amelia, who was still emphatically against the idea of moving with us, actually put a plan into motion for once in her life, packed her own stuff up and moved into her boyfriend's parents' house. I wasn't happy with the idea and had been expecting her to change her mind but, as she had so firmly stated, she was 18 and there was nothing I could do.

Luckily, Huw is lovely; 6' 4" and built like an overly hirsute piece of string, he actually took the time to come and try to allay all my fears and worries, which was very mature for an 18-year-old. It didn't help at all but I appreciated the gesture.

We had met his parents who, strangely, seemed to be so convinced that they were taking on 'a lovely girl, so helpful and polite' that I came away from the meeting wondering if Amelia had paid a stand-in to cover for her as we seemed to be discussing a different teenager.

From the very start of the dreaded boxing-up exercise, Geoff had maintained that this was an excellent opportunity to do a major 'life laundry' and had blithely thrown away anything either he hadn't used for a year or that he hadn't seen me using. In the early days of packing I was more likely to be seen dragging things *out* of the skip than actually putting them in.

Things finally came to a head when he tried squeezing past me in our small hall with two very lumpy black bags.

'What's in there?' I asked, failing to inform him that I had noticed a couple of stiletto heels sticking out through the plastic. Geoff's eyes slid sideways and he took a step backward, ineffectively trying to push the bags behind him.

'Just some last bits and pieces I found under the spare room bed,' he muttered. Picking up the bags he tried to slide past me again.

'Oh, no you don't,' I shrieked, 'those are my shoes!' I lunged toward him and grabbed one of the bags. Not only was it full of shoes, but boots and bags as well!

That was the final straw; I was tired, dirty and miserable. I had the choice of living with my mother-in-law, or on a floating coffin that smelled like we would be sharing it with the resident carelessly interred corpse, and as far as I was concerned that was no choice at all. Now this useless, hairy lump was going to throw my Jimmy Choos in the skip.

It was all his fault we were in this state, and it was his stupid idea that we go and live with his mum or on a boat (reality wasn't playing a huge part in my life at this point), Sam couldn't swim, so he was going to fall off the boat and drown about two minutes after we cast off and even if he didn't die he was going to be so emotionally scarred by all this that he would probably end up with his own counsellor at ChildLine.

Geoff took one look at this wild-eyed and maniacally angry woman lunging toward him and decided that discretion was definitely the better part of valour. He dropped the bags and fled.

A couple of minutes later, he called gently up the stairs,

his voice following the trail of scuffmarks that I had made in the paintwork as I had stamped past, swearing and dragging two bags with sharp heels sticking out, acting the part of expensive grappling hooks.

'Are you OK?'

I stuck my head out through the bedroom doorway. 'No I'm bloody well not, just leave me alone,' I shouted down at him and, turning, stamped back into the bedroom, the angry slam from the door echoing around the bare room.

I leant against the door and stared at the dents and impressions in the carpet; it was as though my beautiful furniture was still there, just invisible, and for a moment I could forget that it was either sold, given away or just dumped.

Sighing, I emptied the shoes out of the bags and watched them bounce across the floor. I spent the next five minutes arranging the 30 plus shoes and boots into their pairs and placing them around the wall of the bedroom. Staring at them I sat on the carpet in the middle of my invisible bed and promptly burst into tears.

I must have cried solidly for a good ten minutes and then, finally getting angry with my pathetic self for being so upset over a couple of pounds of shaped leather, I stood up and walked around the room, picking up each shoe in turn and throwing it with as much force as I could muster against the opposite wall.

It's strange; you can only cry and wail for so long before your conscience starts to metaphorically tap you on the shoulder and every single time, the voice it uses sounds just like your best friend – at least mine does.

'What the hell are you doing?' it scolded. 'Either you stop now or you're going to end up with a nice jacket to match those shoes, one of those popular styles with the arms that tie behind you. You started this, shit happens – either sort yourself out or be miserable, your choice.'

Helen, a no-nonsense paramedic, has been my best friend

for about 15 years and throughout that time I have always relied on her to give me a major verbal slapping when necessary. It has happened so many times in the past that she can now accomplish a good dressing down even when she isn't actually there – not a bad trick.

Geoff had given me the mandatory half an hour to calm down and had finally worked up the courage to brave the shoe- and furniture-deprived psycho wailing banshee-like in the bedroom. He stepped through the battered door carrying two cups of tea and a large bar of chocolate.

Looking around, he took in the shoes scattered around the room and the dents in the paintwork. (I suppose I should apologise profusely to the new owners but, in view of the price they got the house for, I'm not going to. So there!) He put the tea and the chocolate down and then started to gather up the shoes. He handed them to me, one at a time and I quietly placed them back in the bin bags. There was one pair, a beautiful pair of black leather boots, well worn and well loved, that I had real trouble putting in the bag. I stood there, hugging them for a couple of seconds until Geoff came over and gently took them from me. I assumed he was going to throw them into the bin bag but instead he left the room with my boots tucked under his arm. A couple of minutes later he returned, carrying a suitcase. Unzipping it, he placed the boots reverently on the top, and making sure they wouldn't be crushed, he zipped it back up and turned to me with an enquiring look on his face.

For some reason, this struck me as really sweet and started the tears again. I was blotchy and sniffly but managed to give him a weak grin. Through all this, he hadn't said a word. Handing me my tea, he unwrapped the chocolate, broke off a large piece and, leaning down, held my nose until I opened my mouth which gave him somewhere to stuff it. Standing up again he picked up the bin bags and put them outside the door where I couldn't see them. When he returned to sit down beside me, he stole half of my remaining chocolate to go with his tea.

We sat there chatting about nothing; I knew it was just an excuse to give me time to completely calm down. When he judged that normality had returned, he handed me the last piece of chocolate and very quietly stated that he had just got off the phone to the marina, our offer had been accepted on the boat, but that if we went ahead the present owner wanted no comebacks.

'What does that mean? "no comebacks",' I asked.

'It means that if the survey is poor or if there are any issues that arise from the survey, we can't ask him to drop the price any further, although we can still pull out of the sale altogether,' Geoff explained.

'Oh.' I stared into the last inch of my tea and tried to think about what all this meant on a grander scale, but being completely exhausted from my crying and shoe-slinging marathon, I found it really hard to make head or tail of the whole situation.

'So what do you want to do?' I turned to face him. 'If the survey's bad, at least we can pull out.'

Geoff shook his head 'Your call,' he grinned, 'what do *you* want to do?'

I stared at the dents in the wall and ran my finger around one in the carpet. This was, I realised, a very last opportunity to get out of this. I knew it and Geoff knew it.

Stealing his hanky, I blew my nose hard and drained the last of my tea.

'Call the surveyor,' I reached down and, grasping his hand, completely failed to pull Geoff to his feet. 'Tell him we need a quick appointment, the less time I have to stay with your mum the better.'

Twenty-four hours and two crying bouts later, we had managed to pack a desirable four-bedroom detached house (with large garage and a range of outhouses) into one transit van and the boot of my car.

Actually, we had managed to pack the absolute essentials

31

into one transit van and the boot of my car. Everything else was either squashed into storage, cluttering up my father's factory or peering at us mournfully from the top of a very, very overloaded skip. We had also, over the last two months, become very intimate with eBay and a lot of friends had picked up some great, if slightly embarrassing, bargains.

I deliberately didn't hang around to say goodbye to the house. A four-hour drive to my mother-in-law's in Cumbria with a tired, stressed child and an ancient, smelly, narcoleptic dog with a weak bladder was going to be difficult enough without the added trauma of another bout of tears, and anyway, I'd had enough of crying. What was done was done. There was no going back now.

Chapter Five
What Do You Mean, You've Never Driven a Narrow Boat?

LILLIAN, GEOFF'S MOTHER, WAS great. She made us all welcome and did what she could to try and ease the weird transition we were all suffering. The two weeks we spent with her felt like a holiday.

The holiday feeling became a problem in itself, as, although this interlude felt like one of our normal six-monthly breaks, I knew that it wasn't and kept thinking 'won't be long till we go home' except that we had no home to go to, and every time I realised this, I had to go and have a lie down.

We drove back to Braunston to meet up with the surveyor on August 28 and, for once, the gods were smiling on us.

Happy Go Lucky was in a dry dock and out of the water, and she showed every single one of her 23 tonnes; standing beneath her and looking up, she looked huge.

The surveyor went over her with a fine-tooth comb and gave us a monetary value which was worth more than the asking price and far more than our ridiculous offer; she was sound, dry, had a good solid hull, an efficient if slightly underpowered engine, and plenty of ventilation. The only thing he could find that could possibly cause a problem was that there was some play in the tiller, but a set of shims, he explained, should sort that out. He also mentioned that the propeller was possibly a little undersized for the length of the boat. He agreed that it was going to take some work to make her beautiful and she would probably handle like a pregnant cow but really it was only hard graft and a bit of TLC that was needed.

With the survey complete, he asked what we had offered for her, lost his eyebrows in his hairline when we told him and informed us we'd had a huge bargain. He shook our hands and was still grinning as he climbed out of the dry dock and wandered back to the office. How strange, a nice surveyor; obviously house and boat surveyors are a completely different species.

With his departure, silence descended as Geoff and I looked at each other. It was quite a comfortable and hopeful silence and would have been enjoyable if Sam hadn't chosen that precise moment to fall into a large, oily puddle. We dragged him out, dried him off and decided to get some lunch.

If you ever go to Braunston, walk through the marina and take a left turn down the canal, and about a hundred yards up the tow path you will come across a small restaurant boat called Gongoozler's Rest. I suggest you order a bacon sandwich and chips; the bacon sandwich is superb and the chips defy description. They were so good that a year on Sam was still asking to go back and have some more.

We sat on the public seat, next to the canal, the sun was shining, smiling people were wandering past and saying hello. We relaxed there for about an hour, eating bacon butties, feeding the ducks, drinking huge mugs of tea and discussing hare-brained plans for the future of *Happy Go Lucky*. It was at this point I began to think maybe this wasn't such a daft idea after all.

With an end to one kind of vagrancy and the start of another finally in sight, we made the journey back to Cumbria to await the clearance of our cheque and to sort out exactly which articles we could pack into poor Lillian's loft from those which were essential for actually living and would accompany us into the boat.

It was at this point that the problem of finding a mooring

became all-encompassing. Knowing that we wanted to live near Cambridge, we had taken a couple of trips down there to see friends and to view boats that were for sale around East Anglia. One of these boats had been moored in a small marina just outside the city. I had taken its number and from Cumbria I gave them a call.

Throughout the whole boat hunt escapade, every single person we had spoken to had either told us we were bordering on insane, informed us of the impossibility of finding a mooring or just laughed in our faces.

'Get your mooring sorted and then buy a boat to fit it,' one elderly and weather-beaten boater had told us. So, as usual, we were doing everything backwards and against advice. I took a deep breath and dialled the number.

'Hello,' a deep voice answered on the second ring.

'Oh hello, um I wonder if you could help us, we are looking for a mooring.' I held my breath expecting the person on the other end of the line to begin choking or giggling maniacally.

'What size mooring?' was the reasonable response.

Breathe out. 'Erm, 70 foot,' breathe in and hold breath again.

'Phew, big bugger, eh? You a live-aboard?'

Breathe out and panic, oh my God what do I say? We had been told by people, who looked like they knew what they were talking about, that you NEVER, EVER tell a marina that you are a live-aboard, but I'm the world's worst liar. Argh, what do I say? What do I say? Breathe out.

'Erm … Yes?' Deep breath, and hold it …

'Oh, OK, the only one we've got in that size is an in-line mooring but it'll have electricity. We charge £26 per foot, per year, split into quarterly payments; if you want to book the space, you will have to pay the first instalment now.'

Breathe out, panic again, argh! What to do?

'Erm, great, yes, thank you, will you take a card?' Hold breath again, although I'm not sure why at this stage of the conversation – maybe I was expecting a shout down the phone of 'Gotcha, of course there aren't any moorings available, you muppet!' but what I got, was ...

'Yep sure, that will be ... oops, hold on a mo ...' the sound of calculator type clicking echoed down the phone. 'Yep, £460. I'll just get the machine.'

By this time I was completely bewildered and went through the rest of the negotiations in a bit of a daze. When would we be turning up? Two to three weeks? Fine, just give them a call two or three days before we arrived and they would make sure it was all ready for us to move on to.

I gave the lovely, wonderful man both mine and Geoff's details and after dealing with the other bits of red tape, assured him that I would call before we got there and that was it. One phone call, one mooring, completely stress-free.

If I had known at the time how lucky and coincidental the timing of that phone call was, I would have probably become very religious on the spot; however, I didn't find out until some months later that the only reason we got a mooring was that someone had left in a hurry, exactly ten minutes before my call. So instead of becoming a nun, I just became very smug.

I took a few deep breaths (just to make up for the ones I hadn't let escape throughout the phone call) and, acting as nonchalantly as I could, wandered into the living room. Geoff looked up at me from his book.

'No luck, then?' he asked.

I dropped onto the sofa and picked up the paper.

'Hmm? Oh no, it's fine, all organised, one mooring with electricity waiting for us when we get there. I had to pay the first quarter in advance, is that OK?'

'Sure,' he agreed and looked back down at his book. 'WHAT?' he threw the book down. 'You got one? How?'

Laughing at his cartoon-like double take, I affected surprise and shock; this was 'me' we were talking about, Mrs 'Anything is possible' (well, obviously it is if you have no idea what you are doing). As if I could do nothing other than get a mooring at the first attempt, I snorted and innocently continued to scan the paper.

'Immense personal charm, I suppose.' I looked over the top of the paper and frowned at him. 'Um, Geoff? What's an "in-line" mooring do you think?'

September 5 found us all loaded, yet again, into our still overflowing vehicles and after declining a third cup of tea, the offer of lunch and a second offer of cake and biscuits from Lillian, who was obviously unhappy at the idea of us leaving to start a weird, transient life, we were on our way.

We had already said a slightly relieved goodbye to Herbert who was spending a couple of weeks with Helen. I didn't think at his age he would have coped very well with being on a boat. Although being on the boat wouldn't have been any trouble, it was being in any situation that restricted him from getting onto some grass for his fifteen wees a day, which he seemed to need at this point in his life, that would have been the problem. Despite the initial excitement about Happy, Sam wasn't entirely eager to leave Grandma's and head off into some weird and hazy future; he, unlike us, had agreed to cake, biscuits and anything else she was offering and I think would have been quite happy to wave us goodbye from the door of her house. He was a little tetchy for the first part of the journey, but music from the Goodies and a hand-held electronic bleepy game soon raised his spirits. By the time we reached Braunston (for the third time) we were all in quite a hopeful mood, although Sam was a little manic and wide-eyed due to an over-abundance of sugar coupled with staring at little moving characters for three hours.

Leaving our tired-looking, over-laden vehicles in the car park, we wandered into the office to finalise all the bits and pieces. I was in such a good mood that Sam finally got his duck and exactly 15 minutes later we were officially 'Water Rats'.

The marina had allocated us a three-day mooring in the basin; this would give us time to unload the vehicles and generally get ourselves sorted out. Sam and I went to find it, accompanied by Mary from the office.

Mary was an odd character. We had met her on all our previous visits and had never seen her smile; she was also terrifyingly and angrily efficient. I found myself treating her like a headmistress, nodding and smiling at her every instruction, trying hard not to upset her. Geoff had gone off with a very capable-looking man to bring *Happy Go Lucky*, *our* boat, our very own boat, around to meet us.

Mary sat us down on a bench and pointed toward the gap in the basin from where we could expect Happy to appear, and then, spotting a confused-looking family over by the brokerage, she handed me the spare keys and necessary bits of paperwork before trotting over presumably to demand that they purchase something or to run them off the premises.

Sam and I sat in the sun and waited, staring in the direction of the boat shed, just waiting for the moment when she would make her first appearance. A faint 'chug, chug, chug' was our first indication, then *Happy Go Lucky* (*our* boat, our very own boat) gently sauntered into the basin from the canal.

Sam jumped up. 'That's our boat, Mum!' he shrieked, then leaping off the bench he headed toward his dad, who could just be made out, grinning, at the far end.

After six years, experience had taught me to move very, very fast when Sam takes off. I managed to grab him just as he was about to make a, probably unsuccessful, walk-on-water attempt. With this disaster averted we both watched, entranced, as 'our' boat was skilfully piloted between others, coming in very slowly to bump gently against the wharf; she looked large and capable and with her faded livery of grey, black and red, very friendly. I swear if that boat had a tail it would have been gently wagging.

Geoff stepped from the back of the boat onto solid ground and helped the capable-looking man tie her to some concrete posts. He thanked him then waited till he was out of sight before giving us a big smile.

I wandered up to him, keeping a tight grip on Sam.

'Well, how was she to drive?' I asked, ignoring the tugging on my arm and Sam's rising screams, informing me that he wanted to get on to the boat. 'She looked nice coming in.'

Geoff held his hand out to help Sam over the gap and on to the back, stating loftily, 'I think the word you're looking for is "pilot" not drive.'

'Whatever, how was she?' I frowned.

'I don't know, she seemed …stately, but he "drove" her.' Geoff indicated the retreating figure with a nod of his head and laughed, 'I've never driven anything like this – you're the one with the water experience.'

Confusion and the beginnings of panic.

'What do you mean, water experience?' I squeaked.

Having deposited Sam through the engine room doors and safely into the interior of the boat, Geoff looked up at me. 'Didn't you do a lot of messing around in boats with your dad when you were younger?' he said.

Panic becoming more pronounced.

'Dad sails! We had a sailing boat, you know, sea-going, big flappy things and wooden bits that try to knock you into the water when you aren't looking – and that was 25 years ago, I hated it, I spent most of my time hanging over the side being sick.' I took another look at Happy, 23 tonnes of solid steel, engine, not a flappy thing in sight. 'I can't drive this, pilot this, or whatever – I'd kill us or sink us – I thought you had been on boating holidays.'

Geoff shrugged, 'Well yes, when I was about 18 and that was 35 foot, nothing like this great lump.'

I sat back down on the seat. 'So what we are saying here,' I stated, enunciating carefully, 'is that we have just bought 30 grand's worth of boat and neither of us has the least idea how to make it go! How come this hasn't come up, even once, in conversation over the last three months?' I really didn't know whether to be terrified or annoyed and, deciding that neither emotion entirely fitted the bill, I collapsed into a fit of the giggles. Geoff doesn't 'giggle' so he just grinned and then disappeared into the boat calling to Sam that he needed to come out and stop Mummy being embarrassing.

About six o'clock that night we called a halt to the unpacking. As Happy was still in hotel mode, there was no shortage of rooms in which to stack boxes. Sam chose his bedroom (he changed his mind three times) and spent a happy couple of hours playing 'tents' in his quilt and unpacking boxes; I use the term 'unpacking' loosely, what he actually did was open all his boxes and, taking out each toy in turn, he would play with it inside his 'tent' and then discard it by just throwing it onto the floor.

By the time we had, mostly, sorted ourselves out, his bedroom was a war zone, clothes, toys and quilt all mixed together in a big pile on his bed. However, we were so busy running backwards and forwards to the van carrying boxes that we didn't actually notice until his happy chaos had started to seep into the corridor.

We enticed him out with the promise of pizza and, kicking the detritus roughly back into his room, shut the door on the horror and headed out to eat junk food.

Sitting in one of the local restaurants, Geoff poked at his pizza and stared off into the distance.

'Waf up?' I enquired, around a mouthful containing an obscene amount of calories.

'What?' he focused on me. 'Oh, I was just thinking about our lack of piloting experience, and the little problem that neither of us is particularly confident about moving her around.'

'Confident?' I laughed. 'You mean neither of us has any

idea what the hell we're doing, she's huge, and in our inexperienced hands she could be a lethal weapon to other river users or at the very least a snidely amusing inconvenience.'

Geoff grinned. 'Yes, that's exactly what I meant.' He rummaged around in one of his numerous pockets and dragged out a colour leaflet. 'I was in the office earlier and these were on a stand.' He handed it over to me. It was a leaflet for 'Willow Wren Training'.

I read through it, finding they had all sorts of narrow-boat-related courses, everything it seemed, from how to dismantle your diesel engine, to Inland Helmsman (whatever that was), and then handed it to Sam who was desperately trying to read it from under my armpit. 'That seems like a good idea. Which course were you hoping to do?' I went back to my pizza.

Geoff leaned over the table and gently retrieved the leaflet. After wiping the tomato sauce and bits of cheese from it, he pointed to the inland waterways helmsman course. 'This one seems to cover everything we need,' he said.

I struggled with a particularly large mouthful of pizza for a moment and could still feel it sliding down sideways as I pointed out that it was unlikely that we would get a space on a course for months.

Geoff grinned and busied himself folding the leaflet and stowing it away in his pocket. 'We got lucky,' he said and picked up a slice of Hawaiian with extra pineapple. 'There was a cancellation; he's meeting us at the boat tomorrow.'

The mouthful I was struggling with transmogrified itself into a lump of concrete, hit the pit of my stomach and lurked there. Suddenly I wasn't hungry any more and spent the next half-hour poking at the rest of the contents of my plate. Geoff, however, having imparted his 'good' news, cleared his plate in record time and with obvious relish then started on what was left of mine.

After leaving the restaurant, we stopped at an electrical store, picked up a tiny kettle and a small flat-screen television. Sam was suffering from PS2 withdrawal and the sooner we got him a fix the better for all of us. We then headed back to the boat. It took another hour to make some sense of the chaos and disaster that Sam's 'unpacking' had created but we finally got him into bed, where he passed out in the middle of a sentence about how much he didn't like his new bedroom and would never get to sleep.

Making sure that our room was vaguely fit to sleep in, we took a last cup of tea out on to the roof. It was warm, dark and very quiet; the only sound was the occasional 'splosh' or an irritated hiss from a group of four or five adolescent swans, gliding about the marina, casing each boat in the hope of bullying a late-night snack from some unsuspecting resident. We watched them in silence for a while as they moved silently in and out of the pools of reflected light from the boats; it was a clear night and with no light pollution there seemed to be a billion stars.

Tea finished, we lay on our backs staring up into the night sky. It would have been nice to lie side by side but being an aptly named 'narrow' boat we had to lie head to head with our feet pointing towards either end, trying to work out all the constellations that we really ought to know. It was the second recognisable instance since I had had my 'cunning plan' that I actually felt this might have been a good idea.

Chapter Six
Fully Trained – and Still Terrified!

AS FAR AS SAM was concerned, training day was possibly going to be the best day of his short life. His dad had installed the television, he had a new game to play on the PS2 and, unlike every other day, there were no restrictions, he could actually play for as long as Mum and Dad were busy, instead of just the one hour he was normally allowed.

There were snacks provided (all healthy and good for him), a vast amount of drinks (no additives, no chemicals) and unlimited violence (brain-rotting and mind-boggling). So by the time Dave from the training company turned up, he couldn't have cared less. He did manage to say hello, but that's only because I wouldn't let him past me with the huge quilt (nest-making material) he had stolen from our bed, until he did. He was quite obviously looking forward to his day immensely. I just wished that I could've said the same.

Waiting for the kettle to boil, in response to Dave's 'White, one sugar, please', I watched Sam fluff up all his pillows, pull the quilt around him, arrange all his snacks and drinks in easy grabbing distance and, with a grin almost as big as one of his father's, fix a steely gaze on the big-eared character and his robotic sidekick and completely zone out reality. I found myself unreasonably irritated with him. Here we were in the middle of this 'big adventure' and all he wanted to do was play stupid games, but he looked so happy sitting in his 'nest' I had to smile and pushed the growing jealousy to the back of my mind. I grabbed the cups of tea and fought my way through the cramped engine room to the back of the boat, hoping that the tea was enough to put off leaving for a little longer.

Dave was explaining to Geoff about something called 'springing off'. He was a lovely guy who had obviously been around and aboard narrow boats for years, still finding them just as wonderful today as he did 20 years ago. He had run his own hotel boat business so Happy held no horrors for him at all. Unfortunately he had one huge flaw – enthusiasm! He was eager to be off, eager to impart his love for all things wet and sloshy, eager to get us trained and competent. Geoff seemed to be as eager as he was, while I, on the other hand, was eager to go and see how Sam's new game was progressing, help him eat his snacks and drink his drinks and I was pretty sure there was room in that nest for two.

No such luck.

'Right, come on then,' Dave enthused. 'Let's get this lady turned round.'

For a moment, I thought he was talking about me and eyed him with wary confusion, where was I supposed to turn? He was, of course, talking about the only lady he had eyes for and, with a turn of the key, Happy came loudly to life and seemed as eager to be off as the two chattering men.

'Springing off' went surprisingly well. Geoff stood on the bank with the stern rope wrapped around a bollard, with the tiller far over to the right and the engine chugging away. Happy's nose moved gracefully out into the marina in a beautiful 90-degree left curve and, at a nod from Dave, Geoff unwrapped the rope from the bollard and just stepped aboard; we were off.

With Dave at the tiller we moved slowly and gracefully through the other boats; he turned her out of the basin and on to the canal then stepped aside and said to me, 'Here, grab this.'

It is a fact that if someone says, in a casual tone of voice, 'here grab this', you automatically take what they hand you and there was a moment of panic when I realised I had control of 70 feet and 23 tonnes of steel; the panic bubble welled up and then just went 'pop', melting away into a sort of worried, pleased surprise. Happy was doing just as she was told. We were pottering along very slowly, the sun was shining and other boaters were waving and smiling.

There was definitely a sense of slightly dangerous contentment to be in charge of something so big and cumbersome but which also was incredibly stately and graceful.

Our first major encounter with another boat killed off any nerves I might have been experiencing and highlighted the weirdness that I probably would need to expect living on the river. I had the tiller and thought I was doing pretty well, getting the hang of it, puttering along. I was starting to see the draw of this lifestyle, passing slowly and stately around a sweeping bend. Smiling at Mother Nature's decorative style and half drowsing in the sunshine, the throb of the engine was lulling me into a semi-hypnotic state.

Dave suddenly stopped slouching with his elbows on the roof and stood up to his full height, frowning down the canal in front of us. He reached down and pressed the horn, then grabbing my arm, reached past me to throw Happy into full reverse. It took me a couple of moments of complete confusion to work out that something was going on ahead of us and I looked along the length of the roof to try and work out what it was.

About 30 feet ahead of Happy's nose, a much smaller narrow boat was floating sideways across the canal, no one at the tiller. For a moment I wondered if we were seeing the inland waterways version of the *Marie Celeste*, but then I noticed the raised buttocks of two people, leaning over the bow, trying desperately to fish something out of the water.

This is where I learned another, very valuable, lesson. NARROW BOATS DON'T STOP! That drowsy hypnotic drift is one of the most dangerous states to be in. You'd better pay attention to what is going on a good way ahead of your nose – and in our case, that's a fairly long way ahead – because bringing 23 tonnes of steel to a full stop against forward inertia does not happen quickly, if it happens at all.

Luckily, Dave had been paying attention and his quick reactions meant that we just gently kissed the back of the other boat. It transpired that their kitten had taken a suicidal leap overboard and in their panic to get it out of the water they had both rushed to the front to try and fish him out, leaving their boat adrift.

Pandemonium reigned for what seemed like about half an hour but was, in reality, only a couple of minutes. Kitten retrieved, the young couple, suddenly aware that there were queues building up either side of them, rushed about getting their boat underway again.

Putting Happy in forward and taking up the tiller again, I hoped Dave hadn't noticed that I had been wool gathering – fat chance!

'Always best to keep a really good eye ahead,' he murmured, smiling gently.

I smiled, and nodded, damn! Caught red-handed.

Our next odd encounter of the day was with a lady going very slowly in the opposite direction. Geoff was at the tiller and, noticing her lack of speed and that she seemed to be looking in all directions, leaning out over her boat to inspect ahead and around her, he slowed down. Dave nodded in approval, while I sighed and hailed the woman.

'Is everything all right?' We had slowed to a crawl and were nearly alongside. She looked up and nodded.

'You haven't seen a stray man have you?' she called back.

Dave just raised an eyebrow 'Have you lost one then?' he enquired. In his gentle Warwickshire accent he actually managed to make the question sound sane.

'Oh yes,' the woman put her hands into the pockets of her oversized, rainbow-striped woolly jumper and managed to look a little embarrassed. 'He jumped off to walk for a bit and get some exercise but the tow path stopped and I sort of lost him, he said he was going cross country and I'm following him – I think.'

Dave put his hand over his mouth and coughed slightly. 'No, sorry, haven't seen anyone walking.'

She nodded philosophically and waved, returning to her search of both water and hedgerows. Dave waved back and watched her potter past us.

'Lesson to the wise,' he mused, 'this is the one thing that mobile phones are good for.'

For the next six hours, Geoff and I took it in turns to face the *'normal'* day-to-day perils we would likely have thrown at us on the long journey down to Cambridge: locks (don't stand on the gates and look down – makes you sick); winding holes (make sure that you actually have some wind and that it is going in the right direction before you try to turn round); straights (can get boring); curves (anything but boring, can't see what's coming the other way); tunnels (cold, dark, wet and just terrifying); open water turns (three attempts at this); what to do when you run aground (after the second attempt at an open water turn); mooring up (make sure you are actually close to the bank before you jump off with a rope) and casting off (make sure the boat is still within jumping distance when you try to get back on).

We also took it in turns to try and engage Sam in the different aspects of the day and keep him company; sadly I think we just managed to irritate him, although he did enjoy going through the tunnel. However, as soon as we cleared the exit, he grabbed another handful of grapes and a yoghurt, bought some more ammo for his Morph Ray and went back to turning robots into chickens, giggling every time he did it. Kapow! Zap! Fizz!!! Cluck!!! Ho hum.

We returned to Braunston at around four o'clock in a heroic frame of mind and moored up perfectly, without Dave's assistance, just outside the marina on the canal tow path. We were qualified Inland Waterways Helmsmen and there was no peril, no danger that we couldn't face.

We said our goodbyes to Dave, thanking him profusely; it wasn't so much the training, which, in itself was invaluable, but all the information and useful tips that he had also imparted. I can honestly say without that information we would have faced far more nasty surprises than we actually did.

Geoff finished his post-training cup of tea and jumped to his feet. 'Come on,' he said, 'we need to pump out and fill her up with water, let's do it now.'

We informed Sam what we were up to and he waved vaguely at us over his shoulder. He had now been on the game for six hours with only a few breaks and his eyes were beginning to glaze; I made a mental note that, as soon as we finished with pumping out, it would be a proper meal and a long walk along the tow path for him – just maybe we could anchor him in reality again.

We fired up Happy's engine and backed her carefully into mid stream to make the sharp right turn into the marina. Strangely, without Dave there, it seemed much more difficult. I pulled myself together. For goodness sake, I had been doing this all day and with my backbone firmly held together by willpower, I managed to get her around the corner and perfectly positioned by the pump-out for Geoff to step off and tie her up. I was still smugly congratulating myself 20 minutes later when Geoff shouted that we were full of water and all pumped out. I re-started the engine and backed her carefully out onto the canal again.

One thing Dave taught us was that narrow boats do NOT go backwards well, as they lose all their steering. You have to guide the back end by doing short bursts forward and swinging the nose round, then reversing again. I was still watching the bow and trying to get her in a good line to get back on to our mooring when I ran her hard, backwards, into the trees on the other side of the canal. There was a horribly loud, cracking thump, and a handful of pointy twigs impaled the back of my neck.

This is when I learned a lesson that has stayed true ever since: when you perform a perfect manoeuvre, there is never a soul to be seen, but mess it up and you will always have an audience. Size is relative; the bigger the mistake, the bigger the audience. The only exception to this rule is when you actually need help and then it doesn't matter how big a screw-up you make, there won't be a soul around and no one will turn up to point and laugh until you have sorted yourself out.

As complete screw-ups go, this was one of the minor ones, mainly embarrassing, rather than dangerous. It took us three or four minutes to disentangle ourselves from the tree and get back to our mooring. By then, I was so flustered, still trying to stem the blood from multiple scratches on the back of my neck, that I bought her in nose-first and way too fast. As a result, we hit the bank with another resounding thump and Geoff's imminent jump to the bank was aided by a sudden stop in forward momentum, so much so that he was propelled off the bow in a tangle of arms, legs and rope accompanied by a cartoon-like short scream.

Once Happy was all safely tied up, I looked about, wincing, to check just how many people were still standing around, sniggering at our amateur dramatics: not a single one. With the entertainment over, they had melted away, back to their jogging and cycling, leaving the tow path completely deserted.

Chapter Seven
Why is My Kitchen a Cardboard Cut-Out?

AFTER ANOTHER MUCH-NEEDED cup of tea, I decided to make an attempt at dinner. Incredibly, Happy was equipped with a diesel hob, expensive things, but much safer than gas. Leaking gas tends to drop into the bilges and then explode at the least provocation, or so we had been told. It was one of the things Geoff liked about her, as every other boat we had looked at had gas installed.

To install just the hob alone would have cost over £500, hob and cooker together came to a massive £1200. So with budget restrictions in mind, we had decided that, for now, we would make do with just the already installed hob and the microwave, and the diesel oven could wait for our overdue lottery win.

The hob's controls were basic to say the least and, with a certain amount of trepidation, we had dragged the instructions out of Happy's collection of how-to booklets in an attempt to make sense of the wretched thing. Half-an-hour later, we had a pool of fuel in the cupboard space under the hob, the whole boat stank of spilt diesel and every time the hob actually lit, rather than just running through its array of flashing lights, it made this odd whistling, screaming noise before cutting out and dropping more diesel into the cupboard.

Tired and hungry, Sam had hit manic, I had got to the point of screaming and Geoff was talking slowly at me with slightly gritted teeth, a sure sign that he was approaching furious. I was voting to rip the whole thing out and throw it into the canal when Geoff dumped the instructions on the side and said, 'Sod it, let's go to the pub, we can get something hot to eat and Mr Hyper there can run off some of that energy.'

We stared at each other and listened to Sam who had taken to bouncing on our bed, each creaking thump accompanied by rude songs of his own devising. Both the bouncing and the singing were enough to make any parent wince.

Holding Sam down with one hand, I made him eat a slice of bread and butter to tide him over until proper nutrition could be found and we took a walk down the tow path, in search of a peaceful beer garden, some alcohol and someone else to do the cooking.

It was a lovely evening and watching Sam tire himself out on the climbing frame in the pub garden we were happy. Geoff let the peace of the evening, a good meal and numerous cups of tea restore his equilibrium, and I let three-parts of a bottle of decent red restore mine.

The next morning dawned clear and bright. I, however, didn't. Too much wine and the overpowering smell of diesel from the kitchen were just too much for my delicate sensibilities so, deciding that both Sam and my headache would benefit from some more exercise and fresh air, I wandered over to the office with him to see if they had a list of handy diesel engineers that could come out in an emergency.

Sam and I left Geoff with his head in the electrics, muttering imprecations against whichever hapless soul had installed our, in his opinion, 'stupidly small inverter'. What I gathered, from amid the swearing, was that we only had 1.5kW available to us at any one time, which meant that whenever we had the microwave on we couldn't use the kettle, as both together blew the inverter and cut out all the electrics.

There was also a problem with the fridge, which

appeared to be completely non-functional, but Geoff couldn't work out whether the fridge was actually dead or if it was just another problem with the electrics.

This is one area where I neither get involved, nor make suggestions; I am terrified of electricity, so I just made him lots of cups of tea and kept Sam out of his way.

Despite Mary's taciturn personality, she was very, very helpful and spent a good 20 minutes trying to find us someone who could come at short notice; there are very few people who can deal with diesel cookers. Kuranda are the main suppliers of this type of cooker and hob but they are based in Yorkshire and although they were more than happy to fix it for us, we would have had to send it up to them.

Mary finally found us a couple of diesel heating engineers who were willing to have a look at it and would be going past in about an hour.

'There you go then,' Mary growled, putting the phone down. 'Anything else you need?' She bared her teeth at me in what might have been a smile, or a snarl to warn me that there'd better not be.

'No, no, that's brilliant, thanks – you've been really helpful,' I stammered at her.

Narrowing her eyes at me in case I was being sarcastic (I wouldn't dare), she then looked down at her paperwork.

'When they get here, I'll send 'em over.' I had been dismissed; I turned to go, resisting the urge to bow myself backwards out of her office.

Collecting Sam from the wonders of the shop, I spent a couple of minutes telling him that no, he didn't need the Rosie and Jim dolls to go with his duck, and, feeling Mary's steely glare on the back of my neck, I ushered him quickly outside.

Crossing the car park toward the river, the smell of cooking bacon wafted effusively past us and I decided to surprise my poor, deprived husband with one of Gongoozler's incredible bacon sandwiches. While they were constructing Geoff's breakfast, I let Sam coerce me into letting him have a second breakfast as well. My hangover gave my stomach a good talking to about the danger of seductive smells and I decided that coffee was all I was going to get away with.

The restaurant boat was small but nicely set up, with eight tables, some with four chairs, some with two, nothing fancy, but clean and very classic with castles and roses painted on every available surface. I never did find out the owner's name, but she was one of those people who always had a smile; she asked us how it was all going and then bustled off to cook.

Sam had obviously worked out that Mum was not 100 per cent up to par today and he had decided that some good behaviour might get him another chance to turn robots into chickens, so was quietly playing some complicated game with the crucible set. I basked in the sun coming through the window and was busy looking at the same group of young swans that we had been watching on our first night, mugging passers-by for titbits and musing that all they needed was a matching set of hoodies and they wouldn't be that much different from human teenagers, when a group of four well-dressed thirty-somethings stepped loudly into the boat.

They were that arrogant type that usually frequent trains, talking loudly into mobile phones and to each other as though their conversation is the only thing that matters. The owner came out to take their order and, after loudly condemning everything on the menu (your loss, people), they settled for three teas and a coffee.

'Make sure the cups are clean,' one young man shouted down the boat toward the kitchen.

'Isn't this small,' one woman giggled at the other, 'I can't believe people actually live on these things.'

'Well, for the type of people that live on them, it's probably a step up,' the clean-cup man, sitting next to her, lectured. 'Don't forget, these people are basically river gypsies, there's just no space for them on the roads any more so they've turned to the waterways.'

'Yah, well the sooner they bloody get off them the better,' clean-cup's mate sneered. 'My friend's father had a lovely boat and one of these things ran into him, sank him outright, didn't do a bit of damage to the stupid, crappy narrow boat – then they had the cheek to say that it was his fault, pulled in front of them or some rubbish. Why they didn't just stop I'll never know.'

If my hangover had been just a little less aggressive, I might have been just a little more forthcoming and put my oar in there and then, but as it was, I was content to just sit and listen as clean-cup poured out more and more rubbish about the 'type' of people that lived on narrow boats.

In the three months we had been searching for a new home, we had met and talked to possibly hundreds of boat dwellers, and the only thing they had in common was that they lived on a boat. We had met teachers, plumbers, office workers, writers, musicians, all manner of different people; all had different reasons for living where they did.

Our takeaway breakfast arrived just as I finished my coffee and just in time to stop Sam licking his plate clean. Giving one last look at the sniggering group, smug in their ill-informed superiority, my only thought was, 'If your mate's dad was as big an arsehole as you lot, I would have run into him, too.'

As I wandered down the tow path, buffeted by Sam's normal erratic progress, I was struck by a sudden awful thought: was that how people would see me now? Would I be dismissed as a lowlife before people even took the time to find out who I was? It was a depressing thought, only slightly diminished by a short stab of guilt that I too, just a year ago, would have been exactly as biased as those that may judge me now. Ah karmic retribution, it's almost guaranteed to bite you in the arse just when you expect it least.

By the time Sam and I got back to Happy, Geoff had emerged from the electrics and was making another list; he looked worried and harassed but brightened up considerably when he opened the bacon sandwich.

'So, what's the prognosis?' I asked, hunting for yet more coffee.

He sighed around a mouthful of bacon, 'Not good. The inverter is just too small to cope with our power demands, so we need a new one. The electrics have been seriously bodged and added to over the years and now they just look like a big ball of multicoloured string. The fridge doesn't work, and it looks as though the battery bank could do with being replaced.'

'Oh. How much is all that going to set us back?' I picked up his list and winced at the prices that he had guesstimated. 'A grand for an inverter! What's it made of – gold?' Raising my voice had set my headache off again and reaching for my fourth cup of coffee of the day I used it to wash down a couple of paracetamol. 'And what sort of battery costs £350?'

'Six of them.' Geoff finished his sandwich, reclaimed his list and studied it again. 'We could probably get a cheaper inverter but we use a lot of power and the computers will need a clean power supply. This inverter will give us 3kW which is double what we have at the moment. Yes, it's the top of the range but we may as well buy it while we have the money; in a year's time we may not.'

'Good point,' I conceded. 'On an up-note, Mary found us someone to look at the hob; they should be here any minute.'

In actual fact, Geoff had managed to finish his breakfast and we were well on the way to having a full-scale row with Sam about chickens before they arrived. In the sudden flurry of introductions, explanations and tea-making, Sam made good his escape. Blatantly exploiting the situation, he had worked out that I was now too busy to have a family discussion about the dangers of computer games.

Watching him hightail it up the boat, I managed to take cold comfort from the likelihood that his sneaky tendencies would stand him in good stead when he was older; maybe he would have a career in politics.

I never actually managed to remember the engineers' names, as they were immediately nicknamed Tweedledee and Tweedledum, but they were brilliant and an absolute cliché. On hearing about our woes, they set about wedging themselves into surprisingly small spaces for such large gentlemen; as they drank vast amounts of tea there was a lot of swearing and passing of strange tools about, but in due course the hob was disconnected and lay mournfully on the worktop in a puddle of diesel with its innards strewn about what passed for our kitchen. This is the point where the strange sucking-of-teeth noises started and, for every hiss and frown, the pound signs clicked up and up in my mind.

Eventually, Tweedledee extracted a copper something that had obviously snapped (even I could tell that it shouldn't dangle like that).

'There you go, that's the bugger,' he grinned, waggling it to and fro. 'Funny thing, though,' he continued, 'this looks like it was like this when it was put in, it was snagged in the seal.'

Geoff frowned. 'That doesn't actually surprise me,' he said. 'This kitchen is weird, the hob's damaged, the fridge doesn't work, and the microwave is brand new. I've been wondering if this whole kitchen had been thrown in just for the sale of the boat.'

'Why would they do that?' I asked.

'Well, you think about it,' he leant on the wall. 'This was one of a pair, all the cabins were on this one, and the galley and the saloon were on the other one. Why would anybody have a small kitchen taking up space in a boat where you need to sleep as many folk as possible? I don't have any proof, but I think this was a cabin, possibly for the crew as it's next to the engine room, and he has just slung a kitchen in for show and none of it actually works; mind you, we can't really complain, for the price he accepted we should count ourselves lucky that there was anything here at all.'

'Bloody hell,' I fumed, 'it's going to cost a fortune to replace all this lot.'

Obviously a married man, Tweedledee stepped in before I could go off into 'rant mode'.

'Don't worry, it's not that bad, all we need to do is give Kuranda a call and they'll have another one here by tomorrow. We'll pop in and fix it and you'll be on your way.'

I must have looked unconvinced because he continued, 'No, no, really, they're very good, the part will be in the office by tomorrow morning, you watch.'

He looked so sincere I didn't have the heart to tell him that it wasn't Kuranda sending the part I was unconvinced about; it was them turning up again tomorrow to fit it.

The moaning and griping were interrupted at that point by a phone call from my mother to tell us that she and my father were bored and were coming down to see the boat; they would be with us in about an hour and a half.

Argh no, not in this state – hmm ... hang on a minute.

'Great, we'd love to see you ... erm, Mummy darling, sweetie, lovey, most helpful mummy of all...'

Silence, then a sigh, 'What do you want?'

'You know that fridge you've got in the garage, the one you only use at Christmas?'

'Yes?'

'Can we have it please? The one on the boat is a dud – along with every other bloody piece of kitchen kit in here.'

'What's happened?' My mother loves a disaster, and she always likes to step in and save the day – the trouble is she's actually very good at it. (Mind you, dealing with my sister and me, she's had years of practice.)

'Well,' I moaned, 'let's just say, the kitchen was a bit of a cardboard cut-out and didn't actually exist.'

Mum laughed. 'No problem, tell us all about it when we get there, us and the fridge. See you in about two hours – love you, byeee.'

And with that she was off, marshalling my father into action. Thinking about it, he probably didn't even know he was going for a two-hour joy ride, let alone do some major weight-lifting as well. For just a brief moment I felt a bit guilty on behalf of my gender – good grief, it's no wonder men have sheds. Then the guilt was gone in the smugness of getting a free fridge. One more problem solved.

During my phone call to Mum the engineers had made good their escape, and Geoff had his head stuck in the electrics again.

'Mum and Dad are going to be here about 11 o'clock,' I informed him. 'Do you want to have a quick run round to the chandlers before they get here and pick up your solid gold inverter?'

He looked up, surprised. 'Your mum and dad are coming down?' he asked.

'Yep,' I grinned, 'and they have offered us the Christmas fridge, well, not so much offered as have given it up for the greater good – our greater good.'

Geoff was looking at me and nodding, but I could tell his brain was still wrapped in multi-coloured wiring.

'Come on then, let's go and spend a vast amount of money,' I prompted, 'and this thing better look like it's worth it. I need a good paint job and a vast array of flashing lights for that price, oh and the lights better be blue or the whole deal's off.'

Actually the inverter was a mucky yellow and about the size and weight of a large shoe box filled with rocks. It had just two lights (red ones) and didn't look at all like £1,000 worth of kit, but Geoff was ecstatic about it, and buried himself in the instructions, making copious notes until my parents arrived. He showed it to my father who took one look and brightened up as well; both of them disappeared into the engine room to play with their new toy.

'Well, that's got rid of them,' Mum mused gently. 'Right, where's my boy?'

Sam, on hearing Nanny's voice, had turned off the PS2 and was walking slowly down the boat, thus giving him time to formulate a huge list of complaints. He hadn't had any sweets for days and Mum and Dad were always soooo busy, no one was talking to him, and there were no toys to play with, and nothing to eat.

Mum listened to them all, her frown deepening with each wildly inaccurate whinge.

'Aaoow, poor thing, why don't we go out? Now that your mum's got a fridge, I'm sure we should go shopping to find nice things to put in it and maybe some sweets for you as well, poor boy.'

Sam's face fell. Aha, this should be interesting, I thought, he doesn't want to go out and leave his game, but he knows that Nanny is good for sweets. I raised my eyebrows at him, and smiled, 'If you want sweets, you have to come to the shops with us.'

'No, no,' Mum cut in, 'you don't have to come, if you're all comfy, you can stay with Daddy and Grandpa, we'll bring you back a surprise.'

I sighed; that was just what Sam wanted, thank you very much, Mother.

'Thank you, Nanny,' Sam fluttered his eyelashes at her and gave her his best smile (where do they learn to do that?) 'I love you. Could you bring me a comic as well and maybe a toy?' And without waiting for an answer, he whizzed off down to the front to continue his 'chickenation' of the world. I had lost, as usual.

'Cup of coffee, Mum?' I asked. She pursed her lips at the milk gently evolving in the late summer warmth.

'Hmm, no thanks love, let's go shopping.'

59

On our return, we found that Dad and Geoff had installed the fridge. I put everything away and set to making lunch. Sam tore himself away from his game again long enough to collect all his extravagant goodies from Nanny (we 'are' supposed to be going for a simpler life here) then disappeared back into his nest, but at least this time it was to play with toys and not the computer.

'So what do you think then,' I asked, indicating the boat.

'Oh, it's lovely,' Mum looked slightly embarrassed. 'Well actually, it's horrible,' she laughed, 'but I'm sure it *will* be lovely when you have sorted it all out. Do you know what you are going to do to it?' We wandered down the length of Happy and I explained what we hoped would go where. Dad and Geoff grabbed their lunch and disappeared back into the engine room with it. Sam refused to come out of the bow.

Mum and I, left to our own devices, sat on the bank with a picnic. It was strange, I had absolutely nothing to do and I couldn't remember when I had last talked to her without having to clock-watch or be disturbed by phones ringing. We spent a happy afternoon under a tree, just chatting. Maybe there's something to living in the slow lane after all.

Chapter Eight
No More Excuses,
We Really Have to Actually Travel

MUM AND DAD LEFT that evening at about nine. They had treated us to dinner and had generally been helpful and lovely. Maybe this time one of their children had rolled so far left field they couldn't really help and had no advice, so all they could do was just sit back, watch and be ready to catch us if we fell. I know they were worried but had obviously discussed it between themselves and had decided to just smile and be supportive.

Watching them drive away, I was struck with a sudden homesick panic. What the hell was I doing, stuck on this floating bathtub, I shouldn't be here, I can't do this, I need to be looked after, I really, really want my mum. However, I didn't have long to dwell on it, as Sam morphed into were-brat after eight o'clock and had to be coddled back to the boat and into bed. Geoff was in (he claimed) the final stages of getting the new inverter installed so he went back to the engine room.

I hovered about for an hour or so tidying up Sam's 'nest' and trying to find something useful to do but at about ten o'clock I wandered into the engine room to irritate Geoff.

'How's it going?' I asked the soles of his feet. The opposite end stopped swearing for long enough to tell me exactly how it was going in full and colourful detail. 'O...K,' I backed off, 'I'm going to read in bed, do you want anything before I go?' I'd like to believe that what he said was, 'No thank you, darling, thanks for enquiring, you go and have a bit of a lie-down, you deserve it' but I don't think it was. I went for that 'bit of a lie-down' anyway.

At two o'clock in the morning his cold feet woke me up. But at least it was cold feet and a tired smile. I went back to sleep knowing that tomorrow morning it would be safe to ask him about it and not get the wretched contraption thrown at me for my curiosity.

Geoff had been 'telling' me about it since we had got up. When Tweedledum and Tweedledee showed up with the new part for the hob, I was so surprised that they had actually come back, and so thankful that they had provided me with a reason to shut Geoff up for a bit, that I offered to make bacon sarnies for everyone. It only occurred to me after they had all gone to the engine room to make hissing noises at the new inverter that I couldn't actually cook anything until they fixed the bloody hob. Oh well, another trip to Gongoozler's it was then.

Two hours later, the hob was back in place, we were minus an actually rather reasonable sum of money; Tweedledee and Tweedledum, full of bacon and tea, had bumbled off to their next job. It finally occurred to us that we had no excuses left, we had to go.

We chatted for a couple of minutes over *another* cup of tea, both trying half-heartedly to find reasons to stay, but both of us were aware of what was really going on.

'Are you sure you know how to get there?' I made a last-ditch attempt to bury Geoff once more in his waterways maps. It was no good; he knew me too well.

'Come on,' he said, 'it's only one o'clock. We've said thanks to the marina, they know we'll pick up the cars in a couple of weeks, Sam is expected at school in 13 days' time, the hob's fixed, we HAVE to go. Are you ready?'

'No,' I said, beginning to well up, a huge lump forming in my throat, 'I don't want to go, I want my house back. This was fun for a week, but it's still not real. I want my life back, I've changed my mind.'

Geoff gave me a huge hug, and then stuck his tongue in my ear, which he knows is guaranteed to make me scream. He stepped back and looked at me, all pathetic, wet and snivelling, obviously searching for something supportive to say. There wasn't anything, and he knew it.

'Forward,' he said, and then laughed, 'but only at four miles an hour, eh?'

With only a small struggle, we extricated Sam from his 'nest' for the grand departure; pulling expertly away from the bank we started up the same route that we had taken on our training day with Dave, which was nice because it all seemed familiar. The only problem with familiar is that that which terrified you yesterday *with* support is going to overwhelm you today without.

We approached the first lock slowly and with a certain amount of trepidation, but the training kicked in and absolutely nothing went wrong; we entered as someone was coming out and all was well. We planned to do the six locks up and then tackle the Braunston Tunnel which had frightened the life out of me on the training, then on to just past the Leicester arm to where Geoff planned to stop for the night.

From the marina to the first lock I had given myself a severe talking-to. I was fully aware that I wasn't really 'living in the moment' and that all my moping about life, the universe and everything was beginning to not only wear my family down but I was getting bored with it as well. There is only so long that you can wallow in misery and self-pity before people stop being sympathetic and start getting fed up with it.

Helen, as usual, had been my voice of unsympathetic support.

'Oh for God's sake, stop blithering,' she had finally snapped, during one of my hour-long 'I need support' phone calls. 'Most people would give their eye teeth for an opportunity like this – people dream of doing this sort of thing – and there's you wandering about with a face like a slapped bum and moaning on about how bad everything is.' She hesitated for a moment, then carried on in a more thoughtful tone, 'Mind you, I can see why you are upset, the sun is shining, you have no work to worry about, you're off on a weird experience, you have money, you're warm and safe and fed, you have no responsibilities and you only answer to yourself, yep, I can see why you are so fed up, it must be terrible to be you – oh poor you!'

I'd put the phone down on her.

Wandering along, chatting to various people at the locks and watching Geoff bring Happy toward me, I finally understood what she had been talking about. It wasn't bad at all, actually, and as we approached the last lock I found myself sporting a huge grin and was back in my usual frame of mind. The top lock was open and all Geoff had to do was pull Happy into place and we could head toward the tunnel and beyond that into unknown territory. I was almost excited.

As we approached the lock gate, a scruffy narrow boat with a huge generator perched precariously on the back pulled into the top moorings. A couple of teenage lads jumped off, one began to swing the lower gates shut and the other positioned himself at the winch and as the gates swung to a close began to fill the lock pound with water.

Dave had impressed upon us that this was a cardinal sin. To bring a lock up empty, especially when a 30-second wait would have had us positioned inside, wastes a huge amount of water and is just plain rude and selfish. So I was filled with righteous ire as I reached the top step and encountered what can only be described as a 'character'.

He lounged on the back of his boat picking his teeth with a grime-stained digit, occasionally adding whatever he found in there to the interesting multi-coloured array of food debris that was splattered down his grubby vest.

As I came toward him, he missed his vest and wiped his

finger down a hairy stomach that looked as though it was trying to wriggle away from him through a vast gap between unhygienic vest and ageing grey trousers.

'That yours?' He indicated Happy with a wave of the spit-covered digit. I wasn't sure what to say; if I said yes, he might apologise for being in so much of a rush, then I would have to make polite conversation and quite frankly I wanted nothing more than to be as far away from him and his drippy digit as possible. I tried to nod noncommittally, '... Well you want to tell your bloke to pull his f**king finger out, if he went any f**king slower he'd f**king stop.' He stuck his finger into his mouth again.

That was it, I'd had it; he became the focus of all my troubles and woes over the last three months. I am not good with confrontations, in fact I am a complete coward, but I now understand what is meant by a red haze. I was completely and utterly furious, had lost the plot, and was totally enraged.

'I'm sorry,' I snarled at him, 'were you in a hurry? I can see why you have to make up seconds in locks; this thing looks like it would sink at a moment's notice.'

OK, definitely not the most cutting rejoinder in the world, but for me it was nothing short of amazing. I detest raised voices and will pretty much do anything I can to avoid any sort of argument or row. Mr Blobby started to rise from his seat and I suddenly thought, 'Oh dear, now I'm in trouble' – to this day, I'm really not sure which bit of my brain short-circuited at that point. One part screamed at me, 'Run! Apologise! Duck! Scream!' and then shut itself whimpering in a darkened corner, as I glared at the guy and took a step forward.

Incredibly (and probably luckily) he looked around at our growing audience, then sat back down and shouted at me, 'You just f**kin' tell 'im, ya silly cow.'

Emboldened (and surprised) by my earlier success, I sneered at him, 'I'm not telling him anything, you grubby moron. You want him told, you tell him yourself.' Wow tuff grrrl! And, with that, I swung on my heel and headed back down the steps to where Geoff was bringing Happy into the lower mooring. I explained what had happened as I helped him tie her up and then we sat on the top of the boat grinning at Mr Blobby as he came past. He stuck two fingers up at us and we stuck up one each, so that was fair.

As he disappeared into the next lock, we both fell over on the top of Happy, giggling like naughty schoolchildren caught making rude gestures at a teacher.

As we finally entered the last lock, a group of people that had been enjoying the sunny afternoon's entertainment stepped exaggeratedly out of my way as I walked past. One young man apologised for Mr Blobby; I, however, was magnanimous in my victory, and just smiled, saying, 'Well, you just get people like that, don't you.'

A new me! Bold and fearless, tough and feisty, ready to face anything. Geoff gave me a hug and went to make tea. I was still grinning as we rounded the next corner and the Braunston Tunnel came into view.

With Dave at my side the tunnel was merely a curiosity, even if it was a very scary curiosity. You could actually enjoy being scared while you concentrated on what you were doing, knowing that if you messed up there was someone there that could get you out of any trouble.

I had forgotten how difficult it was to get a 70-foot boat down a narrow, bendy tunnel in total blackness. Geoff, knowing that the tunnel was coming up had turned all the internal lights on to give a little more illumination. Our tunnel light was pathetic and I cursed it soundly as we disappeared into the oncoming black hole.

Tunnels are strange, dark, damp, drippy places, where all sounds are exaggerated. In the darkness your sight plays strange tricks on you. Halfway through, when the little keyhole of light through which we had entered had disappeared and the one we were aiming for had yet to make an appearance, I began to feel there was something behind me and kept turning round, staring into the black water foaming from the prop just behind my heels, or staring up into the darkness, convinced that something was running upside down across the dribbling roof.

At certain intervals there were large square holes in the roof that let in light and air. I looked forward to the first one, but thereafter dreaded the wretched things. You could see it in front of the boat, dust particles and midges dancing in the beam of light; as Happy continued her slow and stately progress, the square of light would move over her roof, like a search light, toward me.

Dave had warned us not to look at the light, as it would take away any night vision that you had built up, but this is almost impossible to do, so you look up, then, for about a minute after, you are completely blind. In the time it takes you to regain your night-sight the noises and little hallucinations become more intense. Moving away from the vents, the pressure in the tunnel increases, which affects your hearing. So partially blind and with the only noise your own heartbeat, your brain tries to make the other senses compensate. At one point I was positive something had stroked the back of my leg.

Finally, after what seemed like hours, the keyhole of escape could be seen in the distance, and that was where it stayed ... in the distance. By the time we finally got back into daylight, tuff grrrl had swaggered off to wreak havoc elsewhere and whimpering ninny was firmly back in control.

At the end of the tunnel, the canal was beautiful, overhanging trees swayed gently in a warm breeze shattering the sunlight and creating moving patterns on the water. It was very quiet after the hustle and bustle of Braunston. Geoff had decided that we would moor at the water point which was situated at the top of a seven-lock drop and all too soon the moorings appeared with another couple of boats already in residence.

We brought Happy alongside without too much of a bump and got chatting to the holiday boaters who were already filling their water tank. After my altercation with Mr Blobby, I found myself worried and a little wary of these folk, especially as whimpering ninny was still firmly at the reins, but I needn't have worried. It seemed as though fate had decided it was a day to experience extremes of character and these folk were as nice as Mr Blobby was foul.

After chatting to them for a while, we found out they were youth workers piloting two boats (one of which they had lost) filled to the brim with inner-city teenage boys 'experiencing the countryside'. We could hear lots of screams and thumps from the inside of their boat and, noticing our questioning glances, the youth workers informed us that the lads were getting ready to go to dinner at the pub over the lock for a last evening of revelry before they returned home. They always went to this pub as they had brought kids here for quite a few years and the landlord could 'cope'. It occurred to me at that point that there are two sides to every coin; to allow inner-city teenage boys to experience the countryside, the countryside has to experience inner-city teenage boys and I'm still not convinced the experience is an equal one.

All dressed up and ready for a 'relaxing' evening, the boys boiled out of the boat and hung about looking menacing. Sam chose this point to take an evening stroll as well; it took him all of two minutes to find a soul-mate in the shape of an 18-year-old lad called Jes with more tattoos and piercings than I have ever seen on one person before. Watching them closely, there was a sharp intake of breath from both Geoff and myself when Sam happily poked Jes in a lip piercing, but there was no explosion and after that they spent a happy half hour discussing each piercing and tattoo in depth:

'How much did that one hurt? Does it go right through?'

The youth workers, after watching them both for a while,

smiled and explained that Jes had a little brother who he had been missing, so he was probably enjoying himself, and we could see that Sam certainly was. The pile of clothing and the sounds of pained awe from Sam grew as Jes unveiled more and more of his coloured or pierced flesh. Jes was down to his shorts, when, laughing at something Sam had said to him, he looked up and caught my eye. I raised my eyebrows at him. He blushed and, looking down at himself, called a halt to the proceedings; I felt he had more to show, but had decided to keep it all under wraps for my sake.

I was very grateful to him as I was unsure I could have coped with the subsequent questions from Sam who was obviously in complete awe and had found a hero. I listened to him cataloguing Jes's decorations: 'I'm going to have one of those, and one of those, and one of those ...'

It was at this point we discovered the first of our 'forgotten items'. Trying to fill Happy's tank with our hose, we found that we were missing a specific nozzle that would attach our hose to the tap. Luckily the youth workers came to our rescue and lent us theirs.

Since we had managed to reach the mooring much faster than expected, we decided to press on. As we waved goodbye and headed toward the top lock, their lost boat turned up with the occupants in fine form, waving, grinning and shouting loudly; ecstatic that they had caught up with the other part of their little band, but even in these high spirits they were quite happy to stand around and help us with our first lock.

Watching the harassed youth workers rushing about, trying to stop the high-spirited lads from pushing each other into the canal, it struck me that it was an unlikely crowd to restore my faith in human nature after the earlier confrontation; but restore it they had. Maybe if there had been people like these long-suffering and ever-hopeful youth workers in Mr Blobby's past, his current personality might never have existed at all.

At the bottom of the flight of locks, a cold wind had picked up and it had started to rain. We found the first place into which we could drive a mooring stake and there we stayed, snug in our warm boat, listening to the wind, rain and the occasional grumble of thunder.

Mooring up on a whim had seemed very romantic at the time and it was only when we poked our heads out of the boat first thing the next morning that we found that we had moored about 50 yards away from a bend in the M1. Sticking our heads out of the boat, we were buffeted by the roar of the traffic and deduced that it may not have been thunder at all. But the previous night's weather, real or motorised, was completely forgotten as we settled down to make a full cooked breakfast only to discover that we had forgotten to bring a can opener.

Chapter Nine
A Can Opener – a Can Opener –
My Kingdom for a ...

SEPTEMBER 10 DAWNED BRIGHT and blue, filled with the promise of a completely lock-free day. However, the sunshine lasted for exactly 20 minutes before the rain, feeling it hadn't quite expressed itself adequately the night before, decided to return for an encore. Geoff clattered off down the boat to wade through our boxes in search of waterproof clothing, and I approached the diesel hob with some trepidation. Half an hour later, life on board Happy was ... not.

Geoff had worked out that we had carefully packed all the waterproof clothing in a box, marked it up with fluorescent ink and then just as carefully failed to read it and had stuffed it into storage with, no doubt, other carefully marked-up boxes containing things we needed; the can opener had probably climbed in by itself just to irritate me. I had had a futile 30 minutes trying to get our newly 'fixed' hob to light, then stay alight, and then stop howling, and I had also cut myself trying to get into a can of cheap beans with a chisel and hammer.

'What's going on?' Geoff yelled at me over the screaming of the hob. Biting down another curse, I stopped hopping around the kitchen in pain and waved my bleeding hand at him in a complete snit.

'This stupid cooker won't light and then when it finally does light, it just makes this horrible noise. I thought those two idiots had fixed it – what the hell's the matter with it?'

'I don't know,' Geoff yelled back over the banshee-like howling, 'I'm not a *cooker* engineer.' The howling reached new heights and I took my typical line with technology and started thumping it with a wooden spoon. Geoff reached past me and just turned it off, then wrestled the spoon out of my grasp and held it out of reach. A diesel hob does not turn off quickly due to the glow plug; it should just gently cool down and then turn itself off completely. This one just screamed until it had no more energy and then whimpered out into oblivion.

As the noise dwindled away, Geoff and I stood, alternately staring at the hob and glaring at each other. Sam wandered into the kitchen with a pile of Lego.

'I'm hungry,' he announced.

'Tough,' both Geoff and I snapped. Sam, not at all sure why he was being shouted at, looked up from whatever fantastic monster he had been building, took one look at my blood-covered face (I had used my cut hand to push my hair out of my eyes while shouting at Geoff), burst into tears and rushed off down the boat. Geoff hurried after him to apologise and assure him it wasn't his fault and I went into the bathroom to find a mirror and remove the incredible amount of horror-film-type gore that had plastered itself to my forehead; we had muesli for breakfast.

About an hour later, the rain had abated enough for Geoff to don a normal coat and head us off toward Bugbrooke. We took turns at the tiller for about an hour each while the other either tried to unpack some more boxes, or blackmail Sam to come out of the half-emptied box.

As it was lock-free, the morning passed with very little of note. The countryside would have been pretty if it hadn't been sulking under grey skies and moisture-laden air. The weather couldn't make up its mind so it stayed in limbo – one of those classic English days that just sits there and, imitating a lot of people, irritates you with its indecision and grey apathy.

At about one o'clock we pulled into Bugbrooke. Geoff had noted from his map that about a mile away, in the village itself, was a small shop where we should be able to replenish our dwindling stock of fresh food and, we hoped, obtain a can opener, thus enabling access to our huge stock of canned goods which weren't dwindling at all. Now that I was terrified of losing a limb and had condemned the hob, we were really down to microwave meals which was far from ideal.

The walk from the canal into the village was pleasant and refreshing. Sam, denied a steady downpour in which to get wet, made up for it by leaping gleefully from puddle to puddle.

The village shop was quaint, pretty and utterly devoid of anything remotely resembling real food, so settling on sausage rolls for lunch we spent a fruitless 15 minutes searching through their freezer for microwave meals that at least paid lip service to nutrition. We failed, and began a new search for 'just possibly edible'. Carrying our basket of fake food and chemicals, we wandered dispiritedly up to the counter.

'Do you have a can opener?' Geoff asked. The girl behind the counter glanced up and waved vaguely to the far right corner.

'Hmm, over there,' she muttered.

'We found the place where they should be but there was just an empty space,' Geoff explained.

'Oh well, probably not then,' she started ringing up our goods.

'Do you think you might have one out the back?' I prompted.

'What? Oh no, we won't,' she went back to her till.

'Do you know where we might get one?' I asked, through rapidly gritting teeth.

'No,' she said, without looking up.

'So there's no one here that knows where we can get a

can opener?'

'No.'

I opened my mouth to say more but Geoff trod on my foot. Heaving a sigh that I hoped spoke volumes about poor customer service, I gave up and wandered back down the aisle to look for more plasters.

Being unsure of the state of Happy's water tank, we had elected to drink bottled water and were going through it at an alarming rate. Five litres lasted us about two days; admittedly we were also cooking with it, cleaning our teeth with it and making vast amounts of tea and coffee. We had purchased the shop's entire stock of bottled water; unfortunately this meant that Geoff had to carry it, as, when I tried to lift the rucksack we'd packed the ten bottles into, I failed. Geoff, of course, lifted it with ease *and* took two of the bags of shopping. I still think he had it easy, I had one bag of shopping and Sam, who, like the little yellow bird from the Peanuts cartoon, finds it impossible to move in a straight line. It doesn't matter in which direction you walk, he is always a quarter-step in front of you, causing you to side-step or stop suddenly as he bends over to look at something interesting on the ground. I honestly don't know how he does it.

After about a quarter of a mile of this strange, slow, whirling progression of Sam walking and Geoff and I dancing around behind him while trying desperately not to step on him, Geoff decided that the water was getting a bit heavy and I agreed to meet him on the boat, as soon as Sam finally decided to walk in a straight line.

It took about half an hour, but with his fifteen steps to my one I decided that he was getting a fair amount of exercise and seemed content, so, even if he was soaked up to the thighs and filling his pockets with unidentifiable objects, I didn't really mind. We could see Happy in the distance when the weather finally made up its mind what to do for the day and by the time we arrived back at the boat we were drenched from head to foot.

The rain eased off again by about two o'clock and after a tasteless, slightly plastic lunch we headed toward Gayton Junction. We had planned to stop there and fill Happy with diesel and water; we also needed to purchase the environment agency key and windlass that were required for the next leg of the journey. I was looking forward to an early mooring and a long hot shower.

As we neared the turn into the Northampton branch of the Grand Union Canal, I re-learnt the main lessons from our training; a large narrow boat takes time to get up to a decent speed and then takes three times as long to slow down; and a large narrow boat cannot be leaned at speed around a sharp curve like a motorbike.

The turn into the Northampton Branch is a good, sharp 90-degree turn and I was going way, way too fast to make it, especially as, by the time I worked out that we actually needed to turn, Happy's nose was just past the nearside bank.

There is a lovely plaque that I really must buy at some point that sums up my whole attitude to stressful situations. It sagely states: 'When in trouble, or in doubt, run in circles, scream and shout!' I realised that I was supposed to turn left and, without changing the engine speed at all, just threw the tiller far right. The effect of this ...? Well, not much really, the bow began a slow turn toward the left, so now we were travelling at speed and heading toward a concrete wall on the far side of the turn.

Panic! Slam poor Happy into reverse. Effect? Nothing! At the speed we were travelling it would have taken at least twice our length to slow down.

Panic more! Look quickly at the tiller, hard over, can't do anything there; check accelerator, hard in reverse; engine screaming, can't do anything there.

PANIC! Scream at Geoff through the engine room and just watch the wall rapidly come toward us. BANG!!!

Luckily for the family, the boat and the wall, we hit at a slight angle. I shudder to think what would have happened if I had hit it nose on. The wall wouldn't have given way; Happy is well buffered with a thick rope fender that covers the thick steel bow, so the only things that would have moved would have been us. Even with the bump we took, I was thrown forward into the engine room and both Sam and Geoff were knocked off their feet.

It was very lucky that they had been standing in the bow cabin so had landed in Sam's 'nest', a little shaken but not broken in any way. Unfortunately the same couldn't be said for a fair amount of our poor crockery. Happy's nose rebounded off the wall and out into mid-stream bringing the mid section of the boat into contact with the corner of the wall.

BANG! I was still in the engine room, trying to get back to the tiller, so was thrown sideways into the still screaming engine. I found out later that Sam and Geoff hadn't actually managed to regain their feet before the second impact so they were fine. We did, however, lose the last of the crockery that had been gamely hanging onto the shelves after the first impact.

This last collision straightened Happy back up and also had the secondary effect of slowing her right down, so, bruised, battered and more than a little shaken I managed to climb out of the engine room and take control once more. Geoff staggered out on to the back and asked if I was all right. I showed him the scrapes and replied that I would mend.

He then gave me a ten-minute lecture on the dangers of being a speed freak. How embarrassing, told off for speeding in a narrow boat, I could hardly use it as a getaway vehicle. I could just see the headlines: 'Speed demon in slow-speed chase down the Grand Union Canal'. The police would have to be chasing us in pedalos. Deciding that discretion was the better part of valour at this point, I went to clear up the debris, but before disappearing I completed a quick head count of smirking spectators – about 30, yep, pretty much what I expected.

We finally reached Gayton Marina at four-thirty and filled up both water and diesel tanks. We had a huge diesel tank and £130 later were still filling up. Geoff left me with the diesel pump while he went to the office to sort out the key and windlass.

'Are you sure you can cope?' he asked, and the look that he gave me before he walked away left me with absolutely no doubt that he felt it was unlikely I could do even this simple job without messing it up. He had already spent a good five minutes inspecting our impact points for damage and there had been a fair amount of head-shaking and tutting over the scrapes and the (very slight) dent he had found.

The plan was to moor up for the night just past Gayton. A good night's sleep meant that we would be bright and fresh, ready to face the 14 locks of the Rothersthorpe flight early in the morning.

As we turned toward the flight, it was obvious that the Northampton branch was nowhere near as heavily trafficked as our recent travels. The banks were rough and uneven and the tall river plants grew a fair way out into the main flow of water. Moving at a snail's pace we desperately looked for a suitable mooring, but, being used to man-made wharfs and tow paths, nothing looked right. We were still searching when we hit the top lock of the flight at 5.20 p.m.

'What the hell do we do now?' I shouted at Geoff over the rising wind.

'I don't know, did you see anything that even looked vaguely like a mooring?' he shouted back.

'No, and even if there was I'm not sure we could turn her here.' I looked around. 'And we sure as hell can't go backwards.'

Geoff groaned. 'We're going to have to go down – and as fast as possible.'

Fourteen locks, all against us, oh what joy and rapture. I tried to make the best of it by thinking that at least we wouldn't have to face this tomorrow morning and could probably have a lie-in.

The threatening rain hit us full force at about lock ten. We had been doing three locks each, running ahead to set the next lock while the previous one was emptying. The wind picked up further and Happy was blown about like a paper boat in a puddle.

I have always felt that this is the one thing that is really unfair about narrow boats, 23 tonnes of steel should be able to withstand a little side wind but, the reality is, it can't. Even a gentle wind can blow you about, and, of course, the more wet and exhausted we became, the more difficult she was to control.

In hindsight (always a wonderful thing) we should have said damn the consequences and just spent the night at one of the bigger stretches between the locks; yes, there are big signs telling you that this is absolutely forbidden but in our exhausted state it was more by luck than judgement that we didn't catch the rudder on a lock shelf and get hung up. Big locks in the dark, battling against high winds and heavy rain, are just hideously dangerous. Luckily we didn't know any of that, so like a bumblebee in flight, we carried on regardless.

We pulled out of the last lock at about ten o'clock soaked, frozen, windblown, exhausted, hungry and totally miserable. We were also wallowing in a fair amount of guilt. Poor Sam hadn't had a proper meal. We had rushed down at various points in the descent to reassure him that all was well and to give him some snacks, but he had essentially been on his own for four and a half hours.

When we finally moored up, we were so tired that we just threw her into the side and Geoff used the gangplank to get ashore to set the mooring pins. He returned, sodden and exhausted, to find me, also still dripping, staring down at Sam who had fallen asleep in his 'nest', all by himself, still unfed. The guilt at being a bad, irresponsible and uncaring parent was almost crippling.

I left Sam asleep in his 'nest' while I dried off and put on my warm, fluffy dressing gown, then, picking him up, I carried him to his bedroom while Geoff made the long-awaited cup of tea. Sam, feeling himself being moved, opened his eyes and smiled, snuggling down into my shoulder. While I was putting him into bed, he held his arms out for a big cuddle. Lying down beside him to acquiesce to his unspoken request is the last thing I remember that night.

Next morning I was awoken by a fully refreshed and very hungry six-year-old climbing over me. He was trying very hard not to wake me up (this involved his foot in my face and smothered giggles, *very* loud smothered giggles). Nursing my face, I lay, confused, in Sam's bed waiting for feeling to return in the shoulder that he had been using as a pillow.

As you get older, confusion on waking becomes commonplace and an accepted part of the morning routine, but, this particular morning, I was completely adrift from reality. Waking up in pain in a strange room should have been enough to confound me, but when I sat up and looked blearily out of the window, I couldn't work out why the sky wasn't where it should be and the world had turned green.

As a result of our mad rush to moor up somewhere, *anywhere*, the previous night, we had managed to get Happy in amongst a huge reed bed – the plants were higher than the boat. Sam summed it up, saying he felt like he had been made very small.

There was a definite loitering going on that morning. We created the world's biggest breakfast of cereal, cold meats, fruit, cheese and naughty cake, very continental. Sam was very enthusiastic about having cake for breakfast, even if we did have to eat from the plastic lids of large storage boxes due to the lack of crockery. We then sat about, drinking vast amounts of tea out of a couple of old mugs that were discovered shoved into the cupboard beneath the sink, and listening to Sam chattering on about nothing in particular.

Studying the map, we decided that as the locks were now nicely spaced apart, one of us could stay with Sam, to make up for the previous day. We were also due to stop at a big supermarket in Northampton, where at last we could buy a wretched can opener, get some more water and other bits and pieces; I ruefully added crockery to the bottom of the shopping list.

So with the sun shining and the horrors of the previous night now a mere memory, we backed Happy out of the reed bed and sauntered on towards the promise of gore-free baked beans.

Chapter Ten
I Think I'm Having a Heart Attack!

SADLY, THE CLOSER WE drew to Northampton, the less salubrious our surroundings became. The dirty, overgrown canal hid, embarrassed, under huge broken lumps of floating polystyrene, so reminiscent of dirty, pitted chunks of ice that Geoff started to hum the theme from *Titanic*. The banks were overgrown, covered in litter, and we moved between grubby, off-white buildings that faced away from the canal in a huddle of barbed wire and security guards.

Cautiously feeling our way through the congested water, I held the tiller lightly, waiting for the tell-tale jerk that would signal something was wrapped around the prop, but amazingly enough it never came. Maybe the fates had decided that we had paid for our passage through this litter-choked potential minefield by suffering the trauma from the night before. So, making slow but surprisingly unimpeded progress, we transferred from the Grand Union Canal to the River Nene and moored at lunch time without incident at the Northampton City Quay.

After lunch and a huge shopping trip to the local supermarket, we were on our way again. I had spent a happy hour packing away all the new plates and cups and unpacking our exciting new acquisitions; a slow cooker, a three-tier steamer and a baby George grilling thingy. I had deliberately placed them on top of the hob.

'I won't have to listen to you for a while.' Then, realising that I had finally started talking aloud to inanimate objects, I went and checked on Sam.

Sam had recently discovered the delights of the 'Beano'. He was so engrossed, I had to poke him before he finally answered my questions (talking to the hob had given me just as much response), his eyes sliding back to the colourful characters on the page mid-conversation. I gave up and went back to the kitchen.

After I had prepared a casserole for dinner, smiling at the simple delight of being able to use real vegetables, I took Geoff a cup of tea.

'How can it be,' I sat on the deliciously warm roof with my cup of tea and pondered to my slightly nauseated husband – he had slipped a surreptitious pack of five jam doughnuts into the shopping and had eaten them all over the last hour – 'that a supermarket that size has no bloody can openers?'

I was still enjoying the sunshine on the roof when Geoff pointed out that the fourth lock of the day was approaching. We had become proficient at locks: pull the boat in, close the gates, make sure all is secure and that you are far enough away from the sill at the rear and then start letting the water out or in depending on whether you are going up or downhill. But this was the first time we had come across a 'guillotine' lock.

When training, Dave had mentioned them as being something to look out for, because instead of nice, gentle winding handles, you have to insert a key in a lock, turn it, then wait while a huge metal door rises automatically and lets the water out from beneath you.

We pulled in at the mooring, as Geoff wanted to study the lock mechanism before we brought our monster into the pound. When he was satisfied that he knew how it worked, he signalled me to bring Happy round the corner and into the enclosure on my own. OK, not a problem. It should have been a simple manoeuvre – and would have been – if I had actually elected to turn left into the lock, but instead, and to this day I don't know why, I sailed merrily past and turned right.

As soon as I was past the lock I figured out what I had done and put Happy into reverse to slow her down. As usual, she completely ignored me and carried on, preferring, instead, to take up a central position on what appeared to be a huge lake.

There was open water all around me and a wind had sprung up from nowhere, pushing me further away from the bank. I promptly went into complete panic and did every stupid thing I could think of; first, I put the engine into neutral; now, without propulsion of any kind, the wind had free rein to do what it liked; I dithered, felt sick, put the engine into forward, then changed my mind and put her into reverse, let go of the tiller and stared horrified back toward the rapidly disappearing lock.

Totally convinced that we were going to capsize at any moment I finally pulled myself together enough to put Happy into forward and begin the necessary 180-degree turn. It is awe inspiring to find out, first hand, just how much space is needed for a 70-foot boat to turn half circle.

Eventually, after what seemed an hour but was probably about three minutes, she was pointing the right way again, and I managed to relax. I was quite proud of not killing either myself or Sam and finally pulled into the lock. Geoff, still admiring the architecture of the lock, hadn't even noticed we were missing and was quite surprised when I appeared from an unexpected direction.

Still nervous and waiting for my heartbeat to settle, I positioned Happy carefully within the lock, threw a rope around a bollard and awaited the now expected, gentle pull forward as the water escaped from under the hull and lowered you into a dark wet hole giving you a good amount of time to study the slimy, weed-covered stonework while you waited for the forward gates to open. It's quite nice really, five minutes' peace and quiet to mull over the happenings in your day.

Not this time. Geoff stuck the key in the mechanism and, checking to make sure I was ready, turned it. The great metal door started to lift, pulling a huge amount of water from under the boat, Happy leapt forward as though she had been kicked in the butt and smacked her nose against the far door, her back end swinging around as a bubbling tide cascaded out from beneath us. Geoff took one look at what was going on and hit the emergency stop button. The lock door stopped and although water continued to pour down to the next level it soon settled and Happy stopped trying to climb the lock walls.

'Everything OK?' Geoff shouted down.

'Yes, sort of,' I answered through gritted teeth as I struggled to keep Happy's rear end under control. 'Bit fast that, isn't it?'

'Will you be all right if I open it again?' He put his hand on the key and made ready to turn it.

'Yes, I think so, I just wasn't expecting it to be so fast.' I looked at the huge door, held in stasis.

This time I was ready for it, Geoff turned the key and the water picked up pace. I found the easiest way to deal with the pull was to let Happy's nose rest against the door as it rose; with her big rope fender around the bow it wasn't going to do any damage to either the boat or the lock and it was obvious from long vertical smears on the lock door that others had done the same thing. Just as the lower edge of the lock gate cleared the water, I pulled her back and allowed her to float free. When the lock is empty and the door is at its highest point, the dripping lock door covers you in water and occasional small wriggly things as you pass beneath it ... Lovely.

We had six of these locks to face before the end of the day, three of them were key-operated and the others were manual. The manual locks consisted of a huge metal wheel that has to be turned by hand, which, by a series of counterweights, then lifts the huge door at the end. These locks, being slower to rise, weren't quite as ferocious as the electronic ones but I still got very wet as we exited. They also had the added advantage of giving Geoff an unscheduled upper torso workout. Taking pity on him after the first puffing, panting lock raise, we changed places with the intention of giving Geoff a rest but, as it took me three times as long to raise the door, Geoff decided that it was better to suffer but be quick.

That evening we were scheduled to stop at Billing Aquadome, but it was so crowded with screaming kids and holidaymakers we braved another lock, mooring up a little further on, beside a field full of curious horses. Compared with the previous night's fiasco, this evening was almost holiday-guide perfect. Dinner had been silently cooking all day thanks to the new slow cooker and was eaten and cleared away by six o'clock. We spent a pleasant evening on the bank playing silly ball games with Sam, and just generally relaxing. I called Amelia and Charlie and although I missed them I was too tired to really get upset about it. By ten o'clock we had all peacefully and soundly passed out.

Due to our pleasant and early night we were all up and about early the next morning, ready to face the ten locks that we were scheduled to tackle that day. Geoff, still a little sore from the three he had completed the previous day, was less than ecstatic about the coming day's exercise but a cup of tea or four and he was as ready to face them as he was likely to get.

The locks were about an hour apart, which is just enough time for the non-driving part of a couple to start a project and get really involved before they are dragged away by the pilot screaming 'LOCK!' down through the engine room.

At the fifth lock of the day, our progress was impeded by workmen from the Environment Agency completing some repairs, but, as it was around midday, we made them a cup of tea and settled down to a picnic lunch on the mooring.

About half an hour later, another narrow boat pulled in

behind us and the owner, an older gent who strongly resembled Kris Kristofferson in his *Blade* persona, wandered over to us, wondering what the delay was. He checked out the repairs in the lock and, agreeing that none of us were going anywhere for the next half hour or so, we fell to discussing our separate journeys, taking time to moan about the locks and the 'tourists'. On hearing that we had moored at the bottom of the Rothersthorpe flight he perked up a little.

'Did you hear anything "funny" while you were moored up there?' he asked, raising his eyebrows and leaning forward slightly.

'No, didn't hear a thing,' Geoff shook his head. 'Mind you, we were so tired, there could have been a brass band playing on the roof and we wouldn't have noticed. What was there to hear?'

'Well,' he leaned forward and looked around conspiratorially, 'they say that there are feral children in the woods there, and they'll throw rocks until you give them food.'

'Sounds like normal teenagers to me,' I laughed around a pasty.

'Ah, but they belong to a troop of travelling dwarves who escaped from a circus just after World War II, and it's said they can be heard singing old war songs at dusk just around that area.' He sat back smiling and nodded in the self-satisfied way of one who has imparted great knowledge.

'You're having us on,' I laughed. 'I know we're new to this, but I'm not falling for that.'

He looked hurt, 'No, no, it's true, if you read some of the travel pamphlets, you'll see it listed as a local myth.'

There wasn't much we could say to that, so Geoff just muttered, 'No, didn't hear a thing.' Luckily, at that point the workmen opened the lock again and we all began finishing cups of tea and clearing up. The older man gave us a cheery wave and went back to his boat, whistling 'We'll Meet

Again' as he walked.

Geoff and I just looked at each other.

'Do you think ...?' I paused and looked back toward the other boat.

'No!' Geoff said emphatically. 'I don't.'

Through the repaired lock, we headed on toward Wellingborough. The next lock 'Wollaston' was against us, forcing us to moor up while it was filled. As the water rose, I could see something white bobbing around in amongst the clutter of plant life and twigs that always seem to gather within the pound. Eventually I could make out a very young swan, still mostly grey. It had obviously been stuck there for a while and the poor thing was completely exhausted.

As we opened the gates, it swam out of the lock and, staggering up the bank, keeled over amongst the reeds. Forgetting for a moment how big and scary these things are, I rushed over to it and put a hand out to help it (to this day I have no idea what I expected to do if I had caught it). It leapt to its feet, flapping and hissing, then bit me. This sudden burst of energy convinced me it was fine and probably just needed to rest, so nursing my serrated hand, I backed away from the still hissing monstrosity and returned to the boat. As we pulled into the lock I looked back and was comforted to note that it had settled back down in the reeds and appeared to be already asleep; in my mind, its contented snores kept time with my throbbing hand.

Wellingborough Embankment was the next mooring with shopping opportunities. Geoff needed various bits and bobs: more screws, a hose attachment and some electronic bits that would enable us to connect our stereo into the speakers that were already embedded into the ceiling, and although we were all due a visit to the local supermarket upon his return, he had strict instructions that if he saw a can opener he was to buy it immediately.

While he was gone, Sam and I spent a happy hour in the park. I was very glad that most children were back at school;

I don't think 40-year-old women are supposed to enjoy themselves quite so much on a children's slide.

The visit to the supermarket was more than a little fraught. Sam had decided that he hadn't finished playing in the park and strenuously objected to being dragged away to go shopping; we finally had to bribe him with the promise of new comics.

As we were heading out through the checkout, I remembered the can opener and was about to dash off in search of one when Geoff nudged me and pointed surreptitiously to the lady who was working on our till.

'That's why we didn't hear any singing,' he snickered. 'They are all now integrated back into society.'

I was confused for a moment and then looked at the smiling lady on the till. She was rather vertically challenged, and, laughing, I gently slapped him for being rude. As we got out of the supermarket, the jokes about singing World War II escapees became more and more unlikely and it was only when we had made our way, giggling, back to the boat and were underway again, that I settled down to unpack the shopping. Oh bloody hell, with all his messing about I had completely forgotten to go back for the wretched can opener.

As we headed towards our last two locks of the day, Sam came and helped me to put the food away. This involved him opening a lot of packets and eating a little of whatever he fancied; he ended up scurrying off with a handful of goodies and leaving me to not only put the food away but to clean up his crumbs as well.

About half an hour later he came back into the kitchen complaining that his face hurt. Looking at him closely I could see that he was covered in little pin-prick blisters that were rapidly turning an interesting shade of puce. This got worse as the day progressed so that by the time we reached the Ditchford Radial Lock we were quite worried about him and didn't really have the inclination to marvel as much as we should have at this fantastic piece of Heath Robinson-like engineering with its huge curved gate that, when lifted, curved over the boat. It still dripped horribly, and covered us all in mud and weed, so quite frankly I wasn't that impressed.

Reaching our destination – the moorings at Rushden and Diamonds Football Club – Sam resembled a pink hamster and I rushed about trying to find the antihistamines. Luckily we had decided that an early start the next morning was not on the schedule. There was a Doc Marten's factory shop on the grounds of the football club that I particularly wanted to visit and it looked as though we would have to find a doctor as well. Sam slept badly that night and really looked quite unwell the next morning; still swollen and itching, he was understandably in a foul mood. Seeing the time moving on, I was just about to go and poke Geoff and berate him for being a lazy good-for-nothing, when a groan from the bedroom arrested my progress.

'Argh! Ooo! Ow!' I rushed down the boat and found Geoff holding his left arm and looking seriously worried.

'What's up?' I tried to pass him a cup of tea but he wouldn't take it and just kept holding his arm.

'I think I'm having a heart attack,' he muttered, grimacing.

Strange, in all other areas he looked fine; his colour was good, his lips were OK, and he wasn't sweating,

'Why do you think you're having a heart attack?' I asked, putting his tea on the shelf.

'I can't move this arm, my chest really hurts and so does my other arm.'

Hmmm, not at all sure about this. I've seen someone having a heart attack, and it didn't look like this. 'Where is the pain in your arms?' I asked.

'All over,' Geoff rubbed his arm.

I had a sudden epiphany.

'You don't think this is anything to do with the ten

manual guillotine locks that you did yesterday then?'

'Maybe,' Geoff grinned, 'but I don't get as much sympathy for just being out of shape as I do for a possible heart attack.'

I was as sympathetic as I could be – I slapped him and then took his tea away so that he had to come and get it.

We wandered down to the little town of Irthlingborough and dragged Sam in to see the pharmacist. She took one look at him and asked if he had any allergies. Unfortunately the answer was yes, lots. Starting with hideous hay fever, to maniacal behaviour if he so much as tasted aspartame or acesulfame, we kept him away from colours and additives and anything containing caffeine. It was only recently that supermarkets had started selling sweets with all natural colourings and flavourings which was excellent, as Sam would be a sad and deprived child without them.

Back on the boat I dosed him with the stronger antihistamine that the pharmacy had provided and covered him in calamine lotion. Going back through everything he had eaten the day before, I tried to trace the culprit. I finally tracked down offensive scotch eggs with a colorant in the breadcrumbs and immediately binned them. Sam was much happier knowing that it was just an allergy, even if it was a severe one. Having had these problems from birth, he took each new allergy philosophically. His first teacher was a little bemused that he could recognise the words 'aspartame' and 'acesulfame' but couldn't read 'dog' and 'cat', and now that he can read, he religiously checks every ingredient on any new food. At six years old, he knows what he can eat and what he can't have and is quite rabid about the whole thing.

I often have to smile, watching an adult's face as my son switches to an excellent imitation of his father's 'lecture voice' and tells people at length and in great detail of the damage they are doing to themselves by eating this muck and the damage they are attempting to do him by offering it to him. He hasn't quite accused anybody of nutritional child abuse yet, but I can see it may only be a matter of time.

So with him assured that all the itching would soon stop and sitting happily in his nest with a new Beano annual, he looked a strange little figure. He was so covered in calamine lotion that he resembled the victim of a drive-by custard pie fight, and was unusually content to have a hummus and salad pitta for lunch.

Chapter Eleven
I'm Really Sorry, I'm an Idiot

AS WE HIT THE first lock of the day, we discovered that we had caught up with another boat, a perfectly nice couple who invited us to double lock with them to save water. Their boat was so new and shiny it made poor Happy look like the 'wreck of the Hesperus', and they handled it perfectly.

The wind had picked up and, as usual, it made Happy frisky. I was having more than a little trouble bringing her into moor and getting her into the lock. Mr and Mrs Smile of course had no problems at all. Dave, from the training company, had told us that, if possible, you should always go through locks with another boat. What he hadn't specified was the etiquette. If there is another boat on the pre-lock mooring do you bring yours alongside? If you do, do you have to ask permission first? I decided to play it safe and elected to hold Happy in mid-stream while waiting for the lock to open.

To enter the lock you had to make a fairly sharp left-hand turn, so I positioned Happy with her bum by the far bank and her nose pointing toward the lock doors. She was having some problems with the wind and kept trying to edge sideways toward a weir that was roped off at the right-hand side of the lock. I was starting to get a little worried about this, when there was a gentle bump and she finally stayed in one place. 'Oh good,' I thought, we must have just run aground on the very back of the boat, so with her back on the bank – or so I thought – and her nose just resting gently on the far moorings all I had to do was put on the power and bring her backside around and we would enter the lock with stately grace.

The lock doors opened and John, in the other boat, gave me a big grin and pulled away from the mooring at my wave and entered the lock. 'OK, here we go,' I thought, and moved the throttle forward. Sure enough the prop churned the water at the back but Happy didn't move at all.

Hmm, not what I had hoped for – try again. Nothing ... what on earth was going on? We certainly weren't grounded because if I jumped up and down on the back Happy swayed gently in response. 'Oh well, try again.' Lots of foamy water and thrashing from the back. Forward movement? Not a bit. By this time Geoff, Sarah and John (still smiling) were waving me into the lock. I waved back at them and, putting Happy into neutral, got down on my hands and knees and peered over the back.

'Aha!' I could see what had happened. As I had bumped into the far bank the rudder had just managed to edge a tree root up and over itself; this root was now holding Happy as fast as a well-tied rope. I moved the tiller backward and forward and watched as the big lump of steel just slid along the underside of the root. OK, now there were shouts from the lock.

'Come on,' Geoff bellowed. 'What are you up to?'

I waved at him. 'Oh well, nothing for it but to break all the rules again,' I thought and looping one arm around the base of the tiller I held on fast, leaned out over the water, grabbed the root and heaved it back over the rudder, thinking all the time that if Geoff or Dave knew what I was doing, fishing around down by the prop with the engine still running, they would have forty fits. As Happy's stern came free she resumed her slow, inevitable swing toward the weir again. Leaping up to grab the throttle, I received a smart smack across the head from the forgotten tiller which was swinging about unattended and the blow nearly knocked me into the water. I pushed the tiller out of the way and jumped up, waving at Geoff who was now wandering toward me.

John and Sarah were deep in conversation, their smiles had thinned out, and I was pretty positive they were asking each other how long they were going to have to stick with these numpties.

As we exited the lock, I explained to Geoff what had happened and sure enough, got grouched at, but in the end he laughed and said,

'Oh well, you've still got all your fingers so you're OK.'

By the next lock, it had started to rain. The lock was against us once more and, being the second to the moorings, I again attempted to hold Happy in mid-stream. This time there was no weir but the wind was still fairly strong and, by the time the lock was filled and opened on our side, Happy was being held diagonally across the river. I could see John looking at me and frowning as he watched me put her first in reverse and then in forward to try and hold her in one place. Again the lock doors opened and he pulled forward, neatly and efficiently positioning their boat against the far side of the lock.

Waiting for him to enter, Happy had almost turned herself right round and was facing the opposite direction, so to enter the lock I now had to manoeuvre sharp right and she didn't want to play at all, but even with Happy sulking and the wind egging her on, I managed to get her nose somewhere in the vicinity of the lock doors. I only managed to get her fully into the lock by running our crappy old boat down the length of their beautiful shiny paintwork. I apologised profusely, blaming the wind, and luckily they were too nice to grouch very hard, but their big smiles had disappeared completely. I hadn't done very much damage, but just like the weather, I could see that John and Sarah's mood with us continued to deteriorate. Rapidly!

At the third lock I decided to steal the mooring and maybe, just maybe, I stood a chance of entering with some sort of grace. 'Ha, let's see how *he* fares, trying to hold his boat in mid-stream,' I chortled uncharitably to myself, although I had a sneaking suspicion that he would do it perfectly well. I was beginning to suspect that they had a very quiet bow thruster, which would explain why they were so efficient at manoeuvres.

I moored Happy up and then sighed as John just came alongside and handed me a rope. I stood there open-mouthed and just looked at it.

'Would you mind just tying that on one of your T studs,' his renewed smile evolved into a rather quizzical expression.

'Oh, right, um OK.' I took the rope and wrapped it around the nearest T stud, again forgetting to push the tiller out of the way and smacking myself over the shoulders as I stood up. By this time, we were pretty much out of conversation; within three locks, I had bashed into two walls, scraped his paintwork, turned the boat around and just generally looked like I didn't know what the hell I was doing. I had a mental image of Dave with his head in his hands, crying gently.

At the fourth lock, John and Sarah had a hurried conversation before she left the boat to set the lock with Geoff and, watching them agree on a plan of some kind, I turned to Geoff and moaned, 'I can't believe I've done this so badly, we look like a real couple of hicks.'

Geoff, who just laughs off embarrassment, looked surprised. 'What do you expect?' he said, 'I was talking to Sarah, they've had their boat for over a year and have been travelling all that time, although she did say they had stopped for a week at Christmas. Their boat is 15 foot shorter than ours with a bigger prop, a newer engine and they have a bow thruster (I knew it!) – of course theirs handles better than ours.'

'Humph, you know all that, I now know all that,' I grimaced, 'but I'm fairly sure they think I am the most incompetent boater in the whole of the east Midlands.'

Geoff just laughed and jumped off to help Sarah set the

lock; luckily this mooring was so large I was saved from any more embarrassing incidents and the necessity of conversation by being able to moor behind them. As the lock gates opened, John looked back and waved me forward. This one had another sharp right to enter the gates, and I had to first pull out around him and then swing the nose into the lock, hoping her backside would follow. It did but I misjudged the swing and our back end clouted his nose with a good solid *thwack* – oh dear.

This was definitely the final straw for John. Over the roar of the water, and when he could get my attention in between running Happy backwards and forwards to keep her back end away from the sill and her nose out of the gates, he informed me with a strained smile that this would be the last lock of the day for them. They had decided to moor up just a little further on and get an early stop for the day.

Really? What a surprise! Being fully aware of their motives, I agreed that this was indeed an excellent idea and expressed regret that we weren't able to do the same but, being on a tight schedule, we had another three locks to get through before we could stop for the night.

As the lock gates opened, John again motioned us to go ahead. I gave Geoff just enough time to step onto the boat before I had the throttle down hard, punctuating our get-away with lots of waves and shouting 'Good luck' etc. We were both heartily glad to be away from each other, though for very different reasons I am sure.

Lock number five of the day was a complete doddle. We moored up, Geoff opened the gates, I pulled her in as though she was on rails, she stayed rock steady as the water level changed and then pulled gracefully away on the other side: a textbook lock manoeuvre. I was beginning to think that our boat is possessed by an embarrassment spirit.

As I looked up at the underside of the A14, just outside Oundle, it struck me as odd to think that we had often travelled that road and each time had looked down at the river wondering where it went after it disappeared beneath the viaduct. This time we were looking up at the road, and we still didn't know where the river went; the only thing I knew for sure was that travelling above – on the A14 – we would have made our destination in around 40 minutes, travelling beneath it would take at least a week.

Being the type of person who does everything in a rush, I examined how I felt about this, expecting to find myself disgruntled that everything moved so slowly. It was quite an epiphany to realise that I didn't actually care one little bit. With Geoff driving, Sam and I sat on top of the boat and watched the A14 very slowly disappearing behind us into the distance. After 40 minutes we were still well in sight of the road. It was a very odd but strangely enjoyable feeling.

Just past Thrapston Lock we decided to moor for the night at the Nene Sailing Club moorings. We arrived at about five o'clock and had time to go for a nice long walk before tea. It was a beautiful evening; the wind had dropped to a whisper and, with no lights for miles around, the stars were incredible. We spent about an hour after tea just lying on the grass, once again trying to identify constellations, until Sam stated that looking up into the nothingness was making him feel sick. I fully understood the way he felt, the sky seemed infinite, and against that even a 70-foot narrow boat feels very, very small.

Chapter Twelve
Going Nowhere, Nowhere at All ... a Lot

ALL THE NEXT MORNING we travelled through the beautiful Titchmarsh Nature Reserve, around wide, sweeping bends and, once past Wadenhoe Lock, into the dappled silence of a couple of miles of woodland. Any stress, real or imagined, just drifted away in the sunshine and for the first time on this trip I could honestly say I was thoroughly enjoying myself.

The locks were far enough apart that they didn't really impose on my happiness; Sam amused himself by sitting on the top of the boat and screaming with excitement every time he spotted some odd wildlife. I never once saw what he was screaming at, as by the time I had turned around in response to his wild gesticulations his loud yells had frightened whatever it was away. After the fifth or sixth time that I had failed to spot the object of his excitement, he accused me of not paying attention and stamped off in a snit to point and scream to his father.

In our never-ending quest for a wretched can opener we had planned to stop in Oundle and go shopping, but finding no suitable mooring for our big beastie we just carried on. Fotheringhay was eight locks from our mooring of the previous night and we reached it at a very acceptable four o'clock. As there was no shop Geoff elected to ride to the next village on our ageing bicycle, however as we had taken it apart for ease of transportation, he had to spend an hour digging out the various parts and then putting it back in working order before he could even attempt the ride, he was so irritated by the time he found all the parts that he nearly didn't bother and it was only when I pointed out that we had no milk for his tea that he grudgingly mounted the rickety old thing and pedalled off in search of much-needed groceries.

As he came back through the doors about an hour later, I hardly raised an eyebrow.

'Can opener?'

'Nope.'

'OK.' I went back to reading my book.

Fotheringhay Bridge is on an interesting turn in the river. We had been warned to make sure we only went through where the signs indicated, as with our size boat we would need to keep well over to the left, which would enable a straight run through the largest left-hand arch.

Once again, I was going way too fast and although I had managed to keep so far left that I had partially redecorated the bridge with a fair swathe of paint from poor Happy's gunwales, the sharp turn to the right on exit completely defeated me and I ploughed us, still at speed, straight into a willow tree which wound itself around our tunnel light and held on tight.

Geoff wandered down the roof and disengaged the greenery and as I backed Happy (slowly) out of the V-shaped dent in the bank that we had created, he spent a couple of minutes trying to straighten out our battered and miserable tunnel light. Just to irritate me, he kept one of the willow branches and placed it carefully over the engine room hatch as, he said, a permanent reminder that narrow boats go SLOWLY!

I managed to keep my speed down for a good couple of hours, but the river was straight and plodding along in a straight line is mind-bogglingly boring, so little by little my speed crept up and up. By the time I managed to wrestle her around the first little bend beyond Warmington I was pretty much at full throttle again.

As we scraped around with the engine in reverse, I

noticed from the map that the second bend was much tighter and, beyond that, the river became very bendy and narrow so, sighing, I decided to take Geoff's advice and keep the speed down. As we came gently around the next corner, I spotted a small fibreglass cabin cruiser, apparently motionless, sitting diagonally across the river.

For once, I was able to put her into reverse and slow down with a little grace, without the screaming and panicking that had plagued every other incident. In fact, everything happened so gently and slowly, I wasn't actually sure if what I was doing was correct; it all seemed so lacking in energy. It was the first time I had managed to see a potential trauma at anything other than fast-forward pace.

The reduction in speed wasn't quite enough and even in full reverse Happy continued to inch her way toward the cabin cruiser like a very large dog which, even on a strong leash, drags its owner forward, intent on menacing a kitten. Knowing that we were going to do no harm, I did allow myself a quiet smile as the other owner attempted to fend us off with a small plastic paddle. This merely pushed him backwards, which, while it may not have been exactly what he intended, did succeed in keeping the boats apart.

By the time we actually made contact with the other boat, we were travelling so slowly that the fibreglass boat merely rocked slightly. It worried me a little that if I had been travelling at my usual speed I would have hit them broadside, mashed them thoroughly into the bank and by now would have been fishing swimmers out from amongst the floating flotsam and getting ready to tackle a massive insurance claim.

Alerted by the tapping of the plastic paddle against the front of the boat, Geoff came out to see what was going on. Keeping her in reverse, I pulled Happy backwards, until we were standing a more acceptable distance away, and called over to ask what had happened.

The cruiser's owner, Philip, explained that his steering

linkage had broken and they had just been putting it back together when we had come steaming around the corner (I felt that was a little harsh, if I *had* been 'steaming', as he put it, they would now be boat-less). He explained that, in his fright at seeing the underside of Happy's bow bearing down on him, he had dropped the screws, which had rolled away and were nowhere to be found. We held position for about half an hour, enjoying a nice cup of tea while he cannibalised another part of the boat to find the necessary bits required to get him and his family home.

It was funny at the time and I couldn't help but laugh every time I remembered the look on Philip's face as Happy approached. When Philip and his family were all sorted and had puttered off in the opposite direction, it finally struck me just how lucky we had been. Maybe Geoff was right, maybe it was time to slow down and, shuddering to think of what could have happened if I had been tearing along as usual, I resolved to take it easy from now on. I also resolved not to admit to Geoff that he had been right; there is nothing worse than a smug husband.

Geoff took over the driving. I didn't mind – the weather had begun to close in again, the sun had disappeared and over the next couple of hours the drizzle became heavier, turning to a steady rain. The wind picked up so much that, despite all efforts to keep Happy in a straight line, we were pushed diagonally down the river. Both drenched to the skin, I bemoaned the lack of our waterproofs, which were sitting snug and dry in a box in storage.

Approaching Alwalton Lock just beyond the Peterborough Cruising Club, I was very aware that we were surrounded by moored fibreglass boats. The wind was now so strong and the rain so heavy, I couldn't actually see the bow. Taking over the tiller, I managed to get Happy into the lock mooring just long enough to allow Geoff to jump off with a sodden rope and tie us up. The mooring was extremely small and Geoff was only able to get one mid-roof rope onto a stud embedded into the wooden wharf. Happy, bouncing around in response to the strong buffets of wind, side skipped in a jerky arc and then, literally, reaching the end of her tether would bounce back toward the wooden mooring, hitting it with a boom that would start the whole process again.

I was terrified that we would be ripped from the mooring and sent spinning across the water and into the moored cruisers – one near miss with a fibreglass boat was enough for the day. As the lock gates opened, I disengaged the mooring rope and put her into forward, hoping to just slide her along the left-hand bank and into the lock.

The high winds stopped me from 'sliding' anywhere. Immediately the rope went slack, the wind picked up the back end and spun it out into the middle of the river. I poured on as much power as I could and Happy drove her nose back into the bank, ignoring all the steering from the back end. As she now couldn't go forward, the wind took its chance to push the back end further around. We were now completely side on to the lock gates and had no chance at all of getting in without some major manoeuvres.

I slammed her into reverse, trying to get her into clear water. Looking back over the top of the tiller I noticed that we were about three foot from one of the moored cruisers and began to sweat despite the icy cold rain. Deciding not to worry where the nose would end up I put her into forward, hard. Luckily, the resulting wash pushed the loosely tied cruiser out of the way and as we were slammed by the wind into the wooden dock to which it had been tied, my head jerked with the impact and my clashing teeth managed to take what felt like the end of my tongue off. Now with the stern against a solid object, the bow took the brunt of the wind, swinging out past the lock and moving at speed toward the moorings.

Trying not to gag on a mouthful of blood, I noticed with an odd detachment that if Happy was to be pushed hard against the bank we would take out all four of the small boats that would fit along her 70-foot length. There was absolutely nothing I could do to stop her; it was like watching a slow-motion train crash.

Geoff, seeing the trouble I was having, ran down the far bank and made a grab for the front rope, but he missed, narrowly avoiding ending up in the river by performing a superb mid-air pivot. This didn't deter him from trying again and the second time he managed to snag the trailing rope. Wrapping it quickly around a bollard and arresting the front end's imminent attack on the smaller boats, he threw the rope over his shoulder and, leaning as far forward as he could, physically dragged Happy's front end in through the lock gate. Finally beaten, Happy submitted and with a fair amount of power from the back end, she crept sulkily into the lock.

Inside the high walls and with the lock gates closed, all was calm and quiet and I took the opportunity to find some kitchen roll to stem the blood still pouring from my mouth. Geoff, watching the paper turn red, looked horrified and rushed off to get a glass of hot salt water. Mmm lovely, just what a nervous stomach full of swallowed blood needs. He looked a little hurt when I turned it down and went to make a cup of tea instead. Against all the rules, we stayed within the lock pound, until the rain, my blood loss and our heart rates had slackened to something closer to manageable.

Once out of the lock, there was no danger to anybody other than ourselves and, with what was still a fairly strong wind pushing us diagonally into the banks, we battled on toward our intended destination. Gradually over the next hour the wind died down and the sun reappeared, along with other river users.

To those dry, warm, happy people, out for a nice afternoon's potter in their boats we must have looked completely at odds with our environment. Happy, now very clean and steaming gently in the sun, looked great; but when the eye reached her pilots, Geoff and myself, standing still at the back, wide-eyed, soaked, bedraggled and slightly frazzled-looking (I was still holding a very blood-stained piece of paper to my mouth), it was no wonder that we got some curious looks from the passers-by.

The sun continued to shine as we made our way toward Peterborough and as we gradually calmed down, and dried off, we began to enjoy the trip again. We had planned to spend the night at the moorings just beyond the Sculpture Park and, as we approached that part of the river, it began to drizzle again. It was at this point that we found out that the moorings at the Sculpture Park no longer existed; we really needed to buy an up-to-date map.

Not only were they non-existent, but the riverbank had also been so eroded over the years that, when trying to bring her in to moor at what appeared to be a possible stopping place, we ran aground and, of course, we did it in style.

First there was a gentle thump, then the bow lifted and tilted perceptibly over to the right, followed by a swishing, grinding noise as the whole left-hand side of Happy lifted about three inches up on a silt bank and there she stopped. Oh bugger.

To move a 23-tonne narrow boat when she is afloat takes a gentle push; to move a 23-tonne narrow boat when she is aground is a completely different matter and usually takes a crane. Unfortunately, not having one of these grand machines to hand, we coped with what we had, one barge pole, one plank of wood and an extensive range of expletives, none of which helped in the slightest.

Geoff finally came up with the brilliant plan of emptying the water tank which was situated in the bow, if we could get the nose afloat, he reasoned, we should be able to push her into mid-stream and hopefully get her off the silt bed. Eureka! It worked. Amazing, and off we went again.

The rain became a little more insistent and as we rounded a corner we decided to try mooring again on the bank side.

We had been told that on no account did we want to moor in Peterborough due to the fun-loving kids that had made a name for themselves by kicking in boaters' windows, setting boats adrift or just breaking in and pinching things. With these warnings very much at the forefront of my mind I was absolutely adamant that we were not going to moor in town and there was to be no discussion about it.

So once again we turned her toward the bank. First there was a gentle thump, then the bow lifted and tilted perceptibly over to the right, followed by a swishing, grinding noise as the whole left-hand side of Happy lifted about three inches up on a silt bank and there she stopped – again. Oh bugger, bugger, bugger!

This time there were no water tanks to empty and, being at a bit of a loss as to what to do, the difference in our personalities started to show. Geoff sat and pondered the problem, trying this and that to make a difference. I sat and moaned, although with my swollen tongue most of what I said was probably unintelligible. Finally, while wandering up and down the corridor, Geoff hit upon the solution and instructed me to walk backwards and forwards across the boat while carrying Sam. Slightly mystified, I did what he said, and within seconds the nose was back in mid-stream again. It turns out that while he was wandering about thinking he had noticed slight movement and worked out that if we could rock her enough and he pushed at the right time, he had a reasonable chance of getting her clear.

Clever man – mind you, him being clever didn't make the whole sorry debacle any less his fault – so there!

Pulling into Peterborough, I found myself more than a little depressed; it really had been a horrendous day. We were close to exhausted, I had serious face-ache, we had been soaked to the skin, twice, and had spent the whole day testing out how many different things we could run into: willow trees, bridges, small boats, locks, the bank, and now, here we were in the middle of Peterborough, heading toward twilight and totally at the prey of the infamous vandals.

I was being more neurotic than normal but we had been told by so many people that Peterborough was not the place to stay that I was convinced we were all going to be murdered in our beds. I think it was less these oft-repeated warnings and more the horrible prospect of spending an evening with a psychotic and paranoid wife that convinced Geoff a mooring out of town would be a much better prospect.

The map showed a pub halfway down Morton's Leam that advertised moorings, and during a quick telephone call we were informed that they were more than willing to let us book their mooring for the night, which, we were also informed, could easily take Happy's length. I was so relieved to be guaranteed a pub-cooked meal, a vandal-free evening and a long, warm sleep that I became almost cheerful and positive again, which just confused Geoff and confirmed his concerns about imminent psychosis.

As we turned into Morton's Leam it became very dark, and we could see lightning beginning to flicker on the distant horizon. The rain once again became more insistent and we were pleased to see the pub looming out of the murk on the right-hand side. As we slowed Happy to a crawl, ready to pull her over, the mooring became horribly visible. We stood in silence, staring in growing panic. The mooring was four pieces of wobbly scaffold with some old planks stretched between them.

'Not in a million years,' Geoff shouted over the sound of the rising weather, 'we're going to have to find something else.'

I nodded mournfully and as colour images of hot meals and warm beds fled, I applied the throttle, noticing as I did so that water was running out of my sleeves and my tongue was hurting again. I moved Happy toward the oncoming storm.

Twenty minutes later, still looking for somewhere solid

to moor, the storm hit us with full force. The lightning became cartoon-like; huge, crackling, multi-forked explosions of light and sound that appeared to hit the ground about ten feet away. Ten feet is probably an exaggeration, but in the dark and the rain, they appeared far too close.

'We're going to die,' I thought. 'We're standing on the back of a metal tube in a thunderstorm, the only way we can make this any worse is to stand on the roof, each carrying a copper pipe, both screaming insults at the gods.'

Due to the ferocity of the storm, Geoff and I had taken to communicating in sign language; the rain had become so heavy it had been similar to having a conversation in a power shower (just minus the warmth and all the giggling). Every time one of us opened our mouths, the water would run in and we would choke and cough. The gods not only have a sense of humour, they also have a major sense of drama.

Partially deafened by a roll of thunder, we rounded a corner and the subsequent lightning bolt lit up the huge doors of Stanground Sluice just ahead of us.

This was the biggest lock I had seen so far; the black, glistening, heavy wooden doors rose high above the roof of the boat and, appearing out of the storm, it could easily have been used as a prop in a vampire film. Geoff, on seeing the sluice approaching, immediately put Happy into reverse and swung the tiller to the right, intending to push us away from the doors.

'We can't moor here,' he bellowed over another incredible roll of thunder. 'We will HAVE to go back to Peterborough.'

By this time, I was soaked through for the third time in one day, tired, in pain, totally miserable, and quite frankly the nefarious vandals could have everything I owned, just as long as they left me with a blanket and a cup of tea.

As usual, our next problem was turning Happy, and the incredible weather just made it all the more difficult. In the driving rain we couldn't actually see the bow or either of the banks, so Geoff elected to go to the front and tell me when we were close to hitting solid ground. While waiting for him to make his careful way down the gunwales to the bow, I studied the lock behind me.

As the lightning lit the B-movie horror set again, I stared at the huge doors, waiting for the Scooby Doo cartoon bats to make an appearance (luckily they didn't – I think I would've fainted). Through the gloom I could just make out Geoff waving me on. I sighed and wiped my soaked face with a sodden sleeve, down with the throttle, over with the tiller and here we go again.

Peering through the rain I could see Geoff making frantic hand movements and could vaguely hear him shouting something, but as I could neither hear him nor work out what his hand movements meant, I slowed down slightly but kept on going.

First there was a gentle thump, then the bow lifted and tilted perceptibly over to the left, followed by a swishing grinding noise as the whole front end lifted about three inches up on a silt bank and there she stopped – again, again, again. Oh bugger, bugger, bugger, damn and blast.

'What the hell are you doing?' Geoff clambered back down the boat toward me. 'I told you to stop!'

'I can't hear you, and your hand movements don't make any sense,' I screamed at him. 'What am I supposed to do – and what the hell does this mean?' I flapped a hand at him.

'Slow down, of course.'

'Well it didn't look like it to me.'

'Everybody knows what that means.'

'Well I don't. Look, if you can do better, you drive the bloody thing.'

Geoff looked toward the front. 'Just go backwards', he sighed 'and we'll see if we can get her afloat again.'

By this time we were both squelching as we moved about. After about ten minutes struggling, rocking and revving, I managed to coerce Happy into backward movement, but every time we attempted to go forward, we ran aground in the same place. There just wasn't enough room for her to turn; she needed to pivot. Geoff decided that the only way to accomplish this was for him to jump off at the front, push her around, and then jump back on again.

Brilliant! This actually worked. With Happy going forward and Geoff pushing at her nose, she pivoted and turned back towards Peterborough. It was now fully dark and trying to give us some light to steer by, I turned on our pathetic tunnel light, but all this managed to do was highlight just how heavy the rain was by illuminating each individual drop.

I kept Happy turning slowly, trying to keep her close enough to the bank for Geoff to get back on. I could just about make him out in the gloom, walking alongside, awaiting his chance. As another bolt of lightning illuminated the area, I saw him make the jump for the side, saw him in silhouette pull himself up and then he just wasn't there any more. Training once again took over and I immediately cut the engine.

'GEOFF, GEOFF! Are you all right?' I couldn't see him at all.

It's strange, real fear is nothing like hysterical panic. First you go very cold and it's as though a huge hand takes hold of your insides and begins to twist. Another lightning flash showed him pulling himself up over the gunwales at the front and making his way back toward me. I was so relieved to see him in one piece that, for a split second, all I wanted to do was cry; then I became unreasonably angry with him.

'What happened to you?' I snarled.

'I slipped when I jumped but managed to grab the door, so I just got one leg wet,' he shook the offending limb at me, gazing mournfully at his water-filled, weed-covered boot.

'Oh for God's sake,' I snapped and leaving him staring after me in amazement, I stamped off into the boat where I sat, dripping, on the floor to have that much-needed cry.

Half an hour later, we were back in Peterborough. I had sorted myself out and was, once again, keeping Geoff company on the back as we pulled into a mooring. Although I wouldn't have thought it possible, the rain had become even heavier but at least the lightning had subsided. It was decided (more by me than by Geoff, who quite rightly pointed out that any hooligan stupid enough to be out in that weather wouldn't be able to untie a knot) that to allay the danger of the very absent vandals cutting our moorings and leaving us adrift. We would put down the anchor and, more to shut me up than from any possibility of us heading out toward the Wash, Geoff went out to sling the anchor off its rooftop resting position and into the river.

Sitting in the front with Sam, who was complaining vigorously that I was wet and smelly and that he was hungry, we both watched with interest as the big chain came clattering past the window, a huge splash, then silence.

For just one moment I had the notion that the anchor had taken Geoff with it, and the big hand, again, began to grip my insides, but within seconds he was back inside and wrestling with his soaked boots. We were, by now, so wet that it was nearly impossible to tell which leg had dropped into the river, the only tell-tale sign was a small piece of weed caught in one of his boot laces.

As we were sitting despondently in the boat, trying to work up the energy to move, a knock at the door made me leap nervously to my feet and gesture Geoff to go and answer it. Did vandals knock?

'Hello,' a male voice drifted through the open door, 'we saw you come in. You looked so miserable the wife has sent me round with tea and cake.'

I peered around the corner of Sam's nest room to see who would be so incredibly wonderful. The man standing in the rain was about 50 years old, with bright blue eyes, looking slightly embarrassed from beneath a mop of grey hair. He was carrying what looked like a fruit cake and a big teapot.

'I told her you probably wouldn't need it ...'

I leapt toward him holding out my hands to take the pot. 'No, no, that's fantastic,' I gabbled, 'thank you so much, thank your wife so much.'

He blushed gently and rubbed a hand down the leg of his brown cords, shuffling his big brown boots backwards and forwards. 'Ah, it's nothing, she loves to cook but with only the two of us living on the boat there's only so much cake you can eat.'

'Would you like to come in?' I enquired, noticing that the rain was beginning to run off the bottom of his chin. 'Share some cake?' I grinned at him.

'No, no,' he took a step backwards. 'You enjoy your tea, I take it you have milk and sugar?'

We nodded.

'If you could just return the pot when you're done, we're on 'Rosie' behind you; we're sticking around town for a couple of days so you can just drop the pot and the plate into us in the morning if you like.'

With that, he turned and disappeared into the darkness waving over his head at our shouted thanks.

Two hours later we were warm, dry and full of tea, ham and cheese sandwiches and the most excellent fruit cake; it was so good that even Sam ate it.

We took stock of the situation; from leaving Peterborough late this afternoon, we had been soaked to the skin and almost terminally terrified, we had run aground, we had shouted, screamed and cried, we had courted death by electrocution, we had been travelling, struggling and cursing for over two and a half hours.

The outcome of all this hard work and heartache? Two hundred yards from where we started and facing in the wrong direction. Argh!!!

Chapter Thirteen
What Flaming Landmarks?

MORNING BROUGHT THE SUNSHINE, strange, slept-in hairstyles and a restored sense of humour. As we weren't due to go through Dracula's lock until three-thirty that afternoon, we had the morning to pretty much do as we liked and it was great!

I popped round to 'Rosie' to return the teapot and plate that had been so kindly left with us the previous evening. Knocking on the back window I gave a shouted 'Hello'.

'Hello,' a smiling woman with very short grey hair and glasses poked her head through the window, 'are you from next door?'

'Erm, yes,' I waved the pot at her, 'I came to thank you and return your teapot.'

'I saw you come in last night.'

Her head disappeared into the boat and I could track her progress by following her voice toward the back.

'You looked so bedraggled and miserable. What on earth were you doing out so late and how did you get through the lock at that time of night? I'm Faye by the way, do you want a coffee?'

I sorted my way through her questions, working out which one to answer first.

'I'm Marie, and yes I'd love a coffee and then I can tell you why we were coming back from the lock because I think I need a coffee to go over it again.'

'Come on in,' Faye smiled.

The smell wafting from the kitchen was incredible and

set my mouth watering, vanilla and chocolate, the smell of cooking and fresh coffee was enough to tempt any weight-watcher almost past endurance. We wandered into the saloon and she indicated a small table upon which sat a beautiful oil lamp, which was so polished to perfection that it reflected the room around it.

I pulled a chair from beneath the table and sat down as she bustled off toward the kitchen. The decor matched the smell, warm, homely and inviting, it was like sitting in a perfect doll's house; the walls were varnished wood and had that reddish tinge which warmed the room beautifully; the small sofa in cream with gold-tasselled cushions fitted snugly in one corner; a matching tiny armchair stood on the other side of the boat, with a nest of tables to one side and a wood-burning stove to the other, raised from the floor on a plinth of warm cream stone tiles and surrounded by cut logs.

All of these stood on a red and gold Persian rug that stretched from one side of the room to the other; small hangings and pictures cluttered the walls and the whole room changed colour as the light came through the stained-glass flowers fitted into a porthole. Just to complete the picture, there was a huge fluffy white cat asleep with its feet in the air on the armchair.

It was absolutely beautiful and I really hoped that Happy might one day look like this, but I doubted it.

By the time I had finished telling her all about our trials from the night before I had probably extracted every expression that she possessed: horror, laughter and more horror.

'Oh good grief,' Faye laughed. 'I didn't realise you had a little one on board, that must have been so worrying for him.'

I doubted Sam had even noticed we were missing until he was hungry; he had certainly noticed when we came back because we were wet and horrible and definitely getting in his way.

'He seems to be taking it quite well really, no doubt he's saving up all the parentally induced angst until he's fourteen, and then he will hold it against us for the rest of our lives.' I grinned at her and got to my feet. 'Talking of Sam, I'd better go, I promised him we'd go into town. Thanks for the coffee and I really, really love Rosie, she's beautiful.'

'You're very lucky,' Faye smiled sadly. 'We didn't decide to live on a boat until the kids were teenagers and then they wouldn't have any of it, so we had to wait until they left home before we could buy one. They still gave us a hard time and refuse to visit'. She looked down at the table, and ran a finger through a wet coffee ring.

There wasn't really much I could say to that without bringing up my worries about Amelia so I kept quiet.

'Anyway,' she took her glasses off, gave them a polish then stuck them onto her head, 'at least you have someone that would like a cake.'

'Yes, he loved it.'

'Oh no, not that one.' She stood up and stuck her hands into the kangaroo pouch pocket on the front of her smock. 'Little boys don't want to eat fruit cake, does he like icing?'

I laughed. 'Usually that's the only bit he'll eat on the Christmas cake.'

'Hang on a mo.'

She vanished back into the kitchen.

I looked around at the pictures on the walls; there did seem to be a lot of children, two boys and a girl at different stages of life smiled out at me from behind the glass.

'Here you go.' Faye handed me a large paper plate full of small creamy cakes, covered in white icing. 'They're butterfly cakes, I made a load for a lady I look after in town to take to a meeting, but I've made too many as usual.'

'I can't take these,' I tried to hand her back the plate. 'You were an absolute life-saver last night and I really can't thank you enough, but any more would just be greedy.'

Faye pushed the plate away and firmly turned me toward the doors. 'Rubbish. Anyway,' she laughed, 'they're not for you, they're for Sam. I've written my number on the bottom of the plate. If you find yourself back here again, give us a call, I would love to see your boat finished.'

With that I found myself standing on the wharf, Faye gave me a quick hug which I was more than happy to return, then, with a wave, she'd gone back into the boat, presumably to do some more cooking.

Geoff looked up as I entered and fastened his eyes on the plate. 'More cake?' he enquired hopefully.

'Cake?' Sam appeared and surreptitiously tried to put his bowl of Sugar Puffs onto the table.

I put them in the kitchen. 'After lunch.' I picked up the broom and shuffled them both away from the plate with it. 'If we stop to eat these, we'll never get anything done.'

We wandered around Peterborough for the rest of the morning with no aim or itinerary. We had coffee, Sam discovered that charity shops sometimes held old copies of Beano Annuals and made us visit every single one he could find. We found a great Army surplus store that sold some fantastic waterproofs, we raided the camping shop for decent gloves and hats, and wonder of wonders we actually, finally managed to get a can opener (we bought two 'just in case') and then treated ourselves to a slap-up lunch in an Italian restaurant.

Sam couldn't understand why there were no restrictions; I just gave him the menu and said, 'Order whatever you want.' I think it was more to do with the fact that we were warm and dry and the proud owners of a can opener than anything else but it was a lovely, gentle, terror-free morning and, returning to the boat, we were all in high spirits.

After filling Happy with water and pumping out the toilet tank, we were as ready to go as we were likely to get. Turning her round in this wide river gave us no problems at all and I was eager to head back to Dracula's Lock to find

115

out what the nasty thing actually looked like in the sunshine.

Not much better, to be frank. Staring through the now open, black, wet doors, which still loomed menacingly above us, revealed a walkway far above, which reinforced the impression of moving through a castle entrance-way.

Once again the wind had picked up and we struggled to get Happy inside. Luckily there were some men working on the garden and they cheerfully grabbed ropes and just hauled us into place. Not only was this the biggest lock I had ever seen, it was definitely the deepest and Geoff and the lock-keeper's daughter (hmm, sounds like a folk song) seemed very far above me as I struggled to keep Happy still in the fast-rising waters; I now have a much better idea of what an oubliette would be like. It only took about four or five minutes to get the lock filled, and within ten minutes we were all back on board and out the other side, still not a bat in sight.

The other side of the lock was classed as the 'middle levels' and strangely the landscape changed immediately and dramatically. From thinking of the lock as Dracula's castle I decided that maybe it was a large wardrobe and we were now floating through a very flat, boring Narnia. From being gently curving and occasionally wooded, the landscape was now bleak and straight, with no hills, no trees, few houses and every field set out in identical squares through which the River Nene ran in a dead straight line via man-made drains.

We had taken time to study the waterway map while at lunch in Peterborough and couldn't understand why the map showed overhead pylons as identifying landmarks. Actually travelling through this silent, flat landscape it became very apparent why this was so – there was nothing else to use.

For hour after boring hour we travelled through a landscape that was perfectly accessorised by the weather: grey, cool and monotone. After the first hour I noticed that we had started to converse in whispers; obviously this was due to a subconscious desire not to break the mood. By the third hour, I couldn't stand it any more and took to singing in a loud and tuneless voice just to break the silence.

It then became a game, gaining points by actually going around a corner or under a bridge. By the time we reached the infamous Whittlesey Corner we were quite looking forward to it, *anything* to break the monotony.

The Whittlesey Corner is very sharp, and although easily able to accommodate boats up to 68 foot long, we are 70 foot long – over 71 if you count the fenders. We had discussed our chances with the lock keeper at Dracula's Lock, he had given Happy a critical once-over and shrugged.

'You should be all right,' he laughed. 'Give it a go.'

'Great, thanks,' I sighed and went back to imagining the fiasco that would occur if we failed.

Geoff slowed right down to a crawl and started to ease her round the corner, chug by chug. At one point her nose was about three inches away from the left bank at the front, the far side of the middle of the boat was six inches away from the right-hand bank and her stern was scraping gently on the left bank.

For some strange reason, Geoff, Sam and I were all holding our breath, as were the two fishermen on the bank, who, seeing us coming had grabbed all of their equipment and had moved it well out of the way. We knew that if we couldn't get around we would completely block the waterway until some other boat took pity on us and came to give us a bit of a shove. As we finally cleared the corner the fishermen gave us a short round of applause.

Eventually we were back on open water and allowed ourselves a collective sigh of relief. With the worst obstacle out of the way, we moored early in Whittlesey and, as congratulation for getting ourselves there in one piece, we celebrated with an exceptionally good Chinese takeaway.

With dinner finished and Sam safely tucked up in bed,

zonked after a two-hour game of 'completely fail to kick a ball, fall over a lot and run around shouting' – the family version of football (none of us are very sporty) – and a huge meal, we spread the maps out on our wobbly table. I had spent a good hour on it after dinner and, using a toothbrush, had managed to extricate all the little pieces of food that were stuck under the raised sides. Geoff had wandered up to see what I was doing and stood and watched me for five minutes until I said with great satisfaction. 'There, that's done, that wretched table has been bothering me for days.'

'Oh,' he turned to his toolbox, 'you should have said.' He then picked up a hammer and chisel and within 30 seconds had taken all the sides off, revealing more congealed food. He stood looking at me, smiling, obviously waiting for my heartfelt thanks – I nearly killed him.

Sitting at our now exceptionally clean table, we worked out that we were actually two whole days ahead of schedule. As we had to give 48 hours advance warning to Salters Lode, a large lock that would let us out of the middle levels, we prepared to settle in for a couple of days and enjoy the enforced interlude.

We were so close to the end of our journey that it all seemed a little surreal. Being only half a mile apart, Salters Lode alerts Denver Sluice, informing them that a boat needs to get off the tidal stretch of the Ouse and onto the river. Getting onto that river would put us within five hours of our new permanent mooring, our new home.

After sitting around looking at each other for a bit, we decided that there was no way we could just do nothing for two days, so we decided to make use of that time and journey by train to Rugby (which was the nearest station to the marina) and, from there, catch a taxi to Braunston Marina to pick up the cars.

With a plan in mind, we felt that we could legitimately lounge around for the rest of the evening discussing the extreme events of the past week. All our traumas didn't seem nearly so bad when being discussed in the warm evening, with a full stomach and a bottle of red wine past the halfway mark. They almost seemed amusing, not so much that I would like to do it again, but at least I managed to laugh – well, as much as I could around a still rather sore tongue.

Ten o'clock in the morning, Friday, September 16, and I was on the phone (with a slight hangover) to the lock-keeper at Salters Lode. He was helpful and nice, and told us that, yes we could come through at 11 o'clock two days from now but to make sure we were there on time as there was a neap tide and nothing was going through in the afternoon. Great, all going to plan.

'Just one more thing,' he asked as I was about to go. 'How big are you?'

'70 foot.'

Silence, then, 'Oh dear, there's no way I can get a 70-footer through with this tide up, you'll have to come through in a week's time when it's all gone down.'

'WHAT?' The tinkling sound of breaking plans sounded in my head.

'Yeah, sorry about that, the lock has two sets of gates, the first set is full height and those can be used at any state of the tide but only allow up to 60 foot through, and we have a second set of half-height gates that we use for large boats, which can only be used when the water is low. Give me a ring in seven days and we'll see how we are doing, OK?'

Geoff had obviously heard the panic in my voice and was hovering anxiously, waiting for the phone call to end to find out what the problem was. I cut the call and slumped onto the settle, which, strangely, didn't seem half as cosy as it had the previous evening.

'What's the problem?' Geoff poked me in the knee with a stiff finger. 'What time do we get through?'

'We don't,' I sighed. 'There's a neap tide and they can't get a boat of this size through the lock for about a week.'

'Oh bugger,' Geoff huffed, 'what are we going to do now? While you were on your phone to the lock, I called the school, and told them Sam would be there on Thursday.'

'Why did you choose this Thursday?' I asked, curious. 'Why not the Monday after?'

'Well,' Geoff shuffled a bit. 'It's a new school and I thought it might be nice for him to just do a couple of days in the first week, you know, get him used to it?'

OK, can't argue with that logic; so our plans were to be changed yet again. If this whole boat debacle had proved anything it was that life is like riding a unicycle, just when you think you have got the hang of it, you hit a rock and fall flat on your face; I personally think that strategically placing rocks is the gods' recreational endeavour. When plans fall flat there is only one thing to do: make a new plan.

After yet another cup of tea, we decided that we would stay moored in Whittlesey but would still go and retrieve the car. We could bring the van down another time, but having one vehicle here would make life much, much easier, and after another lengthy pore over the map it was also decided that we would move Happy to March, an easy half-day run down the river, and stay there to await the tide dropping. Taking stock of our life, we had decided that a launderette would become very important very shortly, and we had been told there was a good one in March.

By the time new plans were made it was about 11 o'clock and we decided that lurking around for the day, although nice, would serve very little purpose. As the railway station was only down the road, we spent another ten frustrating minutes trying to persuade Sam into some state other than stark naked and, making sure we had the keys to the car, set off.

The walk to the station, the train ride and then a taxi to Braunston took four hours, which included an hour's wait as we missed our connection somewhere in the middle; it was odd, the same journey by water had taken us seven days and that had been pushing ourselves – we had originally estimated nine. Even odder, the car ride back to the boat took only two and a half hours. It was fun to look over the side of the A14 just before Oundle and see the viaduct that we had travelled under only a few days before. Now we *knew* where that river went, hmm, straight into a willow tree if I remembered rightly.

We got back to the boat at about eight o'clock in the evening and having fed Sam on the road we managed to bribe him into bed with promises of no travelling the next day. We were going to have a day of fun.

The gods once again proved me a liar, as we were woken at 5.30 a.m. by the sound of torrential rain hammering on the roof. Geoff leapt out of bed and rushed around making sure that all the windows were closed, and then came back to bed accompanied by two cups of tea. I thought once more that if we ever became land-bound again, I would definitely miss being tucked up warmly inside, listening to the sound of torrential rain on the roof.

We spent the morning playing silly board games, and then, as the sun finally put in an appearance just after lunch, we all piled into the car and drove out to March, hoping to locate a good mooring for the next week.

I had missed my dose of speed over the last couple of weeks, so I was driving – not that I was likely to break any laws in a 750cc Daewoo Matiz, but I found myself plodding along at 30 in a 60-mile-per-hour limit and worrying that I was going way too fast.

Geoff kept saying, 'Come on, put your foot down,' until in the end, I pulled over and let him drive. 'Slow down', 'Speed up' – one of these days I might actually find myself going at an optimum speed for a particular situation, but, to be frank, I doubted it.

Just for once, we were in luck. Parking the car in the marketplace, we wandered down to the river and found superb moorings just under and beyond the town bridge, beautifully deserted and, apart from a bit of litter, nicely kept. It didn't look as though anybody would mind if we outstayed our 48-hour limit. All the kids were back at school and 'silly season' on the rivers had mostly come to an end.

In a good mood, we spent the rest of the afternoon wandering around the town, buying useless decorative items and being talked into purchasing a small collection of DVDs by Sam, who felt that owning the entire Pokémon series was necessary for him to carry on breathing. After indulging in yet another fast-food meal, we wandered back to the boat. Even Sam agreed it had been a very acceptable afternoon; well, he grunted and waved vaguely at us from his statue-like position in front of the telly.

We pulled into March at about three o'clock on Monday afternoon and the moorings were still deserted. Knowing that we were definitely going to be outstaying our allotted time, we pulled her as far up to the end of the mooring as we possibly could, sticking her nose in amongst the greenery. It is nigh on impossible to make 70 feet of grey, red-and-white painted steel inconspicuous without army camouflage netting and possibly a deep cave but we did our best, figuring that if we left as much of the mooring available for other boaters as possible, we would be suffered for a while. We settled down for an extended wait.

Even with all the rushing around over the last 48 hours, we had at least four more days in which to just to hang about; it was very strange. On the Tuesday we all got up early then stood around, looking at each other, for an hour or so after breakfast, trying to decide what to do with our day. I'm not sure why that morning was so slow to gain momentum, as once we finally got our act together it only took an hour to make a huge list of jobs we could accomplish while stationary.

First – and most necessary – was the washing. We had managed for over a week and still had *some* clean clothes but they were getting few and far between. We had really got to the point where the huge stinking pile was starting to get out of hand, especially as it contained the soaking wet clothes from the 'day of disasters' as it had become known. So, we all agreed, the washing was first priority.

The launderette in March is out on the Ely road and a very poor thing it is too. I hadn't used a launderette since I was at college and had completely forgotten how the etiquette works, or rather the lack of it. I had also forgotten how bloody annoying it is to watch one idiot wander in with a small bag of wet washing and then use three different dryers. I had also completely forgotten how mind-bogglingly infuriating it is when someone fills a dryer and then pushes off and doesn't come back to take their stupid washing out.

In short I had forgotten everything that bugged me about launderettes when I was at college, but even as I walked through the door, the memories started to come flooding back: the smell, the decrepit decoration (or lack of it), the ripped seating and the cheap plastic patio chairs resplendent in their differing shades of nicotine white and fingerprint grey, each complete with a set of wobbly legs that threaten to tip you to the grimy floor at the least provocation.

Loading my washing into three machines (have the machines actually got smaller?) I eased gingerly down into one of the wobbly chairs and amused myself by reading the graffiti; it was definitely more interesting than the aged selection of well-thumbed men's magazines that littered the cigarette-scarred plastic table.

By the time all the washing was finally clean and I had laid claim to a dryer with the simple ruse of waiting till I was alone, then quickly emptying the contents of the machine I wished to use into a washing basket (I had no idea whether the owner of washing and basket were the same person), I was completely exhausted and for some reason felt vaguely dirty. But all our clothes were clean and dry, and, as that was the object of the whole yucky exercise, I had to count the experiment a success, although not one I was in any hurry to repeat.

The rest of the day was spent trying to find space in which to store the clean clothes. Geoff had taken the opportunity of a movement-free morning to reorganise all the boxes in the spare cabins and was also attempting to re-pack some items, thereby getting rid of any box half filled or broken. The boat was littered with escaped contents, strange toppling piles and a small boy intent on box diving.

While Geoff had his mind on other things, Sam had managed to unearth a fair few toys that, given the amount of space available in his bedroom, Geoff and I had quietly put away in the vain hope that he either wouldn't miss, or find, them. No such luck. With the crows of pleased excitement growing with each new 'discovery', he carried all his 'treasures' into his room and dumped them on the bed.

Geoff had made a deal with him; he could keep the 'new' toys in his room if he would agree to return an equal number of 'old' toys back into the storage cabin. He agreed and Geoff had left him to it, desperately trying to decide which toys were doomed to go back in a box.

As I arrived back with the washing, I found the boat filled with flying boxes and toys, and at different ends of the boat, frustrated husband and son were both trying to smother expletives that differed only in strength of meaning.

The arrival of the washing turned disaster into pure chaos. After tripping over each other for about ten minutes, we all abandoned the mess and hid in the front cabin using lunch as an excuse. It took about two hours to restore a certain amount of order and by three o'clock we were all annoyed, bruised and several items had been broken but at least they were broken and back in boxes. Taking a look at our newly organised living space, we decided to make a run for it and went to the cinema.

By about eight o'clock that evening, we returned to the boat, slightly wide-eyed from the big screen and the surfeit of chocolate, popcorn and other less nourishing, but vibrantly coloured, sweets. We were just about to start bringing Sam down from whatever sugar-induced cloud he was currently inhabiting and try to blackmail him into bed, when my mobile rang; it was Helen. Well, as far as I was concerned she was far more important than any wifely or motherly duty, so leaving the lads to fend for themselves, I settled down for a good gossip. After the usual hellos and stuff, she asked, 'Where are you at the moment?'

'In the boat,' I answered, knowing full well I was going to get shouted at.

'No, you silly moo,' she laughed. 'Where are you in the country?'

'Oh right ... March,' I answered and told her why we were stuck there.

'Brilliant,' she said, 'I know March; when are you moving on?'

'Saturday,' I replied, hopefully, 'If we manage to get through the lock.'

'Great, we're coming down – can you cope with visitors?'

'Yes, yes, of course we can,' I almost bellowed at her. 'Are you staying over at all?'

'Yeah, we thought we would meet up with you, deliver Herbert back to you, see you into your new mooring and stay till Sunday if you think you can cope with us that long?'

'Not a problem.' Oh this was excellent, real people, people we knew. I was suddenly really very, very happy.

'OK then,' she said, 'I gotta go, Paddy has just been sick on the floor. I'll give you a ring on Friday and you can tell us if you will be moving or not – byeee.'

And with that, she had dashed off to clean up yet another of her ageing greyhound's misdemeanours.

Smiling at the normality of it all, I wandered over to where Geoff and Sam were having their usual nightly argument about 'why you have to clean your teeth', but before I could tell Geoff the content of my conversation with Helen, my phone rang again. This time it was my mother, who advised me that she had bullied my father into coming to visit us again, they were bringing Amelia and Huw with them and they would be arriving tomorrow.

Wow. A little shell-shocked by the sudden possible invasion of people, I realised that the only person we wouldn't be seeing was Charlie and although we had made sure to call her nearly every night, it wasn't the same as actually seeing her, but for that we had to wait another two weeks which would see us at the mooring and well settled.

'Who was that?' Geoff asked as I sat down.

'Everybody.'

'What did they want?' He got up to put the kettle on.

'They're coming to visit.'

'Who is?'

'Everybody.'

He frowned at me. 'Don't be irritating. Who's everybody?'

'Mum, Dad, Amelia, Huw, Helen and Dave.'

'Oh! Right. When?'

'Tomorrow.'

'Oh dear!'

I did finally get around to explaining that they weren't all actually turning up at once and that the 'Mum and Dad' crowd were only visiting for the day, that it was only Helen and Dave that were staying with us overnight, and they actually wouldn't be turning up until the weekend. So it wasn't as bad as it had first appeared.

My mother never does anything half-heartedly and rang me at 6.30 the next morning to get our 'address' as she put it. They must have been halfway down the A14 when she called because an hour later they were hammering on the roof. It was a very noisy and crowded boat for the next two hours, with everyone trying to talk at once. Geoff and I spent the first hour trying to explain why we hadn't finished

126

fixing Happy up yet and why we were stuck in March, then we had to go into why we had only got this far, and why Sam wasn't in school yet (Sam, by this point, had decided that if they couldn't see him, they couldn't 'organise' him and bolted for his bedroom).

In the end we just gave up, made copious amounts of tea and just listened to the advice, nodding in the appropriate places. It was definitely a coward's way out to treat them all to lunch, but we felt they might just hold back on their questions and advice if we were in a public place.

The day was a complete whirl of loud people and cramped conditions on Happy, but it was nice to see friendly faces. I hugged Amelia extra hard as they left, both of us in tears. But we had arranged for her and Huw to come down again in two weeks' time so we both had something to look forward to.

After we had waved them off from the car park, we wandered back to the boat. Happy seemed very large and very quiet. I missed them, I missed being able to see them, especially Amelia, on a daily basis. I certainly missed Charlie, a telephone call with family is never the same as actually being able to sit and argue with them in person. We were all quiet and a little glum as we made our way to bed that evening.

Thursday was Sam's first day at school. He wasn't happy about it and neither was I. Strangely, I had got used to having him around at all hours of the day. I was puzzled by this, back at the house I couldn't wait to get rid of the kids and have some time to myself, but I knew that I would really miss his high-pitched voice giving me long, involved and completely incoherent explanations of whatever complicated game he was currently involved with. I didn't want to think about the day ahead, quiet and devoid of mass stickiness.

Even though the school run was 120 miles a day, we had elected not to keep him out any longer. If we could have guaranteed that we would get through Salters Lode this coming weekend we might have put it off for another week, but common sense reared its ugly head and we realised that we might not get through till next week, so we elected to drive the 60 miles there and back in the morning and again in the afternoon.

Sam was quite happy to wait another week, and explained his position to us, at length, and became morose when he finally accepted that he did actually have to go to school and couldn't spend the rest of his life in a nest with his computer, or sitting on the top of the boat surrounded by small plastic figures, re-enacting fantasy battles between massed ranks of Pokémon and a couple of Amelia's old Barbies (the Barbies always lost, there had originally been five of them, but he was now down to three, two having plummeted to a watery grave as punishment for losing yet another fight). No doubt we will have the same argument with him in ten years' time (possibly minus the Barbies – or maybe not), but we won this one – for now – next time we may find ourselves in a weaker position.

I listened to Sam's piping voice receding down the road toward the car, and for the first time ever, I had the boat to myself. I managed to cope with the silence for about the length of time it takes to drink a cup of coffee and then, unable to take it any more, I went shopping.

March does not have good shoe shops, so that was a bit disappointing. Their book shop was also less than inspiring and as I was beginning to wonder if anybody in East Anglia read anything other than crime or romance novels, or wore boots – come on, people, winter's coming, surely some of you wear boots? I realised that Geoff, at least, would be happy that I wasn't replacing my hard lost shoe collection, or altering the trim of the boat with another three pounds of paper. So with that reassuring thought in mind, I decided to buy Sam a new DVD for when he got home. By the time I left Woolies, I had five, four of them for me.

When Geoff got back to the boat, I was sitting at our

wobbly table reading a canal boat magazine and doing an excellent job of ignoring all the useful things I could be doing. Sam, Geoff reported, had not gone into school well, he was clingy and upset, and I felt guilty all over again that we had uprooted him from a really good school that he loved and palmed him off on one that was obviously going to make him extremely unhappy.

Geoff went off to pick Sam up at two o'clock and I spent the next two hours worrying about the horrible things that had surely happened to him during the day. I became so creative with the terrible possibilities that the only course of action was to spring clean the bathroom.

While the thought of Sam's possible terrors during his first day upset me, they paled into insignificance when I worked out that I had been cleaning the bathroom for over an hour and had completely failed to make a noticeable difference. That *really* upset me.

Father and son arrived back around four-thirty. I could hear Sam's voice long before they actually came through the door. Rushing over to him I gave him a hug and asked him how his day had gone. He looked at me as though I was mad, shrugged, said it was OK and went to turn on the telly, demanding snacks over his shoulder as he went.

Geoff explained that he had had a chat with his teacher and she had assured him that after the first five minutes Sam had found a friend, and settled down. They had had some ups and downs with him during the day, but mostly it had been either frustration at not knowing the routine or moments of insecurity. They firmly expected that he would be just one of the gang by the end of the next week.

Chapter Fourteen
Moving On

WAKING ON FRIDAY MORNING, I was quite surprised to realise that we had been moored for five days and hadn't expired from terminal boredom – far from it – and it was once again time to phone Salters Lode and see if Mother Nature was going to allow us to continue with our journey.

No authority in March seemed to mind that we had overstayed our 48 hours. All week, other boats had been coming and going and had given us the same worrying news, those that had come from Salters Lode warned that the tidal stretch of the Ouse was running fast, and, without exception, they all cast a worried eye over Happy and had said that we were going to have problems.

One weathered, bearded and be-hatted gent wandered up and remarked, 'You lot going through Salters in that?'

'Erm ... Yes.'

'Got a good engine, has she?'

'No, not really, more like two matchsticks and a rubber band.'

'Phew...' He took his hat off and ran his hand through his thatch of white hair. 'Hope you got some life jackets, you're going to be thrown about like a cat in a washing machine – good luck.' And leaving us with that stunning mental image he turned and climbed back aboard his 40-foot, high-powered boat and puttered away up the river.

Geoff and I looked at each other.

'Did you know there was likely to be a problem at Salters Lode?' I frowned at him.

He, at least, had the grace to look a little sheepish. 'There's only a problem if the section is running fast, you have to make a sharp right-hand turn out of the lock and if the tide is going out, it's a real bugger to turn into with an underpowered boat, and if the tide is coming in then you just get picked up and taken, very quickly, down toward Denver Sluice, and with a boat this size and the engine ...' he paused.

'So the answer is bloody well "yes" then, isn't it!' I snapped at him. 'We're all going to die, aren't we? We are either swept inland or swept out to sea – I'm not sure I want to do this.'

'Look,' Geoff soothed, 'hundreds of boats go through these locks every season; they wouldn't let us through if there was a problem.'

'Geoff,' I assumed the 'I told you so' position. 'In case you haven't noticed, we have been here for the best part of a week, and they didn't let us through.'

Geoff grinned. 'Think of it as going over the falls in a barrel,' he laughed, 'if nothing else, it will be exciting and if we survive we will have something to tell our grandchildren.' He took one look at my panicked expression and legged it before I could pour what was left of my coffee over his head.

I leaned my forehead against the wall and listened to him phoning the lock. Damn. They were going to let us through, first boat through on Saturday. I even gave considerable thought to just staying put and living in March; it seemed like a nice place.

The run to Salters Lode Lock takes about a day and we had been assured it was very pretty. Helen had phoned me that morning and, as she and Dave had found themselves without much to do that day, they had decided to take a leisurely run down a day early and would actually be with us that evening. Good, someone to give my last will and testament to.

Well Creek wanders gently through open countryside interspersed with little groups of nicely kept houses, the sun shone and lots of people waved. With the summer holidays well and truly over, we found that we had the creek pretty much to ourselves. There was only one lock between March and Salters Lode, which, after hearing what we were going to have to face, held no terrors at all.

We were a little nervous that Marmont Priory Lock was possibly closed, having tried to call the lock-keeper on several occasions but getting only a ringing tone. Luckily the lock-keeper, like all the others we had met, was helpful and not in the least perturbed that an odd boat had just turned up unannounced. After a short investigation it worked out that the phone number listed in our old Imray Fenland Waterways map was wrong. He was a nice guy, letting the incompetent nutters through anyway, which was good of him.

There are a series of bridges as you approach the Mullicourt Aqueduct. These seem to take spiteful delight in getting lower and lower, until at one point Geoff was crouched right down on the stern, peering over the roof and reaching up to hold the tiller. I had been getting a little edgy as we closed on the Aqueduct; I'm incredibly terrified of heights and had been having horrible visions of a steel monstrosity along the lines of the Pontcysyllte Aqueduct on the Llangollen Canal, which I had vowed never to cross. The Pontcysyllte Aqueduct stands 150 feet high and your narrow boat has merely inches between you and certain death (a 23 tonne lump of steel, falling that far, is NOT going to bounce... or fly).

The guide book states that the Mullicourt Aqueduct is merely 22 metres high (75 feet). I was breaking out in a cold sweat just thinking about it and had vowed to just stay in the cabin and stick my head between my legs or breathe into a brown paper bag or something.

Geoff was a little confused and kept muttering about the

land being so flaming flat, how on earth could they have a rise of 75 feet, it just wasn't possible.

As we emerged from a very low bridge, I made a break for the bedroom knowing that the monstrous aqueduct was just on the other side. After a couple of minutes, Geoff called me out to have a look; he could hardly speak for laughing.

'Come and have a look at this,' he shouted down.

'What do you mean "come and have a look at this"?' I shouted back. 'You know I hate heights, don't be so mean.'

He laughed some more. 'I think the book got it wrong, come and have a look.'

Wondering what was going on, I emerged into the sunlight and looked around, frowning.

'Where is it?'

I had been expecting an extended, slim, water-filled channel heading off over some huge expanse of nothing. What was actually there was a bridge with rails. Happy was going to have trouble fitting entirely on it without having one of her ends hanging off onto normal waterway *and* the wretched thing was only about six foot off the ground.

'I think they missed a decimal point in the book,' Geoff snickered. It was difficult to categorise the emotion, but I think I will label it 'cheated out of an opportunity to be really terrified'. I looked ahead to where Happy's nose was gently ploughing its way over the bridge.

'I'll go and put the kettle on,' I sighed and wandered off.

We moored up outside Salters Lode at three forty-five. Helen and Dave arrived at ten past four, fantastic timing. Helen leapt out of the car and bounced into the boat, leaving Dave to sort out all the bags. She wandered through the boat making appreciative noises and putting the kettle on as she went. Dave on the other hand peered through the doorway, gave me a wave and then backed out again to talk to Geoff.

After the hugs, I asked, 'Is he all right?' indicating Dave who was still chatting away to Geoff and casting anxious glances at the boat.

'What?' Helen glanced up at her other half and frowned. 'Oh they're probably talking engines and things, he's OK.'

Helen and Dave are both paramedics. Helen is small, with long dark hair and a mouth that never stops, she is full of nervous energy and is constantly on the move, even when sitting down, arms waving in time to the conversation, legs jiggling, feet tapping, most of the time she wears me out just looking at her. Dave, on the other hand, is the complete opposite. A paramedic of long standing, he says he may have fallen in love with her at the moment she left him standing on the side of the road. He was training her in advanced techniques for ambulance drivers. All Helen remembers him saying is, 'Go over there,' and pointing to the opposite side of the field about half a mile away, so she did. Dave had got out of the ambulance to open the gate and she had driven straight past him and stopped just where he had indicated. By the time he caught up with her, he wasn't happy, but he could see she might be interesting to get to know a little better.

Dave is the sort that you definitely want to scrape you off the road after ploughing your car into a tree. Solid, calm, huge grin, about six foot tall with a reassuring girth; a truly lovely guy. However, this is not a man that fits easily into a narrow boat. He finally joined us and stood awkwardly in the gangway, head tilted and body wedged sideways between inconvenient bits of furniture. He looked uncomfortable and worried. Helen, giving his tense body and worried look the once-over, pursed her lips in thought for a moment, then stated with her usual tact and empathy: 'I didn't know you were claustrophobic.' Poor Dave, two days of hell coming up for him (well he married her!)

As it was a lovely evening, we headed outside with a large amount of meat, alcohol and cushions stolen from the boat. Sam didn't actually get to eat much, poor boy, as Helen made him laugh so hard, he kept choking on his dinner. I finally had to call a stop to it all after one particularly vigorous tickling and screaming moment had left him laughing so hard he had actually wet himself slightly for the first time in two years and had to go and have a shower. Helen did have the grace to stop after that.

That evening is still one of my favourite memories. It was warm, the stars were out and the evening was made complete with burnt, unidentifiable barbecue food and good company; we laughed a lot, drank quite a lot (except Geoff who doesn't drink at all – he spent the evening relaxing with numerous cups of tea while regarding the rest of us with amused tolerance) and finally staggered off to bed in the small hours, well, in all honesty, Helen and Dave staggered off to bed – I had to be carried, whoops.

The next morning, while, yet again, I was nursing a niggling hangover, it was decided that Geoff and Dave would take Happy to the mooring, and Helen and I would go ahead and make sure that everything was ready for them to arrive.

Sam elected to stay with Dad, and we all headed off in separate directions. I would really like to be able to insist that I'm not entirely sure why we did it this way, but I know that Helen and I wanted to have a day shopping, drinking coffee and chatting. Getting rid of all the lads was at the forefront of our minds. I have always felt a little guilty about this as I was fully aware that Dave and Geoff didn't actually know each other very well, Dave had never been on a narrow boat and they were just about to face that nasty turn on to the fast-running, tidal section of the Ouse.

I was dreading it far more than I had let on to Geoff, so when Dave offered, with only slight hesitance and a fair amount of prodding from Helen, to go with Geoff, I completely leapt at the idea and walked (we almost ran actually) away without a backward glance. How mean is that?

Helen and I were appalled at our horrific ability to

abandon our loved ones and run away giggling but as we were discussing it, while sitting in the sun, outside Starbucks, over a large Peppermint Mocha, I really couldn't find it in me to care. Anyway, I figured that if they got into difficulties Dave could fix them up and, as Helen said, you should never let guilt get in the way of a coffee and chocolate fix.

An hour later, Helen and I were still sitting in the sun with yet another obscene, cream-covered coffee and I wondered if I should phone Geoff and see how he was getting on. I decided that, if he was in difficulties, a phone call would probably make it worse, so I bravely and charitably decided to leave him to it.

After a couple more hours shopping and a quick trip to the pub, we decided that it was probably time to check out the mooring. I had only been there once before and the 15-minute journey between Ely and Stretham took us over an hour because I kept getting lost and dragging us off down side streets.

We finally managed to locate our mooring just in time to watch Happy, luckily with Dave and Geoff still in attendance, pulling around the corner. Grabbing ropes and hammering in stakes, everybody rushed about 'doing things' and it was at least another half an hour before we finally sat down to take stock and ask Geoff and Dave how their day had gone.

I noticed that Happy had huge smears of mud all over her roof and down her sides; Geoff and Dave had it in their hair, down their backs and all over their shoulders. It transpired that Salters Lode is another guillotine lock, but unlike all the others we had been through, this one, instead of dripping a gentle rain of water and weed, embeds itself into a muddy silty bottom so, as it comes up, it drips huge dollops of mud, water and weed. I can't say I was sorry to miss that, but I did manage to keep a straight face, mostly ... I had to go and find an important job to do – out of sight.

Later, I asked Geoff how the turn had gone. He told me that it had been pretty horrendous but not as bad as he had feared, the tide had been coming in and had whipped Happy's nose out of the lock and into mid-stream, she had travelled a little faster than Geoff was comfortable with for a while, but then had settled down and they had entered Denver Sluice at a pretty normal pace. When asked how Dave had coped, Geoff's expression grew thoughtful.

'I don't think he'll ever do it again; he certainly didn't enjoy it, and oh ...' he looked at me sideways. 'How was your day's *shopping*?'

I winced at the emphasis he had managed to put on the word *shopping* but decided to play dumb.

'Oh, you know same old, same old.' Damn, hadn't got away with that one either.

For the first time since he had arrived, over 24 hours previously, Herbert finally took an interest in proceedings, hauling himself out of his already stinking pit and spending a good half hour pottering up and down the riverbank sniffing and exploring. Herbert, as I have stated before, is old. He smells and dribbles and when introduced to friends and visitors the first question they always ask when they see him is 'what exactly is that?' but however old and stinky he is, we have had him a fair while and he is part of the family (like an ageing, incontinent aunt who you would like to put in a home but no one will take on).

Usually, he will rouse himself for one of only two reasons. One: food in; and two: food out. With these two important things taken care of, he usually flops over in whatever comfortable place he can get away with (we don't allow him on either the sofa or the beds, you can't get the smell out for weeks) and within seconds starts to snore. It was nice to see him obviously enjoying himself.

He had managed to successfully navigate the gang plank the previous evening (he's too old to learn new tricks fast) and we were cautiously confident that he could now manage to get on to the bank on his own.

I still don't know whether it was just a senile moment or he was actually a lot blinder than I thought he was, but on this occasion, he completely ignored the gang plank and tried to get back into the boat by jumping onto the bow ... he didn't make it.

There was a rush of fur and feet, accompanied by four adults screaming as we all worked out simultaneously what he was about to do. There was then a complete kerfuffle of people leaping to their feet and tripping over each other as we all tried to move 70 foot in 0.3 seconds. All of this noise and motion ceased abruptly as, with a muffled grunt, Herbert took off.

He jumped and splattered himself, legs akimbo, on the raised bow of the boat, then sliding down the side of Happy, he hit the water with a loud splash. Sam howled with laughter and there was a horrible moment in which I didn't know whether to laugh with him or tell him off for being so unfeeling.

Dave was the first to reach Herbert, and flipped him, soaked and shaking, on to the bank. Geoff smothered him in a towel and poor Herbert was subjected to a thorough rubbing down, which left him looking like a huge, dirty, yellow and grey puff ball with an ugly little face stuck to one side; he was a very sad sight. We sat him in the sun and waited for him to dry out, all the time trying to keep upwind of him (river water mixed with natural *eau d'Erbert* does not a perfume make).

After about an hour it was decided that, apart from being a little scared, he hadn't suffered major damage and it would be all right to let him go back to his bed. Helen carried him over to the gang plank and placed his front paws on the wood and pointed him in the right direction. He tottered two or three steps up the wide plank and then, obviously deciding that he wasn't quite dry (or that he had been dried beyond endurance), he stopped on the plank and decided to give himself a good shake.

Herbert is not what anybody would describe as graceful, and when he shakes, he does it with all the energy at his disposal. On this particular occasion, he started shaking with his normal enthusiasm and the momentum carried him sideways in tiny little jumps, straight off the side of the gang plank and back into the river. It took us another hour and another towel to dry him off again, and this time we physically carried him up the plank and put him back in the boat. He didn't come out for anything other than the necessary for three whole days.

Other than mud-covered husbands, a stunt-double dog and a small boy who had laughed so hard he had actually made himself physically sick, it was a pleasant afternoon. Martin the marina owner had come down and connected us up to the electricity point, only to find out that it wasn't working, so he'd kindly connected us to another one for free, while he organised for the installers to come back and swap ours for a new one; he assured us it would be done within a week.

It was an odd evening, the family were feeling a bit down, brought on, I think, by knowing that the travelling was finished and now the hard work had to begin. Helen and Dave took us out and treated us to a lovely Thai meal at a restaurant in Ely. We, however, paid them back poorly I fear, by being quiet and contemplative company, except for Sam of course, who, being fed late and having to eat unfamiliar food, went into manic mode and then dissolved into tears as he was told off repeatedly for poor behaviour. Helen understood, but I still felt guilty.

Sunday dawned, complete with beautiful sunshine and mixed feelings. On either side of the river the flood defences rise so high nothing can be seen from the water level. A short climb to the top, however, reveals miles of man-made landscape which stretches flat and featureless to the horizon. Having spent the last five years wandering the wooded

Herefordshire hills I felt as though I was on the moon, exposed and strangely disconcerted by the expanse of 'land' around me.

Dave and Helen left after lunch. We had spent the morning turfing out some boxes and getting them ready to go into a storage unit we had already booked in Littleport, about ten miles away. All the tidying had been done in near silence.

Over elevenses, Helen had stated, 'I'm not going to ask how you feel, because if I do you will probably tell me and then cry all over me, and that's not going to do you any good. Dave and I were going to stay later but we are actually going to leave in about half an hour, to give you all some time to come to terms with what is going on.' God, I hate insightful friends.

'I think it's just me,' I griped, staring into my coffee. As if to prove my point, Geoff wandered past the window sporting a huge grin, followed by Sam, wearing a matching grin and asking an unending stream of questions. 'They seem quite happy.'

Helen lit a cigarette and stared at me through the smoke until she was sure I had become uncomfortable and I was forced to snap, 'What!'

She tapped the end of her cigarette into the ashtray and finally said, 'I'm going to work tomorrow, what are you going to be doing?'

That threw me and I had to concentrate on what I actually *was* doing the next day.

'Um ...' I stuttered, 'I don't know, find the closest launderette, find out where the nearest supermarket is, get some shopping in, take Sam to school, pick him up from school – you know, just stuff.'

She raised an eyebrow. 'And the next day?'

I thought again ... 'I honestly don't know. At some point we will have to start ripping all this out.' I waved an arm vaguely at the sad and dilapidated furnishings around me.

Helen stubbed her cigarette out and leaned back with the air of a spider that has just successfully trapped dinner.

'So what you are saying,' she paused for emphasis and I winced, knowing exactly where she was going with all this but unable to stop her kicking my blues, 'is that, while 80 per cent of the population are trapped in boring jobs and doing things that they "have" to do, you are swanking around pleasing yourself.'

I know when I'm beaten, and it suddenly dawned on me that she was absolutely right; no wonder Geoff had such a huge grin, he had worked it out. No responsibility, nothing we 'have to do', just get on with it and do what you like for a while – hey, this might actually be some fun. The idea so turned my feelings around I even let Helen wallow in smug righteousness for a while.

Helen and Dave left about an hour later and, after waving them off, Geoff, Sam and I were left feeling slightly self-conscious in the peace and quiet to contemplate the next phase of project life. It wasn't so bad; this was going to be easy. All we had to do was rip out all the old woodwork in the boat and replace it with new, move all the electrics and put in new plumbing   piece of cake. We should be finished in about three months.

Chapter Fifteen
I Think We Broke the Neighbour

OUR FIRST MORNING AT the mooring I woke a little confused, unsure where I was. I stood staring out of the window with a cup of coffee, just letting the caffeine pull my brain together and going over, once again, the events that had led to this moment. I found myself watching the river. In the early morning chill, little spirals rose up from the shallow covering of mist and dissipated into the warmer air. It was a glorious sight and I found myself just staring, cold coffee in hand.

Beneath the mist there was less ephemeral movement and, taking a closer look, I spotted a fair number of fish slipping through the weeds, disappearing beneath the boat, and then re-appearing. Occasionally, they broke the surface to gulp at floating specs, their big wet lips causing the mist to eddy and curl, then, leaving only ripples, they would sink back into the spiralling mist, the Piscean equivalent of the Cheshire Cat's grin.

'I wonder if they like bread,' I muttered to myself and wandered over to the cupboard. Ferreting around in the dark, looking for the bread bag, I became infuriated and reached up to open the curtains.

'Ah, that's better.' I reached into the cupboard, grabbed the bag and as I stood up I found myself staring into a pair of big brown eyes above a nose that was pressed hard to the land side window.

I jumped backwards with a bit of a shriek at which the animal threw its head up and also stepped backwards. I had forgotten for a moment that Happy would be floating well below ground level which is why my early morning voyeur looked so huge – that and the fact that it had its huge wet nose rammed against the porthole. I couldn't work out what it was; my mind said 'strange, skinny, copper-coloured cow', but no cow ever had ears like that.

As it snorted and danced backward on elegant, stick-thin legs I worked it out: it was a red deer. Good grief! The thing was huge. Even without my strange perspective, it must have stood five foot at the shoulder, it was obviously female and we stayed staring at each other for about a minute, then, blowing spit-filled steam all over the outside of the porthole, she turned and climbed effortlessly up the flood defences where she continued her unhurried wander down the riverbank.

I stood, with the bread momentarily forgotten, watching her make her elegant way along the river, stopping every so often to climb back down the flood defences, stare into another boat, before climbing back up and wandering onward.

Shaking my head slightly and wondering what she was hoping to find in the boats, I remembered the fish and turned to the other window. As I suspected, the fish were more than happy to be offered an easy breakfast and within ten minutes I had about 30 good-sized freeloaders splashing around the boat. This became a ritual, with all the breakfast crusts and edibles being thrown to the fish, which performed acrobatics to delight Sam and myself every morning.

A week later and we were still no nearer to starting the 'refit' than we were on the day of arrival; we had puttered around pretending to start. This had involved mowing the mooring and clearing out a load of junk from the boat which we then put into storage. Anything more constructive than that we had avoided strenuously.

Sam had settled into school well and Herbert had managed to keep dry, so it was on a Monday morning that

Geoff finally announced that the real work could be put off no longer and, even though we had managed to take procrastination to a new level, we really would have to start on the big stuff.

It was decided that the first thing to go would be the second bathroom; it was situated right where Geoff had envisioned the lounge-diner would go and the wall jutted out, obscuring the entrance to the boat. It would be the easiest thing to start with, as there were no major changes to be made and we weren't keeping any of it – piece of cake.

When I returned from taking Sam to school, Geoff had already made a start. He had removed the front wall, which he informed me had taken about three minutes as it was only joined to the other walls at the side, and I joined in with vigour. It was a lot more fun than I had expected, finally taking something apart.

We were a little surprised to find that the shower tray was actually made of concrete, especially when we tried to pick it up, and whoever had installed it was, like Geoff, devoted to over-engineering. I tried not to laugh aloud at his swearing and cursing as he tried to detach the wretched thing from the wall.

It took both of us to 'walk' the shower tray out of the boat, and looking around at what was left we decided that the next easiest thing to remove would be the wash basin, which was a tiny little porcelain affair.

Geoff capped off the water and removed all the taps and pipes, while I huddled underneath removing any screw that I could see. At the last two screws, I advised Geoff to hold on to it ensuring that it wouldn't fall on me. He took a firm hold and I removed the last screw then gave him a thumbs up, telling him that he could take it away. I watched his muscles flex as he changed his grip on the sink, then he frowned and just let go. Squeaking, I crabbed away beneath it, taking a breath to give him a good telling off for trying to brain me with a sink ... No need, the sink didn't move.

Geoff nudged me with his foot, then reached down and took the screwdriver away from me.

'I think you missed one,' he laughed.

I looked at the sink which appeared to be performing some trick of levitation.

'Must have done,' I frowned. 'I took out all the screws I could see.'

Geoff squatted down and had a good look underneath, then getting up again he wandered out and around the back of the side wall making small humphing noises, before returning and giving me back the screwdriver. Stepping up to the sink, he grasped it with both hands and applied a gentle downward pressure; nothing. He frowned and, getting a better grip, began wrenching it backwards and forwards trying to dislodge it from the wall ... nothing.

'This is ridiculous,' he gave the sink a hard stare, 'there is nothing holding it on, just the silicon sealant around the top.' He flexed his muscles again and went back to wrenching on it. Still nothing.

'Can you pass me that big screwdriver?' He flapped his hand vaguely in the direction of the toolbox, never taking his eyes off the sink.

I passed it to him and he began digging out the silicon. An hour later he admitted defeat and, using a jigsaw, basically cut out a rectangular section of wall with the sink still attached. We made quite a few attempts to remove that sink over the next few months and were defeated every time. Later, when Geoff was looking for a piece of wood to form the base of Sam's new wardrobe, he re-used that wall. One day, someone is going to dismantle the wardrobe and wonder why in hell there is an upside-down sink still firmly attached beneath the floor.

It occurred to me at this point that maybe this wasn't going to be as easy as we had expected. When discussing the whole 'let's do up a boat thing', we had expected to be able to take walls out and put walls in and just generally move things around and have it finished in about six months – it was certainly never going to take more than a year. We had allotted one day to remove this bathroom and now, at the end of that time, we had managed to remove one wall (that hadn't been attached to anything much), a shower tray and a sink. I had a nasty feeling that this was just a taste of things to come.

We stood in our dust-ridden gap and surveyed the damage,

'Oh well,' I turned to Geoff with a grin, 'at least that's probably going to be the worst thing to get out.'

He pursed his lips, looking at me with a very odd expression, then, very gently, reached up, grabbed my face and turned it toward the outside wall, 'No, *that's* going to be the worst thing to get out.' He let go of my head and, taking a step back, hunkered down on his heels and stared into our former bathroom. I stayed where I was, confused. I couldn't see what I was supposed to be looking at, or at least nothing that I would class as a major potential problem, just a little, round porthole and an expanse of wall.

'What am I supposed to be looking at?' I asked eventually.

Geoff sighed. 'You're looking too high,' he said, 'look down.'

I did. 'What, the toilet? That's just bolted onto that step, you can see the big bolts holding it down and look ...' I stepped forward and grasped the toilet bowl and gave it a good wiggle. 'It moves. I don't think it's cemented down, what's the problem?'

'It's not the toilet, you twit.' Geoff stepped forward and gave the step a kick; it made a hollow, metallic bonging sound. 'It's the tank that the toilet's attached to.'

I must have been having a stupid day because I still couldn't see a problem. 'It's not that big,' I said, following its line with my foot. 'Look, it stops here, that makes it about one foot deep by two foot wide by two foot long,

146

what's the problem?'

Geoff rolled his eyes, grasped me by the arm and gently propelled me along the corridor and into the next room, then pointed under the bed.

'Have a look under there,' he suggested.

Shrugging, I got down on hands and knees and peered into the dank recess under the bed. Even after my eyes adjusted, it took a moment to work out what was lurking under there. When I finally grasped what I was looking at, I was *really* confused.

'Why is there another tank under there?'

Geoff looked heavenwards. 'It's not another tank, it's the same bloody one. It comes through the wall, and carries on under this bed.'

'But ...' I spluttered, getting down and having another look, 'that's huge – it's got to be eight foot long.'

'Don't be silly,' Geoff gave me a condescending look. 'Eight foot indeed – you never have had much of an eye for lengths, have you?'

I looked up at him and made a conscious effort to keep my mouth shut as a couple of 'length' jokes ran through my mind. 'Well, how big is it then?' I asked.

Geoff grinned at me. 'Seven foot ten,' he said, and then ran like hell before I could find something to throw.

We decided that the only way to even attempt to get this thing out was to remove absolutely everything around it. So, with that hastily constructed plan in mind, we deconstructed the rest of the bathroom. We removed the plumbing for the shower, the shower itself and the bed in the next room (which at least gave us some more free space to stack our seemingly never-ending range of boxes). By the time we had finished, there was a huge tank with a toilet perched on top of it, looking slightly embarrassed to be so revealed.

Lounging in the corridor, with a cup of tea, we contemplated this strange modern sculpture; I was just about to comment that we could probably sell it to the Tate when a horrible thought occurred to me.

'What's under that toilet?' I asked Geoff.

He frowned, 'The tank.' He pointed at it.

'Yes, I know but what happens when the toilet comes off? Is there just a hole that leads directly into the tank?'

Geoff's frown deepened. 'Yes,' he said, 'what did you think there was going to be?'

'So, let me get this straight,' I took a deep breath. 'We take that toilet off and there is just an open hole, and we have to get this tank up on end and manoeuvre it up those steps and outside with a load of ... poo slopping around, is that right?'

Geoff laughed. 'No, I cleaned this tank out as best I could before we left Braunston and we haven't used it since. Obviously I couldn't get it completely clean – that would be impossible – but it should be OK to move.'

'Right ...' I wasn't completely convinced, but obviously there was nothing for it but to give it a go.

Geoff removed the toilet. It came off so easily that we just knew the next stage was going to be a complete flaming nightmare. We stood at either end of it (Geoff had the end with the hole in it – I had made sure of that) and, taking a couple of deep breaths, reached down, grasped the tank and heaved ... Good grief I had never felt anything so heavy in my life. Geoff managed to get his end off the ground by two inches, my end didn't move at all. Oh dear, oh dear.

After an hour, which consisted of mostly grunting, straining, scuffling, sweating and swearing, we had finally both moved to the same end of the tank and were inching it around the boat to the tune of '1 – 2 – 3 LIFT, Argh! Thump! 1 – 2 – 3 LIFT Argh!! Thump!'

We had managed to get it diagonally, widthways across the boat with one end perched precariously on the first of the steps and the other end wedged solidly into the wall on the opposite side of the boat, and there it stuck solid. The tank was actually seven foot, six inches long, and the width of the boat was seven foot. We were in deep trouble.

It was like some horrible antique comedy sketch. With the tank wedged against the wall, we couldn't move it back, we couldn't stand it up on end because there wasn't the headroom, we couldn't stand either side of it and lift it because the steps were in the way, and we couldn't climb over it and lift it from the outside because it was just too damned heavy. We were completely at a loss.

It's one of those moments where the boating community shows its true colours; these people are absolute diamonds. Don't think for one minute that they won't laugh at you when you are in trouble, because they will, uproariously and hysterically, but even while laughing, they will always pitch in and help.

We had only met our next-door neighbour on two occasions and everybody had been polite and nice and that had been about it. We had been a bit worried about living next door to Steve because everybody referred to him as the 'party boat', which did not bode well for a quiet life, but so far we hadn't heard a peep.

Steve was off work due to having damaged his back, but he limped past at the point where the swearing was loudest, had sized up the situation in one glance and, grinning, enquired whether we were having fun or would we like some help. He then piled in, bad back and all, and gave us a hand. There was a lot more swearing, pushing and lifting and a fair few 'ouches', but eventually the wretched thing lay on the grass outside. Looking back at the boat I noticed that with the removal of the concrete shower tray and this huge monstrosity, she had developed a definite list to the right; obviously Geoff would need to do something about that pretty soon, at least before we took anything else out. I had horrible images of her just rolling over.

With the tank finally evicted, we took stock of what was left behind and, unfortunately, although not unexpectedly, there was far more damage than we had originally expected. Over the years, water dripping out of the shower and probably other sources of wetness, upon which I don't want to dwell, had seeped through and rotted the floor beyond repair. The only course of action was to replace it. At that point I gave up counting both time and money as it was horribly obvious that we were going to end up way over budget on both.

Chapter Sixteen
It's a Floating Bathtub –
No, Really, It's a Bathtub!

I HAVE TO ADMIT that taking out two bathrooms (luckily we only had to remove one pump-out tank, the other one was staying in use) had taken far, far longer than we had anticipated. What with puttering about putting in a new floor, blocking up holes and other such important (prevaricating) jobs, summer had become a cherished memory and we were now well into October.

On a crisp, chilly, autumn morning, with the central heating yet again refusing to work properly, despite me giving it its early morning kicking, we had finally finished building – or rather re-building – our first new room: our beautiful bathroom. This had been created from the one bathroom we had left and half a cabin; the original wall between them had been removed to create a large open space that stretched the width of the boat. The original cholera farm had been banished to the local tip, and a hygienic new sink unit, lots of shiny new shelves and a wonderful rainfall shower had been installed. With another new floor in place (both bathrooms had been similarly soaked through) and all the other bits and pieces in, we had only to situate, fix and plumb in the bath and we would be finished.

One morning, just as I was heading out to Tesco, once again leaving Geoff to swear at the plumbing, he called me into the bathroom.

'Sit on the loo,' he said, pointing toward the toilet,

balancing on top of the pump-out tank.

'What?'

'Sit on the loo.' He gave me a gentle push toward the tank. 'Just sit down and tell me if you feel there's enough space.'

I climbed on to the box we were using as a step and sat down on the closed toilet seat. 'Enough space for what?' I looked around, then leant on the wall. 'It's a bit cramped I suppose, but come on, what do you expect?'

'Hmm.' Geoff helped me down from the tank, then stood staring at the wall. 'You off then?

'Yes.' I watched him walk around the wall and listened to him tapping it gently on the other side. 'I'll only be about an hour – do you want anything?'

'Mars Bars,' came the prompt reply. 'See you later.'

I shook my head at his odd behaviour and left. It was actually about two hours later that I arrived home. Having run into one of the other marina residents in town, we had decided to go for coffee.

'Hello!' I called as I dumped the shopping.

'Here,' Geoff called. 'Come and sit on this loo.'

'Déjà vu much?' I muttered at him as I climbed back onto the toilet. I sat and stared at him. 'What were you expecting – that I'd have lost a couple of inches off the shoulders while shopping?'

Geoff grinned. 'Yes, actually, doesn't it feel better now?'

I stared at him for a moment, wondering if he had completely lost it, then, sighing, I looked at the wall. How odd, it did seem further away, not very much, but certainly enough to make getting to the toilet-roll holder a lot easier.

Geoff's grin got wider.

'How did you do this?' I twisted around on the toilet seat.

'I moved the wall three inches to the left,' he leant on the wall. 'It's surprising what a difference it makes.'

'How did you move an entire wall?' I got up from the toilet and walked around the other side.

'It's really easy,' Geoff laughed. 'All you do is unscrew those battens, then just push it and, hey presto, the whole wall moves. Get it to where you want it, screw the battens back down in the new position and suddenly you have more space. He rubbed his shoulder. 'It would have been easier if you'd been here though. Trying to hold a six-foot piece of wood up and then screw it in place on your own isn't easy. It fell on me twice before I wedged it up with ladders.'

He showed me how the side partitions were fitted into the boat – it was quite ingenious really, the wall was one piece of wood shaped to fit under the gunnels, battens were screwed to each edge and then screwed straight to the side of the boat, the floor and the ceiling. When we had taken out the first bathroom, we had only had to remove the front and that had been easy; I hadn't realised the whole boat was done in the same way, and it opened up a whole new set of possibilities of the size of rooms.

'Ha, you couldn't do that in a house, could you,' I laughed. 'What on earth is all that?'

In the empty space earmarked for the new bath lay a good eight foot of garden hose. It snaked backwards and forwards, fixed with little hoops to the bathroom floor, and had one end attached to a small contraption screwed to the floor, from which ran another small piece of hose and disappeared into the outside wall.

'... and what's this thing?' I tapped the little silver thing with my foot. It had 'Whale Gulper' etched across it.

'That's my new pump.' Geoff tiptoed across the hosepipe, being very careful not to disturb any of it. 'This is great; it can run dry and won't go bang.'

'What's all the hosepipe for?' I nudged the snaking hose. Geoff immediately slapped my foot, fed up with me kicking things.

'That's to get the water out of the bath. Do you remember all that black gunge in the shower? Well, that's because the old pump couldn't get all the water out and it just ended up sitting there.'

I wrinkled my nose and nodded – I still had nightmares about the black slime in the bottom of the shower tray.

'Well, if you don't have all this hose, you end up with a small amount of water left in the bath every time you empty it. The hose acts like a sump.'

'What?'

Geoff sighed and grabbed a watering can from the side. He lifted the loose end which had a funnel attached to it. 'This end will be attached to the bath.' He began pouring water into the hose until he couldn't get any more in. 'So, there's your bath full of water.' He waved at the wall, 'Flick that switch, can you?'

I did so and immediately the pump began to make a distinctive, rhythmic, gulping noise. It sounded like a darts player downing a quick tenth pint before his next game. With every gulping sound, water bubbled up out of the funnel and, with a 'blurp', exploded all over the bathroom floor.

'Oh, that's good.' I threw a towel to Geoff who quickly mopped up the tide.

'Yeah, it does that – whatever you do, don't have the bath too full.' He held the funnel upright and we watched as the water disappeared into the pipe. I could hear a faint 'splosh, splosh' and the water evacuated the boat via one of our many outlets. After only a minute or so the tone of the pump changed and Geoff waved at the switch again. 'That's it, the pipe's empty. Turn it off, can you?'

'Do we have to go through this every time we want to empty the bath?' I looked at the now silent pump. 'Why can't we just pull the plug and let it drain away? This rigmarole is going to take bloody ages.'

'Marie,' Geoff looked at me with a slight frown. 'The bottom of the bath is well below the water level. If you've found a way to make water run uphill please let me know, because we can negate all the laws of physics and make a great deal of money.'

I stuck my tongue out at him. 'Nobody likes a smart-arse, you know.' I went to put the shopping away.

Putting the bath in last hadn't been ideal, as there were just too many opportunities for something to go horribly wrong, but we needed the space that the bath would occupy to move around while working, so it had been sitting out on the bank for the last two weeks. Geoff, unhappy with putting the bath in as the last item, had measured, re-measured and re-re-measured, so was as confident as he could be that the bath would fit perfectly within its allotted outline. I felt he was being a complete 'old woman' about the whole thing and was supremely confident that the bath would fit in the gap.

Oh yes, we had thought of everything and, patting ourselves on the back, we manoeuvred the bath through the double doors at the bow and carried it smugly down the boat (I was just wondering where I had put my secret stash of bubble bath, a good hour in a hot bath with a large glass of wine and possibly half a pound of Thornton's finest would really hit the spot) and I was just about to ask Geoff how long it would take to plumb it in, when we hit a wall. This was not a metaphorical wall; this was a Geoff-built, over-engineered, bloody great, double-skin, wooden wall, complete with sliding door that, very cleverly, slid away out of sight on opening. It was the door that had stopped us dead, as it didn't quite slide all the way into the wall, needing a little bit left out to be able to grab it and close it. It was the 'little bit' that had changed the dimensions of the doorway.

Geoff looked around the bath to see why we had stopped and a look of absolute horror dawned on his face.

'That door ... wasn't there,' he muttered.

When? This morning? Just now? When wasn't that door there? I was confused by the existential mutterings emanating from my suddenly sweating and goggly-eyed husband.

'That door wasn't there,' he said again and putting his end of the bath down, squeezed past me and began measuring up the dimensions of the bath and then the dimensions of the doorway – this did not look good.

Sure enough, the only way that bath was going to make it through was if the wall was completely removed or we could shrink the bath. As shrinking the bath would need an Aztec Shaman and suggesting that the wall should be removed would put my husband on an immediate course of Valium, we turned around and dragged the wretched bath back up the length of the boat, through the front doors and out onto the gangplank.

As usual in a crisis, I made tea while Geoff rushed around with a tape measure and tried to find a way to get a two-foot bath through a one-foot-eleven-inch doorway. My happy thoughts of hot bubble baths, chocolates, wine and a great book slunk off to hide behind that wretched, hated door.

Geoff picked up his tea and put a piece of paper in front of me. My heart sank; more diagrams.

'OK ...' he muttered, 'we can get it in through the back doors but we are going to have to be careful through the engine room. The wall between the bathroom and what will be our bedroom doesn't have the door in it yet and I reckon we can get the bath through there. It will be a bit tight, but we should be OK.'

'All right.' I drained my teacup and gave him what I hoped was a confident and enthusiastic grin. 'Let's do it.'

There is one thing that must be made clear before I explain the horrors of the next hour and a half, the back of a 'Trad' styled narrow boat is small, very small – at its deepest you have about three foot – and the whole back is styled as a curve with the tiller at the apex. To have even half a chance of getting the stupid bath through the engine room, the plan was to balance our bath on that back plate and then attempt to manoeuvre it through small, metal double doors into the four-foot, low ceilinged darkness of the engine room, down a deep step into the space that was eventually destined to become the main bedroom, tip the bath on to its side and just slide it through the door space and into the bathroom. It wasn't the best plan, it left a fair amount to luck, but it was the only plan we had.

At the back of the boat, Geoff leant forward over the two-foot gap between bank and boat, grabbed the lip of the bath and hauled the tap end aboard; it promptly wedged itself under the tiller, but this was easily taken care of by just removing the tiller – ha, one problem surmounted.

At the angle the bath was sitting, with one end on the boat and the other on the bank, it was impossible to get it through the doors so we juggled the wretched thing up on end; now the end of the bath was higher than the roof. We needed to bring the back end down, and unless we suddenly discovered that we could walk on water, that looked like a very difficult prospect.

After a fair amount of shoving and swearing, we decided that the only thing to do was turn the bath on its side and hang a large amount of it past the back of the boat and allow it to 'hover' over the water; we would then try to slide it into the engine room. To achieve this, Geoff, being river side, would have to balance on the four-inch gunwales as the bath was taking up the whole of the back of the boat.

I'm still not entirely sure what *actually* happened, but I have a horrible feeling that it was all my fault. With all the shoving and pushing, I finally lost tolerance and gave the bath an almighty push, no doubt thinking that as planning and manoeuvring were proving a waste of time, I was going to go with outright thuggery. I am pretty sure it was me that pushed Geoff off the back of the boat and into the river, and I'm fairly sure it was me, watching the bath slide off after him, who made no move to save either of them. I know for a fact that it was me who thought, 'I wonder if that bath is going to sink?' I do remember thinking that I didn't want to fall into the river; one of us splashing about risking Weil's disease was more than enough, and I had a new pair of trainers on.

With a certain sense of relief, I realised that, as the plug had been firmly wedged into the plughole to stop us from losing it, the wretched thing was actually floating. Geoff, floating with it, had pushed it around the back of the boat, stopping only when the bath bumped gently against the bank. He then stood up in the scant foot of mud and water in which he had been trying to swim and, narrowing his eyes, looked up at me. I was desperately trying to keep a straight face and still leaning nonchalantly on the roof of the engine room.

'Do you think,' he gave me his patented 'I am just about keeping my temper but one more thing is going to make me lose it big time' face, 'that you could possibly – if you have nothing better to do – come and get this on to dry land?'

I know that face, and, wincing slightly, I leapt off the boat and pulled the bath out of the river. Geoff hauled himself out and stood, shivering, dripping water, mud and weed all over my new trainers; somehow I felt that complaining wouldn't really get me any sympathy. Three hours later, the bath was finally in the bathroom and Geoff was dry and full of tea (which always puts him in a better mood). It transpired that dumping the bath into the river showed us exactly how to get it lined up for the back doors, we threw it back in the river and brought it around the far side of the boat, then (*both* of us dry and on the back plate this time), we dragged it aboard in exactly the right position, where it went through the doors with no fuss at all. There was one minor 'hold your breath' moment when we were juggling it past the bedroom wall but although it scraped on both sides, it went through. I can only hope that no one ever wants to take it out because, with the later addition of the bedroom door, that bath is there to stay.

Chapter Seventeen
Twenty-three Tonnes of Steel,
One Man and a Rope

WHILE ALL THIS HAD been going on, Charlie's first and second visit to the boat had arrived and passed. It would be fair to say that on her first visit she had expected the boat to be bad. I think that by her second visit she half expected it to be completely finished. She loved the new bathroom but felt that, really, if that was as far as we had got, we ought to be putting a lot more effort in. She was willing to be slightly mollified with promises of graceful elegance in the future but we had sorely disappointed her with our present level of activity.

It's amazing really: you can completely ignore your living conditions until somebody points them out to you. I think her exact words were, 'Oh yuck.' I have to admit she was right. With one bathroom dismantled, tools everywhere, boxes heaped haphazardly in odd cabins, Happy was looking a slightly sorry sight. However, even with all the disappointment, we had a fun weekend and at least Charlie agreed to come back. But she did expect it to be a lot better by then. (We had our orders.)

Hardly anything on Happy changed over the next couple of weeks (hoo boy, were we going to be in trouble) and one morning, with Sam safe at school, we decided to head into Ely for a pump out and a full refill with fresh water. It had been irritating to discover that the river had no turning spaces for a boat of Happy's length. To travel into Ely, we had to spend three quarters of an hour heading in the opposite direction and turn her at the 'Lazy Otter', so every time we made the journey Geoff desperately searched for likely spots that might have just enough space for us to squeeze our way around and allow us to knock some time off the journey.

He had spotted one such place where the bank had been eroded over time, forming a nice semi-circle shaped 'bite' out of the bank, where, he hoped, we might be able to jam her nose into the apex and use it like a winding hole. So bundled up in jumpers, woolly socks, hats and gloves, we decided to give it a try.

I have always found it difficult to envisage 70 foot. You look at 'normal' narrow boats – most of which are around 55 foot – and then you take a look at our monstrosity. Well, that day we found out exactly how long 70 foot is ... About three foot longer than the width of the bloody river.

Under normal circumstances being across the river wouldn't have caused us any real problems. There would have been grumping and sighing, but we should have been able to kick off from the bank or use a pole to push her backwards, swing her straight and off we'd go. That day the circumstances were anything other than 'normal'. We slowed right down as we approached Geoff's possible turning place and turned Happy's nose into the bank. All was going to plan, and as she was turning in, I increased the power just to get her turning a little faster and, in a foul and horrible moment of déjà vu, her nose lifted, and came to a complete stop. Oh damn. Well, at least, unlike the other times we had grounded, it was only Happy's nose that was stuck; it should have been easy to get her afloat again.

The river had eroded the bank, but it was actually *only* the bank that had eroded. Two inches below the surface, the original line of the Old West River was still there, lurking under the water, a huge soft mud bank. Happy, like a pig hunting for truffles, stuck her nose in deep and there she contentedly stopped.

For the next hour and a half we did every single thing we could think of to get ourselves free: we rocked her; we got off and pushed from the bank; we stayed on and pushed against the bank with bars. Happy just lived up to her name and with every action made a deeper nest for herself in the mud (oink!). Finally out of options, we sat on her roof, each clasping a cup of tea and thought about our predicament.

Looking back on the incident I have decided that while 'necessity' may be the mother of invention, she also had three other children: Stupidity, Danger and Futility (those three obviously left home early and didn't go to university). Deciding that we needed better leverage it was decided that I would push with a pole from the front and Geoff would take a rope into the river and swim with it to the far bank in an attempt to provide extra 'oomph' by pulling her back end toward him. (It seemed like a good idea at the time.)

Geoff prepared to clamber into the freezing cold, fast-running river. Looking at the speed of the water that day, and knowing that Geoff wasn't the strongest swimmer in the world – he's like a shark, if he stops moving he sinks – I insisted that we attach another rope to his waist, which I would hold, ready to pull him back if anything horrible happened.

Taking a deep breath, he slipped into the river and headed for the far bank. Holding his safety rope, I held my breath until he was safely out of the water, then shouted over to him to untie the rope around his waist, as I didn't want any chance of it getting tangled when, and if, we came free and I had to start the engine.

'Untie the rope,' I shouted across the water.

Geoff was busy shivering. 'What?'

'UNTIE THE ROPE,' I bellowed again. Not sure that he had heard me, I demonstrated which rope by giving it a little tug.

Completely unnoticed by either of us, as Geoff had been swimming, the poorly tied rope had loosened and, as he had pulled himself out onto the bank and had stood up, it had slipped down around his ankles. My 'little tug' pulled him straight off his feet, onto his backside. He then slid, down the muddy slope and straight back into the river. I winced at the splash; at least he was far enough away that all his screaming and cursing were muffled by distance.

With Geoff out of the water for the second time, I took myself and the barge pole to the front of the boat. With a big shout of 'GO!' Geoff pulled, I pushed and Happy grudgingly left her pig wallow and headed backward, swinging her back end toward Geoff heaving from the other bank.

No one can think of everything in a situation like this and we found ourselves with a little problem. With Geoff on the far bank and me desperately trying to pull the barge pole back from where it had sunk into the mud at the front, there was no one at the tiller and before I had time to race down the roof, Happy had run backwards into the far bank, the current sweeping her nose sideways and ploughing it hard back into the mud wallow – again.

As all movement ceased and Happy made happy squelching noises in the mud at the bow, we found ourselves diagonally across the river, and, rather than being a little stuck at the front as we had been, we were now stuck at both ends.

At least Geoff didn't have to get back into the water – he just stepped aboard the back plate and stood there, studying our latest predicament, dripping and shivering.

'Go and get changed,' I said to him, 'we're not going anywhere. Surely if we just wait a little while, another boat will come along and they can push us off.'

Unable to speak through his chattering teeth, Geoff just nodded and went below to find some warm, dry clothes. I put the kettle on.

Waiting for him to return, I sat scanning the river. Surely a disaster of such epic proportions as this should have provided entertainment for a hundred onlookers – an unrivalled opportunity for pointing and laughing; and then it struck me, this was the exception to the rule. We needed help, therefore, there wasn't likely to be a boat down the river for another six hours.

A well-wrapped husband, still slightly blue, appeared at the engine room door and reached, with a shaking hand, for his tea. I gave him a hug. 'Sorry about pulling you into the river, I didn't notice that the rope had slipped.'

Geoff grinned. 'Ah well, I was already wet, so you're one up on last time.'

Studying the back end, it was far worse than we feared. Happy had hit the bank rudder first, this had then sunk deep into the mud, and was acting like an anchor; there was no way we could just swing her off at the back end. We wandered down to the front and found the force of the current had lifted Happy so far up onto the mud bank that she was at least four inches higher than normal; completely and utterly stuck.

So there we stayed, blocking the entire river. We had already been there for an hour and there were only another two before one of us had to go and pick up Sam from school. With the complete lack of onlookers, I was beginning to wonder if a bomb had dropped or aliens had attacked and we were the only ones left in the world; no joggers, no dog walkers and no other boats – it really was very unfair.

Over yet another cup of tea, I stood at the back leaning on the immobile tiller and watched Geoff now trying to dig us out with a spade. Finally losing my temper with the whole situation, I grasped the tiller in both hands and gave it a good wrench backwards and forwards.

What's this? What's this? The wretched thing actually moved, only about an inch but it *had* really, truly moved. I rolled my sleeves up and shouted at Geoff that I had got the tiller to move a bit and that I was going to try and just keep moving it backward and forward in the hope that it would dig its way out of the mud.

It took me about ten minutes, and to this day I hate to think what damage I caused to the already dodgy shims, but eventually the rudder began to move more freely in wider and wider arcs. Eventually, I managed to get it facing in the other direction. Geoff had come to give me a hand about halfway through the exercise and, seeing that we now had a possibility of movement, he rushed off to the front of the boat and leapt off on to the bank to give her another push. I turned the engine on and with the rudder no longer attaching us to the bank, Happy moved her bum elegantly round into mid-stream and we were finally back in free water.

Happy and I were now in the middle of the river, Geoff was on the bank – not the best place for him really. He motioned me to keep going and trotted alongside, both of us looking for a good launch point from which he could jump on. Approaching on the left was a flattened muddy area where cows came down to drink, which Geoff pointed to, giving me the thumbs-up sign. I slowed right down and watched him sprint ahead, readying himself for a big jump.

He jumped. He slipped. Grabbing the gunwales, he only ended up waist deep in the river; he struggled onto the boat and sloshed toward me.

'Oh well,' he said, 'we're all where we are supposed to be and at least I'm only half wet this time.'

With him still dripping on to my feet, we rounded a corner and both watched in silence as a perfectly good, man-made mooring slid past. We looked down at his trainers and jeans gently trickling over the back deck, we both looked back at the mooring, we did *not* look at each other and neither of us said a word.

Chapter Eighteen
Breaking in a Boyfriend

By the beginning of November, we had pretty much become accustomed to our new life. I found myself spending a fair amount of time in the bathroom as that was the only clean, well-decorated area in the boat, but apart from that one small sign of neurosis the rest of life just pottered slowly by.

Geoff had sorted out a lot of the electrics and other minor irritations, such as gaps around the windows, through which the wind whistled, and he had taken our rather fragile central heating system apart in an attempt to toughen it up; even with his intervention, the heating was still temperamental and I had actually become quite handy with a ten-millimetre spanner.

All of these little jobs took a vast amount of time but didn't really make a lot of visible difference to the decorative surroundings. So, by the time Charlie visited again, we had to endure a few quiet comments about laziness and how nothing much had changed. She was charitable enough to inform us that, even though her living environment was no better than a kennel, she did enjoy her visits and would continue to grace us with her presence for a little longer, but really we ought to be putting a lot more effort in.

As the weather grew colder, we had to move a couple of jobs to the top of the 'urgent' list. Inside the boat, the temperature plummeted at night and we desperately needed to install a wood-burning stove. The ridiculous central heating system was even more at the mercy of cold weather than we were and although Geoff dealt with the cold in his normal stoic way, I was completely fed up with going to bed fully dressed.

The dropping temperature had also highlighted several extra external problems. Since arriving at the mooring we had been clambering down the steep flood defences, trusting that, if we fell, the late summer grass was soft and lush and the most we could suffer was a slightly bruised bottom and maybe a bag of spilt shopping. As the weather turned, the bank become muddy or icy – in either state, it was hideously slippery. With the dark nights drawing in, it became imperative to construct a set of steps before one of us ended up in the river. A wide, strong and safe gangplank was also needed for pretty much the same reason.

Huw and Amelia were due to visit and it was decided that, with their help, we could actually moor the boat near the builders' yard and just pick up all the wood required for steps and gangplank in one trip. There was far too much to fit in the car and, with our savings dwindling rapidly, delivery charges were a luxury we weren't about to indulge in.

Like Charlie, Amelia and Huw had some comments to make about the state of the boat when they arrived, and were understandably not too ecstatic when they realised this was not going to be a weekend's holiday and they were expected to actually do something to help us out. We all set off toward the builders' merchants. It's not as if you can park a boat right outside a shop, well not in Ely anyway, so there was an approximate ten-minute walk to get the wood, which Geoff said would be an 'easy saunter', even with Huw and himself carrying five lengths of 12-foot by 2-inch by 8-inch pine between them.

It didn't sound easy to me, so Amelia and I left them to it and took Sam shopping; a good excuse to drink coffee and have a chat. Arriving back about an hour later, we were a little concerned to find that Geoff and Huw were still out. Amelia tried to ring Huw but there was no answer and we hung about in the boat waiting to find out what had happened. Another half an hour and there was a thump, a groan and the sound of voices. I stuck my head out of the door and was relieved to see Geoff loading the wood onto the top of the boat.

'Where's Huw?' I asked.

Geoff nodded toward the ground and grinned. Poor Huw was flat on his back on the grass and breathing hard.

'Tough trip?' I asked.

'No, not really,' Geoff laughed. 'These teenagers have no stamina.'

I'm not sure whether or not teenagers have stamina, but what I am sure of is that Geoff and I have toughened up considerably since starting this trip. I can now carry a 25kg bag of coal on my shoulder, from the car, up the flood defences and down a flight of steps. In my previous life, I would have been lucky to get it off the ground.

Geoff definitely has more lumpy bits (more bruises and bits missing as well), but the accumulation of muscle and good health is most noticeable; it's amazing what you take for granted living in a house, a simple thing such as bringing in a week's shopping is now an exercise in weight-lifting over distance. Gone are the days when you leave your car boot open and just scuttle backwards and forwards with one small bag in each hand.

With the wind blowing rain into your face, you only want to make one trip, four bags in each hand, out of the car park, up the road, a three-minute walk over the flood defences (usually in the dark) then down the other side, and a logistics exercise trying to get all the bags of shopping off the bank and into the boat without dropping anything in the water. Every single simple job takes far more effort. The silver lining to this cloud? More exercise, better health, actual muscle, greater stamina and weight loss. There are also: wet feet, mud covering everything and a whole new range of swear words from which to choose – ah, the good life!

Little things mean so much more. The wood that Huw had sweated and griped over made the most fantastic set of steps I had ever seen – they weren't particularly pretty to look at, being plain, functional and over-engineered like most of Geoff's creations, but having those steps meant that we could just walk down to the boat without the death defying slide, fall and drop that was rapidly becoming the bane of our lives. In the dark, the whole exercise had been doubly dangerous.

The day the steps were completed, we treated ourselves to four small, solar-powered, garden lights which we positioned, two at the top and two at the bottom, one at each corner of the steps. Standing in the gathering darkness, we watched them come alive and light our path – it was magical; no fancy light display ever received a better reception.

Herbert particularly liked them, as they warmed in any small amount of sun, and he would sit for hours soaking up that warmth and guarding 'his steps' from the hated dog next door. New neighbours had pulled up about a week previously, and Dion and Charlie brought with them a spaniel puppy called Jake who, quite frankly, was a ball of over-friendly energy. He just never stopped – how they put up with him in a confined space I'll never know – but for all his energy he certainly didn't have a mean bone in his body.

Herbert took one look at Jake's obvious, frivolous youth and abundant energy and loathed him on sight. He would guard the steps, lifting his head as Jake approached, attempting to fix him with a gimlet stare and snarling the dog equivalent of 'come and have a go if you think you're hard enough'. With one wall-eye and only three teeth, he didn't look nearly as menacing as he thought he did. As Jake passed by, Herbert would wait until he was level, then would leap up, hair afluff, and scream at him, so it was slightly ironic that his much loved and guarded steps caused his next major dunking.

It was a beautiful morning, cold, with a weak sun that caused the frosted banks to glitter. Sam and I had decided to take Herbert out for a drag, thinking it might be one of the last sunny days that we would see. So, muffled up in coats, wellies, hats and gloves, we had been walking for about ten minutes when Herbert did his usual trick of flopping over on to his side and playing dead, which means 'I've had enough; I want to go back to my nice warm bed.'

Sam was complaining about cold feet and I really couldn't be bothered to argue with either of them, so we turned and headed for home. I gave the lead to Sam to hold, as neither of them moved very fast. However, as soon as Herbert realised where we were headed he leapt up and shot off ahead, his extendable lead whirring as he bounced through the long grass with Sam crashing along in his wake, giggling furiously.

He stopped and kindly waited at the top of the steps for us to catch up, then took off again. The steps being comparatively new, Sam and I were still negotiating them with care and probably didn't move as fast as Herbert was hoping we would. So when he jumped for the back of the boat, Sam was still at the top of the steps.

The lead reached the end of its roll and Herbert reached the end of his tether ... literally. He was jerked, cartoon-like, back in mid air; Sam was pulled forward down the steps and I grabbed his hand in an effort to prevent a headlong fall. I held my breath and lurched us both toward the boat, in the vain hope that Herbert would still be capable of some forward momentum. No such luck. Straight down and into the river; again. Making sure that Sam was on flat ground, I rushed down the steps and hauled Herbert out by the lead. It was at that moment that a man walking his own dog along the flood defences stopped and studied poor, dripping, freezing Herbert dangling from his lead.

'I didn't realise there were dogfish in this river,' he calmly stated. 'What are you using for bait?' Oh ha ha bloody ha.

With the steps and the new gangplank in place, the next job was to install our wonderful and hideously expensive new wood-burner. We had purchased a Morso Squirrel, having heard good things about them. This wonderful contraption had been sitting (cold) in the boat for about a month, and I was beginning to get tetchy about the whole thing.

Geoff had been putting off the installation, knowing that he would have to cut a circular hole in the top of the boat for chimney access. So, as usual, we had faffed about, putting down the tiled stand for it and arguing about where to locate it and so on. But we had got to the point where there was no logical reason to put it off any longer. With our building problems in the bathroom and the issues we were experiencing with the central heating, we were honestly expecting something horrible to happen and were quite amazed when the whole thing went off without a hitch.

Geoff measured where the flue was to go, drilled a pilot hole, and then cut a circle out with a jigsaw (he actually went through about six blades, the metal on the roof of a narrow boat is pretty thick), attached chimney to flue, flue to stove, sealed around it and that was that, completely painless.

With winter breathing down your neck, a roaring fire is great on so many levels. Obviously it is warm, but it is also living and moving and creates a homely glow and a great noise. It added a whole new level of luxury to a boat that, apart from a wonderful bathroom, had nowhere near enough.

A good wood-burner can really kick out some heat and, within days, we had worked out how to bank it overnight, ensuring that even when we woke up early, the lounge area was warm and inviting. We had actually managed to get it all installed and working two days before Charlie's next visit was due – aha changes that could be seen and felt; a weekend of approval, how nice.

Chapter Nineteen
Christmas

AS I AM SURE I have said before, Geoff is a man of lists; he likes to have a plan. Unfortunately, we were now so far off our original plan, we had to sit down one evening and completely write a new one, and that sort of thing just upsets him. He kept veering back to the original plan and I had to 'look' at him for a while, until he concentrated on the new one.

We were also beginning to understand why we had been told time and time again that it was a bad idea to live on a narrow boat while you are restoring it; there are just too many problems, especially when children are involved. We had discovered a whole list of things that are problematic with a child: there's the school run; there's the fact that at the end of the working day everything has to be cleared before Sam sets foot back into the boat as he can do a fair amount of damage to himself and his surroundings with power tools, especially when he's trying to 'help'; there's the fact that living on a boat means just that – *living* – quality time with your child, nutritious meals at regular intervals, going out, friends, birthday parties, etc. All the 'stuff' that goes on in normal life doesn't stop just because your parents have fallen out of the sanity tree and hit every branch on the way down.

We tried very hard to keep firmly in mind that Sam never asked for this, he never wanted it, and he had given us very little in the way of trouble about it, a fact for which I will be forever grateful. So these were our excuses why, with two weeks to go before Christmas, we still only had one room completed.

Geoff had built a new sofa in the saloon where we could sit by the fire. It was an ingenious thing which lifted and moved, revealing compartmentalised storage space; there are obviously times where being a pedantic, obsessive compulsive is an asset. With the new sofa, which had been installed a little to the left of the front doors, the original bathroom space had become a distant memory and we had finally reached a point where we knew the upheaval was going to become vast and poor Sam would be moved about the boat like a pawn in an extreme chess match.

The new layout of Happy would mean that the old kitchen, which was at the very rear of the boat, would become our main bedroom, one of the old bathrooms and half the next cabin had already been made into the new bathroom, the other half of that cabin and half of the next one would be merged together to make Sam's new bedroom (half of which we were currently sleeping in), the next three cabins were scheduled to become an open-plan kitchen, dining and lounge space (Sam was currently sleeping in the first of these). So, the dilemma was: how to move people around to give them some living space while each of these rooms was being destroyed and walls were being moved.

It was finally decided that we would start with Sam's room. We did this for two reasons – firstly, it was in the middle of the boat and we figured that we could work out to each side; secondly, and probably the more important, was that it would give Sam a place of his own where he could escape the noise and fuss that was consuming the rest of the boat. There was also the odd little room right at the very front of the boat, but as we hadn't come up with a decent use for that yet, we decided to just leave it as a nice warm 'snug'-cum-television room, yet another place that Sam and his toys could escape to, without being in danger of having something fall on him.

But, as it was only two weeks to Christmas, we convinced ourselves that it would be better to wait until the New Year before starting anything major. We were away in Cumbria for the best part of the holiday and then, moving back down the country, were due to visit my parents in the Midlands. There seemed no point at all in starting anything new.

We spent the next week filling Happy with tacky fairy lights that flashed and changed colour; we also managed to find the smallest Christmas tree in the world, I think the sad-looking little thing only stood 12 inches high. We over-decorated it and balanced it on a box. From the outside, and with the curtains open, Happy looked like a floating brothel. Sam loved it and would curl up under a patchwork quilt in the front cabin listening to a Christmas carol CD and watching the lights flash.

I have never faced a Christmas with so little money. With three children to find presents for, Geoff and I set a firm budget, decided to forego presents for the two of us and just concentrate on the kids.

Amelia, although disappointed that this year wasn't going to be full of useless, expensive presents, each one forgotten and cast aside in the excitement of opening the next, seemed to understand and accepted our reasoning. I was so proud of her when she tentatively asked for a new coat, but I felt really sad as well. I *wanted* to buy them rubbish, I *wanted* them to have the piles of useless glittering presents that they had come to expect. Damn it all, *I* wanted the piles of useless glittering presents that *I* had come to expect.

I spent a miserable Saturday afternoon Christmas shopping in Cambridge and, after spending a couple of hours battling with the rabid, unhappy shoppers and another hour battling with equally rabid but more homicidal than unhappy drivers on the A10, I squelched over the darkening flood defences with a scant few bags, a headache and a very heavy heart.

As I approached the boat, I noticed how pretty she looked with the lights twinkling in the front cabin; the fog gathering around the windows changed colour with the reflected lights, giving Happy her own front-end aurora borealis; the scent of wood smoke wafted toward me through the damp air and I could hear Sam and Geoff, singing loud, mostly off-key, carols. With me out of the way for the day, they had been packing up the books left by the previous owners to make room for our own and had taken them to a second-hand book store. They had made more in book sales than I had spent on presents, so they were righteously happy when I clambered in through the door.

Over the next couple of days, Sam and I had a fantastic time making Christmas cards on our wobbly table. By the time Charlie arrived on Saturday, we had a complete range of glittery, tasteless, blobby and unidentifiable cards. These we made envelopes for and sent them on their way to unsuspecting friends and family. With Charlie's help, we spent that weekend making fudge and hijacking a friend's cooker to bake Christmas biscuits and other poorly shaped goodies. It was a lovely weekend; we were all sticky, glitter-covered and felt slightly sick from too many 'taste tests'.

I was surprised to find that, when pushed, the kids didn't actually want anything much for Christmas; Charlie wanted some roller skates and Sam a new computer game. They were far happier just puddling around making things, laughing, throwing things at each other and making a mess. We discovered that Sam can really cook and Charlie has a superb eye for package design. By the time Sunday evening rolled around, they both plonked themselves onto the sofa, next to a huge pile of homemade presents that we intended to give to the family. Exhausted, and even after a bath, still slightly glittery, they both proclaimed it the best weekend ever.

Christmas and New Year sped past. It was strange to spend time in a house again and I found myself staring out of the window, missing my early morning dose of fish lips in the mist. I also found myself automatically throwing the toast crusts out of the window; luckily my mother thought that I was feeding the birds.

'We do have a bird table, dear,' she grouched, as she rushed around sweeping them away from her immaculate patio.

Within days, it seemed, Sam was back at school and we were faced, once again, with *the plan*. The weather was cold, wet and grey. Snuggled up together in front of the fire, we just couldn't bring ourselves to do anything more than make tea and sit around discussing what we ought to be doing.

As we were retiring to bed after yet another fruitless evening of watching mind-numbing rubbish on the telly, Sam woke up from a nightmare and, as he was unwilling to be consoled, I settled him in bed with Geoff and prepared to sleep in his room for the night.

I couldn't get comfortable – the whole bed felt clammy and damp. Putting this down to Sam being frightened and probably a bit sweaty, I didn't really give it much thought, but it felt so horrible that, eventually, I decided to get up and change the sheets.

Stripping Sam's bed down was always a bit of a pain as the mattress had to be standing on its side to enable the sheet to be put on, so, at two in the morning, I was buried under a heavy mattress struggling to replace a fitted sheet. I lifted it up on to its side and, leaning it on the wall, bent down to pick up the sheet. As I began to stand up the mattress toppled and landed across my back and shoulders.

It didn't hurt, but it was absolutely soaking. The whole underside of the mattress was completely sodden, and turning the main light on to get a better look I noticed that the wooden board that made up the mattress base was also covered in water; it had obviously been like this for some time as dark patches had appeared on the underside of the mattress and it had a mouldy, musty smell. I picked the whole thing up and, after dragging it through the boat, slung it as far as I could down the gangplank, leaving it in the dark to be dealt with in the morning.

Grimacing and trying not to give in to the need to wash my hands in Lye, I wandered into our bedroom and poked Geoff awake. I dragged him into Sam's room and showed him the still soaking but mattress-less bed base. He decided that, as the base was solid, the moisture had nowhere to go and no way to evaporate and this had probably been building up for ages. He was far more sanguine than I about the whole thing and, yawning, gave me a kiss, assured me that we would deal with it in the morning, and staggered back to bed; I slept on the sofa.

The mouldy bed pushed us into action again. The next morning we examined all the mattresses and found each one to be in the same condition as Sam's. I was amazed that we hadn't noticed this before, then had minor hysterics and refused to sleep on any of them.

Geoff, stoic as usual, went straight to the room and a half that were to be made into Sam's new space and began to dismantle them. Eventually, after spending another ten minutes moaning about the diseases we could have caught from the beds, I joined him.

Unsurprisingly, we encountered all the same problems that we had when dismantling the bathrooms. Firstly, there were screws with no grip or with heads that broke off the second you touched them with a screwdriver that had to be drilled out. There was no pump-out tank to remove – thank God – but being a hotel boat, every room boasted a little corner sink, and we knew they were going to be trouble.

The wall holding the sink was the very last to be removed and Geoff had been building up to another long struggle. Having nothing to do at that point, I made tea and, wandering in, I leant against the wall sipping it, intent on enjoying the show.

As before, Geoff removed all the screws, dismantled the taps and pipe work and just as before, the wretched thing just hung on the wall and mocked him.

'What are you going to do this time?' I asked, leaning over and giving it a little wiggle. It felt completely solid.

Geoff grinned at me. 'I have a cunning plan, Lord Blackadder,' and with that, he picked up a lump hammer and hit it – hard.

Watching the hammer's descent, I winced and backpedalled away from the expected explosion of porcelain shards. He obviously hadn't hit it hard enough because, apart from making a sound like a broken bell, nothing happened. Geoff frowned and, taking a deep breath, he braced his feet apart and raised the hammer for another blow.

It never fell. Without any sound at all, the sink just dropped to the floor where it hit with a dull thud and lay there, leaving Geoff with a confused look on his face and the hammer held above his head. To this day I have no idea why it was so funny, but I laughed so hard my face hurt and I had to go and sit down for a bit; even now when I think of him standing there with his hammer I still laugh. Over the course of destroying the cabins to make way for a more open-plan living area, we removed seven sinks in all, and not one of them gave up without a fight.

Within two weeks, Sam had a bright new bedroom and we were all looking forward to him moving out of our makeshift room and back into his own. He was enchanted with the new room: a bed just his size, new mattress, massive amounts of ventilation, desk at the end with a light, wardrobe and drawers. His new bed was high enough that all his toys fitted beneath it in big storage boxes. The whole room was decorated in cool blue and white, and a new dark blue, deep pile carpet, which nicely matched the curtains, covered the floor.

The weekend before it was finished, we had let him loose

in B&Q and he was allowed to choose whatever additional decoration he liked. He chose a frieze of Scooby Doo and Mystery Incorporated; it was huge and had the added attraction of little sticky figures that could be placed on it to complete certain scenes of ghosts, monsters and general mayhem.

I had winced slightly; it was so ridiculously far away from the traditional rose and castle narrow boat decorations that it felt like putting fake black oak beams in a spaceship, but it was his choice and he loved it.

When the room was complete, he moved in amidst much celebration and furore and refused to emerge for two days, even to the point of demanding all his meals be served on a tray – this he would place reverently on his desk, turn on the overhead spotlight and settle down to some serious eating. He got away with this for 24 hours, but as part of our new family lifestyle, we had decreed that at least one meal a day should be eaten together around a table, and, lovely though his room was, it was way too small to hold two adults, a small boy and a pot of spaghetti Bolognese.

Chapter Twenty
She's a Narrow Boat, Not an Ice Breaker!

WITH ONE ACTUAL BEDROOM completed, a bathroom and the space where a room used to be now holding a rather comfy sofa, we felt we had actually made some progress.

One morning, after dropping Sam at school, I staggered back into the boat and threw myself down on to the sofa, causing Geoff to look up in surprise. He had a large hammer in one hand and was obviously preparing to hit something, hard.

'Are you all right?' He put the hammer down and, taking a closer look at me, walked into the bathroom and grabbed a bottle of Night Nurse. 'You look absolutely foul,' he informed me, holding out a shot of glowing green yuck.

'Gee, thanks,' I sniffled at him and, turning, prepared to throw myself face down on the sofa. 'Believe me, I probably feel worse than I look.'

'Oh no, you don't.' Geoff grabbed me before I could settle myself in comfort. 'Why don't you go and have a long sleep in Sam's room, you can shut the door to the end of the corridor and I can carry on working.'

'OK.' I downed the disgusting medicine and shuddered. 'Don't let me sleep for too long.'

Geoff looked around what was going to become our saloon. 'Two hours at most,' he promised.

True to his word, Geoff woke me with a nice cup of tea two hours later. Sam's bed had been surprisingly comfortable and I really could have stayed there for the rest of the day.

'Come and have a look at this.'

Ho hum. I got up.

Sam's bedroom had been created from one of the old bedrooms in the corridor, and the saloon had been partially created in the space where the old toilet and one bedroom used to be. There were another two unused bedrooms, which were due to be all knocked down to make a through kitchen, dining room, saloon and, while I had been asleep, Geoff had done it all.

In my strange, fluey state I couldn't quite grasp what he had done, only that there was suddenly a huge area of just, well, 'space' really. He had taken out two sets of side walls, two fixed beds and some other little bits like bedside tables, and all that was left was our little sofa fixed on one wall, which looked a good 30 feet away.

It was an amazing and huge change. Happy went from being one long, dark little corridor to all airy, light space. It was rather empty, it echoed and the whole place looked a little odd as there was just a void with a sofa and the wood burner stuck at the end.

'Wow,' I mused, 'this really makes a difference. Now that you've got it all cleared, what's going where?'

Geoff spent the next 20 minutes showing me drawings and pointing out exactly which part of the new space those drawings pertained to. By the second drawing, I found myself beginning to drift and couldn't remember what was on the previous one. Luckily Geoff finally noticed that my eyes were glazed and I was beginning to slide down the wall. He put the drawings to one side and helped me back to bed. By the time I awoke for the second time, he had cleared all his tools away, vacuumed the mess up, been out to pick up Sam and had made dinner.

About eight o'clock that evening, I was curled up on the sofa with a hot water bottle, which he occasionally re-filled for me.

'How are you feeling now?' he asked. 'Is there anything

you need?'

I sniffed and smiled up at him from beneath my blanket, 'No, I'm fine. I feel a lot better actually.'

'Good.' Geoff reached behind him and brought out a sheaf of papers. 'Shall we go through these drawings now then?'

I suddenly felt really ill again.

Throughout February, the vagaries of the central heating system became more and more irritating until Geoff finally took the whole thing apart for a second time and swore at it for another couple of days. When he put it back together, it certainly was more efficient but still not perfect; every three or four days it would just stop working, and we would have to bleed it and go round the boat bleeding all the radiators which took about an hour and a half, fill the header tank back up with water and restart it.

The wood-burner was a godsend and, as temperatures plunged below freezing, it was often too cold to do any work at night, so we spent a lot of time just huddled up in quilts by the fire. Being very new to all this, it took us some time to work out that in temperatures like these you NEVER let the fire go out, because if you did, it could take up to ten hours to get the boat warm again.

We had learnt that particular lesson very early in our ownership, when, having been out at a birthday do at Arwen and Carl's, we had let the fire go out before we left, at around ten o'clock that morning. By the time we had returned, 11 hours later, the boat was bone-achingly cold.

Sam had been sent to bed with hot wheat bags and, with a fine disregard for the electricity bill, he also had a heated blanket; he was soon warm, cosy and fast asleep. Geoff and I fared less well, the heating went off at about 11 o'clock and refused to come back on again, no matter what we did to it. Even with the fire roaring away, the temperature at the front of the boat was still finger-, toe- and mind-numbing.

With all the old beds still out of bounds due to the damp,

Geoff and I had taken to sleeping on the saloon floor and at two o'clock in the morning, with the fire still on full, we huddled together, fully dressed, under two quilts and gibbered gently at each other. I got up once to check on Sam but even with his blanket now turned off, he was still completely toasty (I think that small boys have some sort of inner nuclear reactor). Pausing only to put on yet another pair of socks, a woolly hat and some gloves, I went back to join Geoff, and we finally fell asleep.

At four o'clock in the morning, we woke up, sweating and soaked. The ambient temperature had finally risen and everything was back to normal – in fact, it was so hot that Herbert had taken himself off to sleep in the bathroom.

We turned the fire down and, after divesting ourselves of all layers of clothing and dumping one of the quilts, we managed to sleep well for the rest of the night, but it was a major lesson learned; the Morso did not go out again until May.

Two days later, we woke up to dead silence, broken only by odd crunching sounds. Thinking that maybe it had snowed; I peered out of the window. No, no snow, just a very heavy frost.

I woke Geoff up as I went to put the kettle on by the simple act of tripping over him as he lay happily asleep on the floor (you would think most men would be happy to have a beautiful woman fall into their laps; maybe he would have liked me to fall from a lesser height).

Anyway, with Geoff up and about, if still wincing and limping slightly, I mentioned the odd noise. He looked in all the usual places that produce odd noises: central heating, water pump, engine room, but couldn't find anything. I was a bit concerned as I am not a great fan of odd noises, they never lead to anything good, and, by the time Geoff gave up, I was getting quite tetchy about the whole thing.

'Good grief! Come and have a look at this.' Geoff had pulled the curtain aside and was staring out over the river. I joined him at the window and was amazed. The whole river was frozen from bank to bank.

'Now there's something you don't see every day.' Geoff slid the window open and gave the ice a poke with our broom.

'That's fairly solid,' I said, watching the broom handle bounce off the white river.

'It's thin close to the boat, look.' Geoff bashed the ice close to Happy's side and it gave way with a crack, the same cracking sound we had been trying to track down.

'Oh it's the ice. As the boat moves, she's breaking the ice,' I shivered. 'Eugh. Close the window, it's flaming cold out there.'

Over breakfast we discussed our day's plans.

'We were going to Ely today. Are we still going to go?' I devoutly hoped he was going to say no but didn't really think there was much chance of that – it would take more than an inch of ice for Geoff to change a 'plan'. Sure enough...

'Yeah, it'll be fine, the sun's out and, more to the point, there's no wind. We might not be so lucky tomorrow.'

Irk! I just knew he was going to say that. Oh well, better go and find the thermals.

An hour later found us both bundled up in whatever warm clothing we could find, standing at the stern, ready to go. Herbert had been forced out for his last wee; I finally had had to chuck him down the gangplank and then stand guard on it to stop him sneaking, still un-emptied, back on to the boat. He had finally given in and with an odd hobbling and tiptoeing movement had made his way over the frozen grass to relieve himself. When I finally let him back on to the boat the ungrateful little gargoyle dived into his bed and lay there staring at me in mournful accusation.

Standing freezing at the tiller, I waited for Geoff to go through his cast off checklist and stared mournfully at the cup of tea he had placed for me on the roof. I had so many pairs of gloves on I couldn't actually pick it up and was just wondering whether we had any straws, when Geoff, finally finished, jumped aboard with a big grin and a puff of breath. I put Happy into forward and with a huge plume of water from the prop we stayed exactly where we were.

'It's the ice,' Geoff inched his way along the gunwales to the front of the boat and, sure enough, the bow had moved enough to make a beautiful 'V' shape in the ice which then held us fast.

The next half hour was spent bashing the ice with anything we could find. The best implements, we found, were a barge pole and a spade. As we smashed the ice away from the river side of the boat, Happy moved away from the bank and toward the middle where the ice was thinnest and actually started to make a little headway of her own. Of course, once we had started moving, the ice began to break away from her bow in big chunks that went skittering off across the frozen surface of the river, which was great fun to watch.

It wasn't quite so enjoyable to sit inside and listen to the amplified cracks as the ice broke and the horrible scratching noises as she brushed gently against any ice that refused to break. It struck me at the time that similar noises, obviously many times amplified, may have been the last sounds that some of the passengers on the Titanic ever heard. I shuddered and went back outside to stand with Geoff.

After about an hour of fairly slow but steady headway, I looked back at our progress: it was quite impressive. Beyond our wake, a huge crack in the ice stretched straight down the centre of the river. I laughed, watching the flock of rather relieved-looking swans that floated, in rather more restricted width than they were used to, behind us.

It took a little longer than usual but we finally made it to our normal turning point at the Lazy Otter. Forgetting the ice (I was driving at this point, Geoff had gone in to warm his hands) I took the usual route of swinging her nose over to the right and then around in a wide circle to the left, which usually meant we only had to perform one backing manoeuvre to get her turned completely around.

In all fairness, I did manage to get about halfway through the turn before she came to a complete halt, stuck in the ice again. It was much harder to get her underway this time. Getting her to go in a straight line with a fair amount of power at the back had worked well, but we were trying to turn her within her own length and the ice was having none of it.

Eventually, Geoff broke the ice to the left of her nose and I broke the ice to the right of her stern. Sweating and occasionally swearing as the ice failed to break, causing the implement in our freezing hands to vibrate painfully, we slowly pirouetted on the spot; it took us nearly an hour of smashing away at the ice to get her under way again.

Getting back to the mooring was much easier, as all we had to do was follow the break we had made on the way down. Our only issue was the seemingly millions of waterfowl that had taken refuge in the crack that we had created on our outward trip – we had to take it very slowly or risk crushing the birds up against the side of the ice in their panic to get away from us.

We managed to get back to our mooring three hours after we left. Pulling Happy back in, we gave up. We were cold, tired and were still suffering from painful, blood-returning tingles in our bashed hands. There was no way that we could make it to pump out and then back in time to pick up Sam. I sighed, another day wasted. But as I sat by the fire with yet more tea, I thought of the swans and ducks all happily swimming in exposed water that wouldn't have existed if we hadn't passed by, and decided that maybe the day hadn't been wasted after all.

What with bad weather and other such traumas, we didn't manage to get to pump out until the weekend, so early on a nearly windless Saturday, with a weak and watery sun doing its best to cheer us all up, we headed out toward Ely.

The journey was pretty much incident free and, as we pulled in to pump out, we were all in good moods and had decided that we would turn around after pump out, find somewhere to moor and go into town and do some food shopping.

About 200 yards downriver there was a fantastic 100-foot mooring free, with just one lone angler sitting right in the middle. As boats have the right of way on moorings in Ely, we did as we were supposed to, slowed right down and shouted to him.

'Coming in to moor!' We began to pull into the space; the angler didn't move. We slowed down a little more and shouted again, but he neither moved nor looked up or gave any sign that he was alive at all. I began to think he was a mannequin that someone had put there for a joke. By the time we actually hit his keep net we were running about, panicking and screaming, Happy was in full reverse and desperately trying to slow down, Geoff had his back against the boat and was 'walking' her front end along the wall in a desperate attempt to stop us from squashing this guy's equipment.

When we were about two foot away from him (and still going forward), the angler jumped to his feet and stuck out his hand in a policeman type 'stop' gesture. Erm, nice to see you are actually alive, mate, but no ... I can't stop. In the immortal words of Mr Scott, 'I canna change the laws of physics, Captain'; we're coming in whether you like it or not.

Well, quite frankly, the guy went loopy.

'What the f**k do you think you are doing?' he screamed, leaping up from his little stool-type box thing and beginning to literally dance with rage. Now I had read about this in books but always thought it was a literary plot device, but obviously not – this guy was really 'dancing'. OK, he wasn't about to be drafted into the hallowed lines of *Hot*

Gossip but he could have definitely been put to music. It certainly didn't help that he was wearing an all-in-one purple waterproof suit thingy so the whole scene looked very similar to a disco dancing, angry, purple Teletubby on 'E'. I was having serious problems keeping a straight face.

'We're mooring,' I shouted to him. 'We did tell you we were coming in, but either you didn't hear us or ...' I let the sentence trail off, as the only other choice was to tell him that he was an ignorant bastard and even though I felt that would add fuel to his Teletubby dancing, I didn't feel I had the moral fibre to be responsible for someone having an aneurism first thing on a Saturday morning.

'You can't just pull a boat in here, you stupid bitch,' he screamed, stamping his way down the mooring toward me. 'You've just squashed my net.' He stamped past Geoff, who was still holding the boat off the wall with his body, and came toward me with one fist raised.

I watched him come down the boat, pure aggression in motion – even if it was purple and ridiculous motion – and had a momentary indecision. If I backed off and apologised, would he feel he had the upper hand and carry on with the aggression or would he calm down?

'Look, I'm sorry about this,' I shouted down to him. 'We did tell you we were coming in and your nets are fine, the boat hasn't touched them.' I pointed to Geoff who was in danger of disappearing into the river, and waited to see if he would calm down a little.

No. He just got redder in the face (ick, blood-red really clashes with purple – he now resembled an overweight teenage blueberry with an acne problem).

'You stupid, fat bitch' (hey, I'm NOT fat), 'nobody has the right of way here.' (Wrong, actually, this is a mooring and if he had bothered to read his fishing licence – if he had one – he would have noticed that boats have right of way for moorings.)

OK, the guy was spoiling for a fight and he obviously felt

that I was an easy target; time to bring out feisty grrrl again.

'Listen, I'm sorry if we have squashed your nets, which we haven't. I'm sorry if you decided to ignore us when we said we were coming in. I'm sorry you decided to sit in the middle of 100 foot of mooring like king shit. I'm sorry we won't acknowledge you, Lord of the River. But we're here, we're moored where we should be, and it's *you* who's in the wrong – now get lost. We will move her back in the spirit of cooperation but we're not leaving.'

Out of the corner of my eye, I noticed, with a huge sense of relief, that Geoff had moved the guy's nets, had fastened Happy's front ropes to one of the rings and was now walking towards us. Mr Purple Teletubby also noticed this and began to back away, shouting as he went, 'Spirit of cooperation? I think we are well past that. I was having a lovely day until you turned up, you stupid bitch. I don't want to fish any more.' And with that last ringing, adult rejoinder he turned and stamped past Geoff back toward his equipment – his undamaged equipment. Geoff and I looked at each other and got on with tying the boat up.

All was quiet for about five minutes until Geoff went inside to look for his coat. Mr Tubby looked up and, noticing that I was on my own again, stamped back up the length of the boat to have another go. Seeing him coming, I nonchalantly stepped back on to the back plate and opened the back doors.

'Nobody has right of way here, you stupid cow. Anglers or boats – we are all equal you can't just pull in and push people out of the way.'

His voice was rising and so was my temper. It was so obvious that he had deliberately waited until he could have a go at me without Geoff there and I was absolutely damned if I was going to let some puffed-up (literally), middle-aged banker think I was an easy target just because I was female.

For each one of my children I have always had the same advice: violence proves nothing, shouting, screaming and swearing does no good, there is nothing that cannot be solved by quiet conversation and a little give and take on both sides.

Right, good advice. Well it would have been if I had taken it, but all that went out of the window completely. We stood there and screamed at each other like a couple of fishwives, with much swearing on both sides I am sad to admit, about the rights and the bylaws, and the fact that he was in the middle of a huge mooring and wouldn't move and that I was a stupid bitch. Eventually I gave up. He just kept repeating the same boring insults, I was called a stupid, f**king bitch so many times that I even considered suggesting some more interesting insults for him to use.

This carried on, to the vast amusement of a growing audience, until Geoff stuck his head out of the back of the boat and, as expected, Mr Tubby put his head down and scurried off with his parting shot: 'Oh I'm not discussing this, you've ruined my day.'

Geoff made sure he hung around me and kept a firm eye on Mr Tubby as he stamped about packing his kit up and complaining loudly about horrid, nasty boat people, to anyone that would give him half an ear. I did notice that none of the other anglers had come to his defence, but were all sitting, very quietly, as far away as possible.

By now it was past midday and, unable to put it off any longer, I grabbed Sam and steeled myself to walk past the still ranting angler on my way to the supermarket, which had been the original reason for the stop here.

Geoff and I agreed that he would stay with the boat – not that we really expected Mr Tubby to do anything to it in such a public place, but better safe than sorry. Sam and I put on our coats and, taking another deep breath and Sam's hand, I prepared to walk past the angler, as he, very slowly, packed up his equipment.

He looked up as I approached and opened his mouth, but I got in first. Very quietly and with as much dignity as possible, I explained, 'I'm not going to discuss this any more, and certainly not in front of my son.'

The deep colour crept up his face again.

'Your son should know what type of person you are; you are a stupid, inconsiderate bitch ...'

I grabbed Sam's hand and firmly walked away from the now almost apoplectic angler, knowing that he would stop screaming as soon as he noticed Geoff walking toward him, and, sure enough, as he spotted him stepping off the boat, he grabbed the last of his kit and scuttled away.

Unfortunately the car he was loading it into was parked just past us. I slowed in indecision for a moment. I really didn't want to break into a run in an attempt to get around the corner and away from another confrontation; it would look stupid and would frighten a small boy. Sam, as helpful as ever, decided at this point that he didn't want to go shopping and grabbed the step rails of the local pub, which he held onto with a death grip, bringing us to a complete halt, and allowing Mr Tubby to catch up.

Deciding that I really couldn't deal with another stupid screaming match, I ignored him completely and bent down to explain things to Sam, as Mr Tubby stamped past. He deliberately allowed his fishing box to swing round and hit me on the back of the head. There were a couple of men sitting in the small beer garden, boaters, from the look of them (they are the only type of people who would sit in a beer garden in minus-degree temperatures) and while one shouted 'Hey' at the retreating Mr Tubby, the other stood up, raising his eyebrows at me, but I just shook my head, asking him to let it go and mouthing, 'Thanks, but no.' The last thing I wanted was a Western-style punch-up between boaters and anglers, ranging across the packed Saturday morning riverfront of Ely; that sort of escapade didn't even bear thinking about.

Finally disengaging Sam from the steps, we stood together, watching, while Mr Tubby backed his car angrily on to the road and powered away. I wondered if he knew how close he came to being thrown into the river.

I would like to think that he had a blow-out on the way home and ended up in a ditch, or his engine exploded, or that he was a miserable little misogynist that still lived with an overbearing and man-hating mother who blamed him for her husband leaving, but I know that life isn't that kind. He was probably the accountant for a large company and suffered from stress. Whatever he was, I hoped he wasn't married – I would have to feel really sorry for his wife.

For the next couple of weeks I was worried that we would run into him again, but he obviously felt that fishing elsewhere would be a good idea. Personally, I agreed with him totally.

Chapter Twenty-one
Why is the Rum, Ahem, Money Always Gone?

BY THE BEGINNING OF March, we were still making slow but steady headway on the refurbishment. We had purchased that last large item, which was a much-needed set of kitchen units, but, in doing so, had spent the last of our money. The new kitchen was proving more than a little challenging to fit, due to the curved walls, the diesel lines and many other little problems that wouldn't have occurred if we had been attempting to fit it into a nice square room.

We had argued about the kitchen for weeks, changing the design, even at one point changing the location, until, finally, we decided on a plan that neither of us was entirely happy with but that was as good a compromise as we were likely to get.

This purchase put us firmly in the red and, knowing what the outcome would be, I had been trying to avoid any sort of 'money' discussion for weeks, until one evening Geoff physically sat me down and said, 'We're out of money. We can exist for about another two months but after that we are totally stuffed.'

Great, 'stuffed' again. Obviously this was one problem that wasn't going to go away by ignoring it. I knew it was going to have to be me that went back to work, but I was completely adamant that I was, under no circumstances, going to resume my former position as a contract Helpdesk Manager; the whole prospect, with its huge amount of paperwork and long hours was just too horrible to contemplate. I did, however, have everyday skills such as typing and office admin that would get me a nondescript position that would just keep our heads above water until the boat was finished, and Geoff could go back to work.

The other reason it had to be me was that Geoff didn't damage himself when using power tools, which was something I did with alarming regularity, much to Geoff's horror whenever he saw me pick up a drill or a sander. The idea of me using a circular saw was just anathema to us both.

On one memorable occasion I had been using the drill with a sanding brush wire thingy on the end to clean pipes and had somehow missed, and the sanding brush had entwined itself into my sock and most of the way into my shin before Geoff rushed up and hit the off button. (I have been handed manual sandpaper ever since and I don't think he was convinced I was actually safe with that.)

One week later, I had a job. Manpower, one of the employment agencies in Cambridge, had found me the perfect position; they had taken one look at me and sent me for an interview just outside Ely. It was a great job, well actually it was a really rubbish job, but it suited me down to the ground: a small maintenance company had opened a satellite office and there was only me and one other woman, Bev, working there – she was as acidic as they come – but we got on well. After such a long time of really doing 'not a lot', it was very odd to be back at work again, odd but rather nice. All I had to do was chase gas engineers about and dish out jobs to them, making sure that all the details were entered into the company's antiquated computer system.

Bev didn't really care what time I got in or if I came in early and went home early, as long as the work was done, so we were both happy. With a regular source of money finally arriving in our bank account every month, we could relax a little and spend the last of our savings on things that the boat needed and not on the tedious business of actually staying alive.

By the end of April, the kitchen was definitely taking up space – I would like to say it was completed but we were still missing the worktops, which made cooking a meal rather difficult. The worktops had, in fact, been installed once but Geoff had made a slight miscalculation and had cut the hole for the sink in the wrong place, so new worktops were required. These, of course, were out of stock so we had to wait. Yet again, we lived on takeaways for a couple of weeks.

When the kitchen was finally complete, the last item to be installed was the water purifier, which dispensed water via a third tap at the kitchen sink – real, clean drinking water; after months of living on bottled water – it was the luxury I was most looking forward to. When it was finally flushed through and ready to be used, we all lined up with glasses. I was reminded of a bunch of excited youngsters and their first taste of alcohol. It was an amazing feeling to just press a button and have real drinkable water flow into a glass – fantastic.

I now know why boat people are so different to your average Joe living in a house; it's because the things that are so normal to Joe are a source of wonder and amazement to us.

'Water! Water from a tap!'

'Yeah, how cool is that!'

Good grief, we're back in the Stone Age, next we'd be saying what a wonderful invention the wheel was.

It had been so long since we tried to cook on the horrible hob that we had completely forgotten how noisy and awful the stupid thing was, and it came as a crashing disappointment to be reminded in such an audible way. We turned it on and a whole minute might have actually elapsed before we had to turn it off and vacate the kitchen until it had whimpered itself into silence again. Geoff sighed, grabbed his tool kit, dug the wretched contraption out of the worktop and, with the look of a man on a mission, disconnected it from both electrical connection and diesel feed before proceeding to strip the despised thing down to its component nuts and bolts. He figured that, as we couldn't use it in its current state, there was nothing to lose and we would probably have to buy another one anyway.

There is something quite endearing about a very, very smug husband. A couple of hours later, he had worked out that one particular widget, component thingy had been put in back to front. He had taken it out, turned it around, cleaned everything up and re-installed the hob back into the work surface. He turned it on and we stood and watched it light and heat up, all in blessed silence.

I had to remember to be extra nice to hubby for the next 24 hours and make sure that I kept telling him what a clever lad he was, especially as a new hob and installation would have cost us well over £500. What with all the savings and Geoff in a great mood, probably due to being able to wrap himself round one of my speciality triple-decker, fully fried egg and bacon sarnies, something he hadn't been able to indulge in for over six months. I felt entirely justified in buying a celebratory pair of boots the next day (they were in the sale and too good a bargain to miss out on – honestly), so everybody was happy.

Chapter Twenty-two
Visitors on the Way

AMELIA RANG JUST BEFORE Easter to inform us that she and Huw were coming to visit, and, I have to admit, with the kitchen now working, and with a small amount of money coming in we had become lax yet again and were happily concentrating on the easy minutiae rather than making a start on the next big job. We were still sleeping on the floor of the saloon next to the fire which was very nice.

However, Amelia's news brought on panicked rushing about while we tried desperately to think of a place we could stash them for a long weekend. Unfortunately, the only answer that we could come up with was to get off our lazy butts and get on with transforming the main bedroom into a liveable space.

It was a horrible mess. Over the last three months it had taken on the dubious title of 'the garden shed' and we used it to store everything that wasn't actually required for everyday living. It took us 12 full hours of running backwards and forwards, making odd piles on the bank before we even had an empty space and another week for Geoff to construct the skeleton of a bed, wardrobes and shelves.

As he was destroying what was left of the original kitchen, a loud shout of 'Oh bloody hell' brought me scurrying down the length of the boat to see what had gone wrong this time. Geoff was standing with his back to me. 'What's up,' I asked, trying to peer round him to see what he was holding. I saw a flash of dark red and wondered where I had stashed the first aid kit.

'Do you remember the trip here,' he asked, turning away from me, his voice muffled and slightly shaking.

'Erm ... yes? It will be forever etched in fire across the span of the file marked painful memories.'

'Do you remember that we had a little problem getting into the canned goods?' He twisted away from me, again keeping whatever he had in his hand out of my sight.

'I have the scars to remind me.' I tried to duck under his elbow and, as he turned away again, only succeeded in running my face into his back.

'Look what I found at the back of this cupboard.' He turned and flourished an ageing red can opener at me.

Dawning realisation. 'You mean that was in that cupboard all the time?'

'Yep,' he grinned and gently poked me with it. 'You obviously didn't look hard enough.'

There was really nothing I could say to that, well nothing adult anyway, so, summoning as much dignity as I could, I merely turned and walked away. I shouldn't have bothered trying, I only got as far as the bathroom before, giving in to my more childish tendencies, I turned and blew him a raspberry over my shoulder, 'Pttthhhp to you and your stupid can opener.'

With Amelia and Huw due in 24 hours, Geoff finished putting the last of the slats on the bed and showed me how it worked; bless him, he really is ingenious when he puts his mind to it.

By its very nature, a narrow boat has a six-inch overhang all around the walls which is the gunwales on the outside; this six-inch overhang is exactly the right height to smash you in the forehead when you sit up after taking a nap. So to combat Happy's insistence on presenting you with a migraine every morning and to give us a little more space, Geoff had designed a bed that slid out the required six inches when we wanted to sleep but could be pushed back under the gunwales to give us six inches of extra walking space during the day.

I know it doesn't sound much, but in a seven-foot wide boat, six inches can make an awful lot of difference. And, unlike some narrow boats, the bed could stay, in its entirety, 100 per cent of the time and not have to be folded out and remade every night. We had seen this feature in other boats and quite frankly, while it certainly gave you some extra room, when I want to go to bed I want to just fall face down and start snoring; 20 minutes making up a bed every night just seemed to be one more trauma that we could live without.

The only problem with the bed was that the side came up to within an inch of the top of the new mattress, so when you sat down to put your socks on, the side cut into your thighs and cut off your blood supply which made your feet go numb. It was one of those jobs that got put aside, as being 'not important enough to do now, but we will definitely get round to it'. We never did.

Easter was great fun – even with Charlie also down for a visit, we just about had room for everybody. Charlie was stashed in the tiny front room, Amelia and Huw lounged about on the floor in the saloon and we all spent the week pushing past each other and getting in each other's way. Even the non-boaters in the family soon learnt to leap into any available space as someone came toward them, it was either get out of the way or risk being covered in whatever the oncoming person was carrying.

Even though it was unfinished, the new bedroom became our sanctuary. It was lovely to just hide in a real bed first thing in the morning and listen to poor Amelia attempting to referee the daily breakfast arguments between Charlie and Sam.

My little job was boring and underpaid, but that week I loved it. It was quiet, and after the four-day Easter weekend, I dashed off every morning for the rest of the week, stepping

199

over slumbering teenagers and snoring dog and breathing a sigh of relief as I stepped out into the silent early morning sunshine.

I did feel slightly guilty as I kissed Geoff goodbye. I had to work, so by default he was child-sitter for the week and by Thursday the strain was beginning to tell. His need to get on and do useful things was completely hampered, either by the older children trying to help, or the younger ones demanding food.

On Thursday night, I came home to find Huw in charge of the circular saw, happily cutting his way through all our waste wood to make it into fire-sized chunks, and Amelia stacking it into a wood pile. Sam was stealing it for Charlie and Charlie, having stolen blue barrels and a length of rope from God only knows where, was attempting to build a raft. I waved at them all contentedly attending to their 'chores' and went in to find Geoff, face down, snoring softly on the sofa, with a spilt cup of tea on the floor beneath him. Oh dear, hard day obviously.

Chapter Twenty-three
Another Child on the Way

WITH ANOTHER CRISIS PASSED and another room complete, we yet again settled into just living. We did discuss that maybe we should get on and finish the boat, *before* another problem had us running around like loonies, but, with the weather steadily improving, life on the boat became almost idyllic in its monotony. Long weekends spent travelling around. Long evenings, either spent with friends or just sitting on the warm steps with a good book and a long drink, often chatting with Charlie and Dion from next door who were also taking advantage of the sunny evenings. It was going to take something pretty monumental to get us moving again. Luckily for us (God forbid we have a chance to get bored), Charlie graciously took it upon herself to provide the next source of impetus.

We had noticed that during her last two visits, she had been very quiet when it came time to leave and had been desperately trying to carve out a place of her own on the boat. While this was expected, it had been difficult to accommodate her needs with the boat incomplete and in such a state of disarray.

One Sunday in early June, I had loaded us both into the car and we had prepared for the journey back to the Midlands; we usually left early and made a stop on the way back to see my mum and dad. Charlie was again quiet and uncommunicative, which was a little worrying, but I put it down to turning 12 and starting on that long slippery slope to becoming a teenager.

Mum asked if she was OK just before we left and I shrugged, not really knowing what the problem was.

An hour later, close to home, Charlie asked, 'Do I fit in with the family?'

'Yes, of course,' I answered, worried where this was going. 'We miss you when you're not there and whatever we do as a family would always include you.' I was horrified to realise that there were definite tears behind that curtain of hair she always hid in when she had to talk about something that bothered her.

'You've had something on your mind for a while now, haven't you?' I asked, worried that I was going to breach the unwritten rules of teenage-adult communication syndrome, but feeling that something really had to give. Maybe she really hated the boat and didn't want to come and see us any more.

She didn't answer and stared miserably out of the window until we pulled up outside her house, where she got out of the car without a word. I joined her at the back of the car and, after getting her bags out of the boot, was surprised when our parting hug went on far longer than normal. She finally stepped back and with a defiant last sniff ran her hands over her face and pushed her hair back. She looked horrible, she had obviously been crying quietly for a lot longer than I had realised, but without giving me a chance to stop her or ask her why, she ran away and into the house.

I stood there for a little while, not knowing what to do. As with any marriage break-up, it is very difficult to put personalities aside and do the right thing for the children, however hard you try. There was nothing I could do, as I certainly wouldn't be welcomed if I knocked at the door. I had to walk away.

Rather than my usual routine of driving straight back down to Cambridge, I called Amelia and wandered over to Hereford to see her and Huw and to see if she had spoken to Charlie at all, hoping that she had more information than I did.

It was a lovely warm evening, so we decided to go for a drink at their local and it was when we were sitting in the beer garden with a large orange juice that the fatal phone call came. Charlie asked to come and live with us.

Thoughts under this sort of pressure lose adhesion. I always wonder if there has been a psychological study regarding the fracturing of thought lines when your world turns upside down. What? Great!! Fantastic!! Oh my God, great!! When? How? Why? I can't ever remember being so pleased and so terrified all at once, but then reality struck – where the hell were we going to put her? AAAARRRRRGGGHH!

I called Geoff and repeated the conversation to him and laughed when he verbalised exactly the thoughts that I had just experienced.

We had been told to expect her in four weeks. Just four weeks to create a teenage-friendly space on a half-built narrow boat. Oh well, there went the hedonistic summer. I was just glad I had managed to enjoy as much of it as I had.

I don't honestly remember much of the next four weeks. There were quite a few loud, angry phone calls and moments when we thought she would change her mind, but she had far more backbone than I had possessed at 12 – possibly more than I had at 30 – she had made her decision and even with the full force of certain members of the extended other family pushing at her, she never budged an inch.

Her immediate family gave her the space to make the decision for herself, but they also defended and supported her decision when it was attacked. Strangely unexpected really, but very much appreciated. We rushed around finding a school and doing all the things one does when an unexpected near-teenager falls into your lap, but most of all, we concentrated on her room.

The odd-shaped room right at the front of the boat

seemed an ideal teenager pad. So we set to work ripping things out. Not only did the walls curve top to bottom in this room, as they did in the rest of the boat, but they also curved left to right, coming to a sharp point at the bow. Every single piece of furniture had to be built by hand; the bed, the shelves and the wardrobe, the wood cladding had to be shaped and fixed. It was, quite frankly, a logistical nightmare and Geoff went almost entirely grey while he was building it. However, we did experience a rather surprising breakthrough – he gave up with his lists and drawings. With a box of tools and a serious amount of wood, he just made it up as he went along. Even if it hadn't worked out, I would have applauded his break from pedantic normality.

Three weeks and six days later, 3.52 a.m., we put the last brushful of paint on to the walls and hung the curtains at the seven small windows that ventilated the room and then collapsed, hoping that it would all be dry by the time Charlie turned up at midday.

By 11.30 a.m., both Geoff and I were on tenterhooks: what if this all went wrong? How would Sam cope with having a full-time older sister? What if she decided she hated us and hated living on the boat full-time? What if she hated her school? What if, what if, what if ... and so the questions just kept coming. My phone rang at 11.55 a.m. and set my heart racing. They were at the end of the marina's drive, so we wandered over the flood defences to meet them.

Discussing the meeting, while covered in paint the previous evening, we had decided to take the mature route and I had laid on drinks and nibbles thinking that they would obviously want to see where she was going to be living and see her room. I felt that we could all be very adult, grit our teeth and for once, just for once, we would try to get on for Charlie's sake.

The car pulled up and Charlie and the other parents got out. Without a word spoken, her stuff was unloaded from the back of the car, dumped unceremoniously on the grass and, with a perfunctory hug, they climbed back into the car and drove away, leaving her standing with a pile of boxes.

Geoff and I stood there open-mouthed; the whole thing had taken less than three minutes. The group of us stood and watched them disappear, not a word was spoken. When at last the car was out of sight, I turned to Charlie; she was pale and tired looking. Oh dear, standing here in silence was not going to do her any good at all. I wandered over and, putting my arm around her stiff little shoulders, gave her a nudge with my hip.

'Typical of your dad,' I tightened my grip and grinned at her. 'He just goes on and on, never knows when to shut up. My goodness, these long goodbyes are so tedious, don't you think?'

Charlie looked up at me and laughed. With the stress barriers finally broken, she burst into tears and we all stood in a big three-way hug, until Sam, wondering what had happened to us all, came to the top of the flood defences, and seeing Charlie, started to run down, shouting hello and wanting to know what was in all the boxes. He slipped and ended up in a heap at our feet, covered in little sticky grass balls – at least that gave her something genuine to laugh at.

The huge decision she had made, the arguments over the last four weeks and the three-hour journey had been painful for all of us and certainly way too much for someone who was only 12. She was stressed to the point of mental incapacity and we had been left to deal with it. In the 11 years Geoff and I have been married I have never seen him so angry. It was unfortunate, really, and utterly frustrating, as he couldn't say anything without upsetting Charlie further, so after making sure that we were busy making refreshments and that she had calmed down into wide-eyed silence, he decided to take it out on the reeds and other vegetation with our strimmer. One angry man with a weed-whacker is something to be left alone for a fair while.

After about an hour, numerous cups of tea and at least a pound of chocolate, we had all calmed down enough to start sorting out her stuff. One consolation was that she loved her room, purple and white, just as she had asked for. By seven o'clock, she had occupied 'her space' and carefully placed all her things, then had promptly passed out in her new bed, completely exhausted by the extremes of the day. One more room finished, one extra occupant. Seemed only fair.

With Charlie finally aboard, we decided that although the temptation was to treat that weekend like a 'visit' weekend, this wouldn't do her any good and she needed to experience 'normal' life as soon as possible. So, Sunday morning, we pulled up the ropes and headed toward Ely for a pump-out and refill.

The normal hour and a half turn phase down to the Lazy Otter went without a hitch. Geoff had finally given in and let Charlie drive Happy and, even with the strong wind that had begun to really get its teeth into doing what wind does best, she seemed to be enjoying herself, showing an amazing knack for driving – especially as she had problems actually seeing over the roof and had to peer around the side of the boat. At the turn, the wind was in our favour, blowing straight onto the bow, so, as we turned Happy around, the wind gave us a bit of a push and Happy whipped about as though she had a pin through the middle, and within seconds we were facing the other way. Congratulating Charlie on her superb piloting skills, we headed back up the river, past our mooring and out onto the wider Ouse toward Ely.

During the next hour, the wind became stronger and stronger, blowing in short, sharp gusts across the port side against which Happy was completely powerless. Ignoring our rubber band engine, the wind had a great time blowing us about and we moved diagonally down the river toward the first turn.

We considered it lucky that we got on to the pump-out mooring without having to wait or queue. In hindsight, I think that all the other boaters had been sensible and, after taking one look at the weather, had decided to leave any movement for another day, only creeping out to check and tighten their mooring lines.

Within an hour we had filled up the main tank with water and had run a deep hot bath for one of the kids – whichever one fancied bathing while moving; there is often a bit of a scrap over this as it is, without doubt, one of the most odd, but decadently pleasurable, experiences I have ever had. You get into a hot bath in one place with a glass of wine and a good book, and by the time you emerge prune-like and slightly tipsy, you are somewhere totally different. Lovely! If I ever live in a 'normal' house again, I know I will be slightly disappointed to get into a bath, relax and emerge an hour later to find it still in the same place.

Sam won the coin toss on this occasion and settled into his bath with about 30 small, plastic, bobbing friends. Leaving him to happily soak and play, we coiled up the mooring ropes and set off upriver toward Littleport. There is an excellent winding hole at Ely, but all too often it is completely blocked by inconsiderate muppets parking their day-boats around the edge of it. I have lost count of the times I have wished that I could just power Happy's nose into the hole and then cheerily count the bits of debris as we leave, but Geoff keeps telling me that that would be very bad for my karma.

With the winding hole once again unavailable, we took her about a quarter of a mile down the river and then prepared to turn. I noticed, with a sinking feeling, that, unlike the previous turn, the wind was now in the worst possible place it could be, blowing straight up the river. So, as we made the turn, it hit us broadside, and, bored with exploring its gusting abilities, had now built up to blowing steadily and strongly.

We had a real problem. Every time we tried to turn, as soon as we came broadside, the wind just picked us up and shoved us further down the river. We went backwards and forwards, but there was absolutely no way that the engine was powerful enough to push the boat round against the wind and the water flow. Once again I wished we had installed a bow thruster as, although considered cheating by some of the old hands, it would have made our lives at that point very much easier.

An hour later, two miles downstream, and as we were still no nearer to turning Happy back towards home, we decided to take the dangerous action of ramming her nose into the rock pilings at the side of the river and hope to use the engine to bring her back end round; this isn't an ideal solution, as you never have any idea of what is under the water, and if we grounded now, in this wind, we were going to be stuck for a very long time.

Geoff grabbed one of the poles and, heading to the front, braced it against the bank, all the time praying that the pole would just bend with Happy's weight and the pressure of the wind, not snap. The whole thing worked surprisingly well and we were more than relieved to find that there were no nasty surprises lurking under the waterline. Some deity must have become bored with playing with us: the wind slackened off and we finally completed the 180-degree turn. Breathing a huge sigh of relief, we headed back through Ely and toward home, thinking that we would be home for tea and wouldn't have to go to pump out again for two weeks.

Half a mile out of Ely, on the open river, the wind, with absolutely nothing – not even a scabby little bush to stand in its way – once again regained full power. The river now sported six-inch waves rippling and breaking around the bow; Happy hit each one with a thump and a groan. Once again travelling diagonally, we limped and bounced toward the mooring and, for the very first time since owning her, I felt terribly, horribly nauseous, although I wasn't entirely sure whether it was terror or motion sickness; narrow boats just weren't meant to move like this.

The normal travel time was, at its worst, an hour and a half. This trip took well over two hours and I never want to repeat the experience. As we finally pulled into our mooring Charlie came out of her bedroom and staggered out of the front doors, before throwing herself down on the steps and turning her face into the wind to take great lungfuls of air.

'The world's spinning,' she complained. 'I never want to have to do that ever, ever again.'

I laughed and gave her a hug, 'Where's your sense of adventure? Oh and by the way ... welcome to the family.'

Chapter Twenty-four
A Grand Day Out

IT MAY SEEM THAT every time we went to pump out something awful happened, and I have to insist this wasn't the case. We have had many visits where nothing of any import has happened at all. We have pumped out, found a mooring and spent many happy hours wandering around the town, usually on market day, just spending our afternoon lounging around on the boat in the sun and chatting to various boaters up and down the wharf. Many trips were accompanied by either friends or family. On one particular occasion, we had Arwen and Carl, their two boys Kaelan and Ashwyn and Ian, a friend from Geoff's university days.

Arwen and Carl both work within academia and I have a hard time understanding what they actually do for a living, especially as they both seem to harbour a deep and abiding distaste for their jobs. Every time you ask them exactly what it is they do, they both just change the subject with a sad shake of their heads. Arwen, tall, dark and overly organised on behalf of other people, rebels on a daily basis at home, preferring to wallow in what she terms 'applied patheticness', giving the false impression that she is completely dippy and allowing Carl, who isn't fooled for an instant, to do what he does best and organise her.

The only fair description of Carl is that he seems to have fallen out of a Viking picture book, lost his horns and picked up a pair of glasses en route – possibly a Superman-like disguise, it's hard to tell. Tall, well built, with long, thick blond hair, unless he has let Arwen cut it for him, when he sports a sort of hairy bob for a couple of months until it grows back. He has a sideways sense of humour and is quite happy to participate in long and seemingly incomprehensible conversations which are likely to encompass ley lines, religion, spaghetti monsters and chaos theory all within about two sentences; you tend to come away from a conversation with Carl needing to lie down and gibber gently for a while.

Sam, Kaelan and Ashwyn have known each other since birth and getting them all on the boat together was a sure recipe for an afternoon of pounding feet and flying toys (not to mention flying small boys). Charlie took one look at this ball of punching, screaming humanity heading at a fair speed toward her and immediately took refuge on the roof with a book.

Ian, while being one of the most amusing people I have ever met, is never going to live on a narrow boat. At six foot four, he has to walk carefully, with his head on one side, down the very middle of the boat where the ceiling is at its highest. If he sits down, in an attempt to take up less space, his great long legs create assailable barriers for small boys to trip over, giving them the opportunity to scream louder.

He is gently spoken and usually fairly elegant, but when stuffed into a small space becomes ungainly and gangly. If he has chosen to wear black that day, he bears an uncanny resemblance to a large spider in a small test tube, a collection of knees and elbows held loosely together by an equal mixture of sharp, biting sarcasm and genial equanimity. We have found, from experience, that Ian is often the best person to keep Geoff company at the tiller, where at least he doesn't suffer a crick in his neck, spotlight burns on his head or lumps taken out of his lower limbs.

On this particular trip, we had all decided to make a day of it, have lunch at the pub and then take a gentle stroll through the French market that occasionally lined the streets of Ely. We all piled on to the boat, which had been turned around the previous day, in readiness for the onslaught, and headed off toward the city. As we passed under the first bridge, we noticed a small holiday cruiser coming from the opposite direction; the occupants, young and happy, replete with beer and warmth, were all singing along to music, while lazing in the sun on the top of their boat. They waved to us with big smiles as we chugged past.

One young man stood up on the top of the boat and reached for the underside of the bridge as they started to pass beneath.

'Hey, look,' he shouted at his friends, 'I can reach.' Laughing, he grabbed the underside of the bridge and swung his feet in mid air. It was inevitable, his boat just carried on and even from our distance we could see his laughing expression change to one of complete and utter panic as he realised that there was no longer a steady surface beneath, just cold, cold water. His friends, also laughing, realised at about the same moment and, leaping into action, they scrambled about the boat kicking beer cans and chips into the water in their panic to get the boat turned around.

Luckily for him, the small fibreglass cabin cruiser was light and manoeuvrable and, after a couple of minutes during which they had to make three attempts to get into a good position, they had him safely back on board. Now suddenly sober they resumed their journey with the sound of our laughter chasing them down the river.

Sitting outside the pub an hour later, Arwen commented on the mentality of people with boats, 'Are they all mad?'

'Not really, it's just a different set of values.' I tried to think of an example. 'How often do you worry about running out of water, or that your toilet is going to overflow, or that your electricity is going to run out and you won't be able to cook a meal?'

Arwen considered these bizarre circumstances, 'Erm ... Never.'

'Exactly, but these are the things that are on a boater's

mind all the time, so it may seem as though they are all a little eccentric, but, really, the children's ballet lessons or getting involved in the school's PTA really aren't that important.'

Carl frowned. 'You say "they" – don't you mean "we"?'

I thought about it for a moment. 'Nearly, but not yet, I don't think we've lived on a boat for long enough – we are still newbies. Some of these people haven't lived in a house for over 20 years, I wouldn't presume to even guess at some of the changes they've seen. I still have problems turning my boat around.'

We fell silent, watching the colourful ebb and flow of tourists, locals, anglers and boaters along the waterfront, all of them stepping around the huge flock of ducks, geese and swans that Ely attracts. Despite their name none of these waterfowl seemed to want to be on the water, preferring, instead, to wander quacking and honking along the wharf where the pickings were much better, getting under people's feet and menacing small children.

Arwen looked around at us all lounging indolently in the pub garden and decided that it was time for a picture.

'What do you think?' she asked, showing me the screen of her digital camera.

I recognised the group immediately, but had to take a close look at one woman. 'Is that me?' Arwen looked at me, confused. 'Yes, of course.'

There was no full-length mirror on the boat, so for the past year I had only seen myself from the shoulders up – and then only long enough to put a dash of make-up on. I couldn't remember the last time I had really looked at myself.

The woman in the picture was recognisable but only just. Gone was the sharp business suit, the slick blonde bob, the permanently worried look, the harassed career woman. In her place sat a relaxed hippy type – dark, short, spiky hair, flowing skirt, purple Docs, a faded Indian shirt rolled up to the elbows, grinning under a baker-boy hat.

The clothes I knew, but the expression was one I didn't recognise at all. I looked happy and relaxed, sitting behind a half-finished pint of real ale, with Sam hanging, grinning, over one shoulder and Charlie in mid sentence to Geoff, who was laughing at whatever she had said. He sat next to me with a faded T-shirt, faded jeans with holes at the knee, salt and pepper hair dragged back into a ponytail; he, too, looked relaxed, healthy and happy. It was a huge eye-opener at how much we had changed – when on earth had that happened?

'Look,' Charlie nudged me, dragging my attention away from the camera; she pointed toward two elderly gentlemen making their way slowly along the wharf toward us. One had a ferret in a harness and lead and, as he shuffled along, the little animal danced around at the end of its tether in time to the music of its own imagination.

Charlie was enchanted. We all watched as they shuffled toward us, and smiled to see the tourists leaping out of the way of their furry and dentally well-endowed yoyo. As they came abreast of us, we heard one say to the other, 'Are you a duck man?'

His friend considered the question and they moved off into the crowds. We never did find out whether he was a duck man or not.

'Are you a duck man?' Arwen stared after the odd group. 'What does that mean, "Are you a duck man"?'

I laughed. 'We may never know,' I said, turning to Charlie who was pounding me on the shoulder. 'What?'

'Can I have a ferret, please, please, please, please? I'll look after it and take it for walks – oh please, please, please can I have a ferret, pleeeeeeeease.'

Hmm, time to go I think.

Charlie never did get a ferret, but she did become the proud owner of three fancy rats. She had been pushing for a pet for some time and had made huge advances in trying to tame a crow that would land on our boat. She had got it feeding out of her hand and it was costing me a fortune in meat. This happy friendship unfortunately came to an end when a delegation of other boaters came round to complain.

Evidently while Charlie was at the boat, the crow (Eric) was perfectly happy to stay with her and be fed. While she was at school, however, it amused itself by ripping open the bin bags of every other boat and strewing the contents over each individual mooring. The friendship had to stop, so, in an effort to stop her feeding it, we purchased Tonks, Pipsqueak and Dangerous Beans, three of the daftest animals I have ever had the misfortune to deal with, but very sweet.

Tonks was a black and white Japanese hooded rat, quite normal-looking compared to the other two. Pipsqueak and Dangerous Beans were hairless, which made them look like freaky, long-tailed, big-eared, miniature, oven-ready chickens. Dangerous Beans had the added misfortune of being a 'Dumbo' rat, which meant that her ears where completely round, twice as big as a normal rat's, and stuck out at 90 degrees to her head, which gave her a slightly goofy appearance. Despite their unfortunate lack of pulchritude (they were pig-ugly and made people scream), Charlie loved them. She did attempt to put harnesses on them and take them for walks but they resisted and complained so vigorously that she gave up. I know we haven't heard the last of the ferret.

The next trip was also classed as one of the 'good ones' with only one member of the family terrorised, which, by our standards, was pretty good going. Unfortunately, it was Herbert who managed to get himself into severe trouble this time.

We had decided that, as the Maltings was hosting a good exhibition on the Sunday, we would stay at Ely overnight, treat ourselves to lunch the next day, visit the exhibition and then take a steady chug home – the perfect weekend – and, by seven o'clock on the Saturday evening, for once, everything seemed to be going to plan. It was a beautiful late July evening, warm and still – gorgeous – and we had a great time in the park. Even Herbert had managed to walk that far, although he had still managed to do his dead-dog impression on the way back and I had had to carry him for the last 200 yards to the boat.

Herbert was becoming an increasing worry to us. Getting on and off the boat was definitely more of a chore these days and his eyesight was getting worse and worse. He had mostly recovered from a stroke he had suffered two years previously and the vet had said (examining him to make sure he was a dog and I wasn't pulling his leg with a bit of old rug) that, by rights, he really ought to be dead and there wasn't much they could do for him, but if he seemed happy, then just wait it out and see how long he lasted.

We had to be very careful when letting Herb out of the boat every time we were away from home, as if one of us didn't chaperone him at all times, he would wander off and then when he had finished performing whatever necessary function he had to, he would just jump onto the nearest narrow boat that he could find. Luckily, most people were very amused by this and just handed him back. Finding himself back with me, he would sort of peer up at me and sigh, then permit himself to be carried back to the correct boat. (I think he was trying to find better owners, ones who didn't think that doughnuts weren't suitable for an old dog with blood pressure problems.)

On this occasion, we all went through the same old routine, and, as we were slightly out of town and it was a lovely warm evening, we just let Herbert wander maybe a bit further than we should have, while we were all collapsed on the grass. Another boat pulled in behind us and tied up. I saw Herbert wander towards it and started to drag myself to my feet, aiming to grab him before he made the usual mistake.

Too late. Much to the surprise of the woman standing at the bow, he executed a beautiful jump and landed smartly at her feet, and at the feet of the three German shepherds that were also occupying his landing space. I'm really not sure who was more surprised, the woman, who screamed, Herbert, who took one look at his predicament and screamed, or the three shepherds who, I'm sure, were convinced that God had dropped a furry plaything amongst them.

Herbert is a fraud; I now know this for a fact. He turned, jumped again, straight out of the boat with all the other dogs hot on his tail, and took off toward me at about 30 miles an hour where he shot behind my legs and keeled over into his usual dead-dog pose. I scooped him off the ground and had to hold him shaking above my head, while our new neighbours managed to get their dogs under control.

Putting Herbert safely into the boat, I went over to apologise. They were very good about it, and apologised right back, although what they had to apologise for I have no idea, but I thought it very British the way we all went about it. Herbert didn't move further than three inches off the gangplank for the next week. Poor old thing.

Chapter Twenty-five
Roast or Drown – Your Choice

THE SUMMER OF 2006 was a scorcher. By the end of July we were enduring day after sweltering day of temperatures that were well into the nineties and began to wonder if we would ever be cool again.

Steve and Jude with their three-year-old son Charlie (another Charlie!) had moved into the marina the previous year and after a couple of months of tentative hellos that gradually lengthened to 'chats', it was delightful to find someone who was happy to have a good laugh at misfortunes, both ours and other people's, and we began to have the occasional coffee.

Sam was quite happy to play with smaller children, so he and Charlie (little Charlie), got on quite well, both of them owning huge amounts of small plastic figures which would be dragged out to wage loud and raucous games while Jude and I sneaked a quiet half an hour, well, relatively quiet anyway. Their second child was now on the way and as the summer moved on and the temperature skyrocketed, poor Jude, suffering from extreme morning sickness, became more and more unwell.

We would often see her sitting in their mooring watching Charlie play. Incapacitated and unable to join in, she would be huddled under the gazebo looking rather green, with any conversation punctuated by her rushing off to be unwell. She must have lived almost entirely on ginger at that time. We all felt so sorry for her, but apart from giving good-natured and no doubt completely unwelcome advice there was absolutely nothing anybody could do to help other than offer to fetch and carry for her.

Because of the way we live, everything we do tends to be a chore. We carry water, we carry shopping bags for miles, we lug small children around and every trip becomes almost like a military campaign to get items to and from the car and boat. Doing this when hale and healthy can be a pain. Doing it when pregnant must have been almost unbearable. Adding into the equation the heat, the insects and the nausea, I found myself constantly surprised that we never found Jude sitting in the corner of the washing block, giggling and rocking gently – maybe she only did it at home. If she didn't, I want to know why because I flaming well would have in her position. Usually I get quite broody when someone else is pregnant, but not this time. I didn't envy her at all.

Eventually, when the temperature reached 30 degrees, they pulled out of the marina and took their boat downriver where they parked under a tree for three days until the heat wave finally broke. I personally think it was that or wait for Jude to break.

As Steve and Jude had pinched the only shaded spot for about ten miles (not that anybody begrudged them having it in the slightest) and, even with the windows completely removed and the doors open, we basically found ourselves living in a metal oven. It was a no-win situation. Although Geoff had been around fitting mosquito nets to all the windows, the little darlings still managed to get in and, like every other live-aboard occupant on the river, we were all covered in itchy, bleeding bites. There was no way to get round this and it was a relief to get to work, which offered air conditioning and massive respite from the rabid flocks of tiny little vampires all trying to suck my blood. Geoff suffered the worst of all of us; he seemed to have a particularly delicious flavour which the mozzies really couldn't get enough of – both legs below the knee were swollen and in a horrible state. A year later, he still had the scars.

We had also been experiencing some really spectacular storms, and, even though these could be terrifying for poor Herbert, who would hide under Sam's bed, or leap quivering into my lap at the first low rumble and stick his head under my arm, we began to look forward to the next one as each storm settled the dust and got rid of the mozzies for a brief time.

Geoff had been working on the boat each day while the kids were at school and I was at work and we were now 90 per cent through the refit. The soft furnishings had all been changed. My fantastic mum had gone well beyond the call of duty by making us eight sets of fully lined curtains and *Happy Go Lucky* was beginning to look absolutely stunning. We were well on our way to having her fully finished; she was really beginning to feel like home.

On this particular Friday, the local radio announcers had been giving ever-increasing weather warnings and by three o'clock the rain was coming down with such force it was filling up the car park at my office. With the wind howling we decided to close early; all the phones and computers were down, we couldn't do any work and we just wanted to push off home.

Three trees had already fallen and it was beginning to look pretty bad on the roads. Geoff had rung earlier and, with the weather being so bad, we had decided that he and the kids would stay at Arwen and Carl's for the night and they would see me in the morning.

I was really looking forward to it: a whole night by myself. I stopped in at the garage on the way home and treated myself to a pot of very naughty, expensive ice cream and, although nervous about the howling weather, set off toward the boat down the A10.

As I came down the drive I noticed that there was a queue of cars waiting to go into the marina – odd, we were usually lucky if we saw one or two. I could see a lot of movement ahead and then realised that a tree had come down and was blocking the drive. Oh, just great!

The one thing that is bad about this lifestyle is that there is an unwritten rule that you absolutely cannot get away with being a girly girl, so waiting in my nice, warm, dry car for the big, strong, burly men to get the tree out of the way wasn't going to cut it. With a big sigh, I clambered out of the car and over toward the hustle and bustle. Sure enough, there were already two other women there, both dressed in office clothes, pulling branches out of the way as one man with a chain saw and another with a hacksaw were cutting a passage through the tree.

Within 20 seconds of being out of the car I was absolutely and completely soaked to the skin; the rain was so heavy it was actually difficult to take a breath without being in imminent danger of drowning. If the afternoon had been dark and bat-filled, it would have been reminiscent of the night at Dracula's Lock. With us all working together, we managed to get the tree cleared in about a quarter of an hour. Spluttering water and unable to talk, we smiled and waved to each other and carried on down the drive. Those of us with log burners took a couple of extra minutes to gather up as many burnable logs as we could; another rule, never turn down free burning material. (I have been known to drag trees out of the river and wrestle them on to the bank with a huge grin – something for nothing – always useful.)

I wasn't looking forward to the battle of walking the flood defences, but I was fortified by the knowledge that after only ten more minutes of battling I could get dry, fix myself a huge mug of hot chocolate, settle down in front of a DVD and maybe have a little nap or, wow, an uninterrupted bath ... Yes! That was the plan: bath, hot chocolate, snuggly dressing gown and a film. Oh, and there were about two shots of Scotch in that bottle left over from Christmas which would go very nicely in the hot chocolate. Oh bliss.

By the time I reached the mooring, I may as well have thrown myself fully clothed into the river; I just couldn't have been any wetter. Steve and Jude had arrived back and Steve had waved and laughed at me as I staggered past their boat. Head down into the wind, I managed to lift an arm in response but I wasn't going to hang around and chat, and anyway, Jude was probably enjoying the respite from the constant, draining heat.

My shoes squelched and my black skirt and top were misshapen dish rags. Appearing, wind-ravaged, out of the pre-storm gloom, I would have terrified small children and could easily have been mistaken for Jenny Greenteeth, a mythical hag that appears out of running water to drag people to a watery grave. Hoping that my teeth were still white, I picked my way carefully down the slick steps, humming some well-loved lyrics by Cloudstreet:

> *Her emerald smile in the sunlight had captured his fearful eye,*
> *She slid like a seal in the wash of the stream and he felt the bank slipping by,*
> *No time to cry that he could not swim, no time to draw in and breathe,*
> *With her hair round his ears and filling his mouth and her long fingers twined in his sleeve.*

I headed down the steps, toward the dry warmth and that hot chocolate with a splash of Scotch, the thought of which had kept me going for the last ten minutes.

Even though I wouldn't have thought it possible, the sky became even darker, and black and purple cumulonimbus clouds, eerily backlit, gathered in a grumbling crowd on the horizon with the first flicker of lightning. I decided that enough was enough. Leaping over the final steps and fumbling with the keys, I entered the boat with a speed that belied my oft-voiced statement that storms didn't worry me in the slightest.

As I stepped into the boat, I turned hurriedly to close the top hatch, intending to shut out the terrible weather. It was only after the doors and hatch were safely closed that I sagged, soaking, against the wall and my thoughts, trying to turn once again to that bath, became arrested by a further cold, wet sensation seeping into my shoes. Looking down, I was horrified.

At least two inches of water covered Happy's floor. Her movement in the storm created very small waves that sloshed around the Morso and the television cabinet and broke happily against the side of the sofa. I noticed with a strange detachment that a couple of Sam's plastic Pokémon figures actually appeared to be surfing.

The windows! Oh no! It had been such a hot day that Geoff had taken the windows out and forgotten to put them back again when he had left to pick the kids up from school. It wasn't only the floor that was covered in water (thank God the laminate flooring hadn't been put down yet), but every curtain, the beds and the sofa were also soaked, and the water was still coming through the window openings, increasing in volume as the storm built up force.

I sloshed around and replaced all the windows – at least that would arrest the deluge – then, waving goodbye to my evening of luxury, I started on the cleaning-up operation. It took me four hours to mop all the water into buckets and throw it out into the river. By the time I had managed to actually dry the floor, the sun had reappeared and all our furnishings were on top of the boat, gently steaming: we were creating our own fog.

Geoff and the kids turned up, worried by the half-garbled message I had managed to get through to them before the mobile network had given up. It had gone something like:

'Argh the boat's full of water, and there's a huge storm and everything is soaking and argh ...'

And of course, at that worst possible moment, the phones

had died. I assumed that Geoff had just turned me off mid-rant; he thought I had drowned or had been struck by lightning.

We had actually been quite lucky. We had spare bedding and I had got to the mattresses before they became soaked, but even with this small reprieve it took the whole of that weekend to dry everything out and another week before the windows stopped steaming up. So much for a quiet night in.

Chapter Twenty-six
Christmas Again

OUR SECOND CHRISTMAS ON the boat was planned to be a little different from the first. Arwen and Carl had decided to go to New Zealand for a month and we had asked if we could borrow their house while they were away. They had recently become the proud owners of a small flock of fussy, fluffy hens and the most spiteful and aggressive cockerel you could wish to meet, so they were happy to have someone to look after the scary group.

We were all approaching Christmas with wildly differing views. One minute I would be looking forward to it, the next I didn't want to leave the boat, and the kids argued and bickered more than usual. Sam, of course, was ecstatic; Sky TV, computer games, Internet and all the lovely things that he felt he was being denied and were his right. Charlie swung her views from one day to the next. She hadn't long left a house, and this was to be her first full Christmas with us so she was understandably a little tense.

Geoff and I had decided that with us all off the boat this was going to be a perfect opportunity to do all those jobs that were smelly and definitely not child-friendly; there is nothing more irritating than finding a seven-year-old stuck in your gloss paint. These jobs also included laying the new floor and completing (well, starting actually) the huge amount of painting that had to be done to finish Happy off completely.

With the car full of clothes and Christmas presents, we headed over to Arwen and Carl's at the beginning of

December. As we were heading down one of the little country lanes, trying to find a way to avoid the A14, a deer crossing the single-track road in front of us was lit briefly in the headlights. Geoff slammed on the brakes, accompanied by the children (and me) screaming. Going so slowly down the tiny lane it had been no problem to stop and we watched the deer disappear into the ditch and across the field.

As Geoff put our ageing Audi into gear and began to pull away, another deer crashed out of the bushes, saw the obstacle that we presented and just took off in an attempt to clear the car. All I can remember thinking is 'Wow, deer really can fly'. But it didn't quite make it. The back legs crashed down onto the bonnet and the animal, while twisting in an attempt to regain its footing, crashed sideways through the windscreen. For a couple of seconds there was only the sound of screaming children, cracking glass, heavy breathing and hooves screeching across metal as the poor thing struggled desperately to get itself out of the windscreen and back on to the road.

Luckily it had fallen with its back and rump through the window so at least we weren't in danger of being decapitated by flailing legs. Finally, it made it off the bonnet of our now horribly battered car. It staggered about in the road for a moment in full view of the only headlight we still had in working condition, then, shaking its head, took off at full speed after its friend, leaving us to examine the state of our totalled car and attempt to calm two wide-eyed and terrified children (and me).

We limped to Arwen and Carl's and made a call to the insurance company. They were less than helpful, and over the next week sent an assessor to study our car. He arrived with a condescending expression.

'A deer jumped onto your bonnet while you were almost stationary,' he sneered. 'What type of deer?'

'A red deer.'

'We don't have red deer around here,' (funny, that was

226

the third one I had seen since we had been here) 'are you sure it wasn't a reindeer, little bells, fat bloke in red attached behind it, ha ha ha.'

'Let's hope not because if that was Rudolph there are going to be a lot of disappointed kids in a couple of weeks' time.'

He sneered again and said, 'Well, lead on, lead on. Let's see if we can find any *evidence* of your so-called *deer*.' He gave a derisive sniff and indicated out the door.

Keeping my evil tongue well under control, I preceded him outside and pointed out the Audi, parked two or three cars down the lane. He wandered over to it, still sniffing, and I could have laughed aloud as I saw him walk round to the front and watched his jaw drop.

'You could have been killed,' he muttered, taking in the perfect hoof print embedded in the bonnet, the smashed lights and the decimated windscreen which sported ginger hair and clotted blood all down one side.

I nodded. 'Yes, we were just lucky he didn't come through feet first.'

He ran his fingers over the dent, 'How big would you say this thing was?'

I shrugged. 'It was nearly fully dark, but I would have said four and a half, maybe five foot at the shoulder, it made a hell of a thump when it landed; it was trying to jump the car.' Then I just couldn't help myself. 'Mind you, the thump could have been that fat guy that it was dragging, I'm fairly sure I heard him screaming, "Blitzen, stop, ya bugger!"'

He whipped round and narrowed his eyes at me. I just smiled back at him, keeping my own eyes wide open and innocent looking. Then he laughed.

'Yes, OK, I agree it was almost definitely a deer, or at least a big animal of some sort – you have to admit that, as a story, it sounded fairly unlikely.'

I nodded. 'I think if I was going to make something up, I would have come up with something more believable.'

He smiled again. 'You wouldn't believe the stories we get told.'

Over a cup of tea he gave me the bad news that the Audi was probably going to be a write-off; she was so old and there was so much damage that it really just wasn't going to be worth fixing her.

I had to agree. I'd been expecting this, and she certainly had been playing up for some time now, overheating and making strange noises, even when she didn't have Rudolph embedded in her radiator. So obviously it was time to get a new car.

Watching the tow truck load our poor, bloody, hairy Audi onto the back of a car trailer, I was not that sad to see it go. It was a really expensive car to run, although it did have a huge boot and I was going to miss that. Now all we had was our tiny little Daewoo Matiz; the children had named it 'pod' because it was bright green and looked like a mobile pea. Arwen and Carl had left their car behind and said that we were perfectly at liberty to use that while we were staying, so at least we each had transport.

While the entire trauma with the car had been going on, Geoff had taken full advantage of us all being off the boat and had been working steadily through his list of jobs. It wasn't only laying the new floor and the glossing that needed to be done; there was also some tiling to do, some emulsioning, lino to be laid in the bathroom which also now needed re-decoration (good grief, had we really been on here so long that the first room was now due for re-decoration – the mind boggles) and, finally, the finishing off and decoration of our bedroom.

Christmas Eve and the new floor was down. It hadn't taken as long as I expected as I was under the impression that the old floor would have to come up before the new laminate went down. When I suggested this, Geoff stared at me in amazement.

'You can't put laminate flooring over a void.' He flapped

a bit of it at me. 'Look, it's all floppy; it would just bend and break.'

'A void?' I frowned at him. 'What's actually under this floor then?'

He shook his head at me. 'How long have we lived on this boat?' he asked. 'Are you seriously telling me that you have never looked under the floor?'

I couldn't understand what the problem was; why on earth would I want to look under the floor, so I just shrugged at him.

'Look.' He put his finger through a drilled hole and lifted up a wooden panel. The gap he revealed appeared to be full of concrete paving slabs.

'What are those?' I poked one; they actually were concrete paving slabs.

'It's the ballast,' he put the floor panel back down and frowned at me. 'You know, those things I have to lug from one side of the boat to the other every time you put a new piece of flaming furniture in and we end up leaning over?'

Realising that I had obviously missed something important, I tried to make amends for my complete lack of observational skills by showing some interest. 'So what's under the concrete blocks?'

'Nothing.' Geoff frowned. 'Well, obviously there's the bottom of the boat, but that's just the steelwork and the struts to lay a floor on. Without those blocks we'd be floating a good foot higher and her prop would be out of the water.

'Good grief!' The extent of the weight and the amount of these things suddenly dawned on me. 'How many of these blocks are there?'

'I don't know, I've never counted them.' Geoff gave me a pointed look. 'But I feel like I've moved hundreds because you keep changing your mind about where you want things to go and every time, I have to drag up the floors and push them from one side to the other.'

'Yes, you already said that.' I thought back over the last few months and reddened slightly, remembering all the changes I had made and how many mornings Geoff had woken up with muscle pains 'Oh ... sorry, you should have said.'

Geoff gave me a kiss on the forehead. 'Never mind, you're happy with it now, aren't you?'

'Well, I did think that maybe the sofa would look better on the other side.'

Geoff's eyes widened and I grabbed a paintbrush to fend him off.

'Don't you dare, I have a brush here and I'm not afraid to use it.' I brandished it at him with a grin.

'Just remember,' he snarled. 'I'm sure I can find a wife-sized space under this floor if I have to.' He gave me an innocent smile. 'Cup of tea ... darling?'

Although the new flooring took less time than I had feared, there were so many cuts to be made, avoiding furniture and other built-in obstacles, then creating lift-up panels so that the dreaded ballast could be accessed, that it had taken far longer than Geoff had hoped.

But while he was completing the floor, I had been working on the tiling that needed to be finished in both the kitchen and the bathroom. So with two of the scheduled 'big' jobs finally crossed off our list, we settled down to a good, old-fashioned Christmas with Amelia and Huw. Being away from the boat we were forced to relax; we had a wonderful time.

Geoff was taking Sam up to see Grandma for New Year and with Charlie heading back to the other family for the same period, I had decided that I would use that time to complete the glossing. Then we had a week left at Arwen's after New Year, which would give the paint a good time to dry, and we could move back into a totally finished boat.

I spent so many hours trapped in the boat with the paint fumes that by the time I had finished each day, I would happily weave my way back to the car and have to spend a good ten minutes breathing deeply on top of the flood defences until I felt that I was safe to drive. On New Year's Eve, I did actually make it to a friend's party that was being held just down the road from Arwen's house, but I was so tired and so high on paint fumes that I left well before midnight and I probably wasn't very coherent company while I was there – sorry about that, guys.

Chapter Twenty-seven
90% of the Work Takes 90% of the Time
The Last 10% Takes Another 90% of the Time

WE MOVED BACK ON to the boat on January 5 2007 and, I have to admit, I was surprised by the attitudes of the kids – they were both anxious to get back aboard and settle back into 'normal' life. There was actually still a fair amount of work to do, but really nothing that couldn't be done at weekends or in the evenings. So, with this in mind, Geoff started to search for a job. My job had changed and with my boss leaving and my previous experience, the main company had offered me management of the Cambridge office, along with a suitable pay rise.

I enjoyed my job. It was a little bit mad, the engineers were great and the office staff were competent and fun to be with. So I never really minded getting up in the morning and, of course, the money was particularly useful. But Geoff was the one with the major money-making skills, he was qualified up to the noggins and was very good at what he did – project management for IT companies. So we didn't really expect it would take that long to find him a job, and we started the New Year with high hopes of getting some decent money in. I could stop work and go back to what I liked doing best: writing, messing around with art and taking useless college courses.

What I really wanted to do was spend some quality time with the kids. I was very aware that as my responsibility at work had grown so, exponentially, my time with the family had diminished, which had been niggling away at me for some months.

By the time spring was in the air, Geoff had been to over 20 interviews and hadn't actually managed to get past the first post. We knew what the issues were but had real problems facing them. One was that, by IT standards, he was just too old. He was competing against graduates and people that really loved what they did – the crème de la crème of geekdom – and that highlighted the other major problem. He just didn't really want to do it any more and I think that was coming over in his interviews.

At the beginning of April, we sat down late one evening and decided to look the problem straight in the eye. Geoff had been becoming increasingly morose over the last month, and from seeing him so happy when he was building the boat, it was horrible to watch him now, battling with the knowledge that he really ought to go back to work, and really trying to get a job but not really putting himself into it. I decided to let him off the hook.

'If you could do anything for a job, what would you do?' I asked.

'Sparky,' came the surprising and very prompt reply.

'Really?' I casually drained my coffee cup and asked, 'So why don't you re-train then and do something you would actually enjoy?'

That was the moment that plan no. 37 was born. Over the next two weeks we looked into training courses and were horrified at the price of changing a career. Geoff already had most of the expertise and experience to become an electrician so he didn't want to spend two years at college, he just wanted to take the exams and start work as quickly as possible. It was a good idea, especially as he wanted to take his air conditioning qualifications as well, but the bill was still going to come to over £7,000 and that was money that we just didn't have.

We wallowed about for a couple of weeks, coming up with ridiculous plans to get the money, plans that didn't include borrowing it from the bank or my father, but there really seemed no way around it. We were bracing ourselves to make that call to Dad when Charlie tried to knock herself out and the plan changed yet again.

To get into Charlie's room there was a foot-high step that continued inside, which meant that the head room in her bedroom was that much diminished. This step was cleverly hiding the huge water tank that sat at the front of the boat, running under the entire length of Charlie's bedroom.

That evening, as Geoff and I prevaricated about calling Dad, she had been sitting in her room, playing her new guitar, when there was a sudden scream, a thump and then silence. I went to investigate and found her sitting on the floor holding her head, her guitar lying face down on the bed above her.

The cardinal rule is that if you don't like spiders don't live on a boat. How they get in, I will never know. The ones we get aren't very big, but they are persistent, and it doesn't seem to matter how many you put out of the windows, there are always others to take their place.

It has amused the kids on no end of occasions to watch a spider come dangling down from the ceiling to hang revolving slowly in front of one or other of them; they then get together and give it a gentle poke on the bottom which makes it scurry back up its web again. Then they sit and wait for it to come back down at which point the whole process starts again. They call it spider yoyo. As it makes them laugh and certainly doesn't harm the spider, I have never seen a problem with it.

It was one of these spiders that had caused Charlie's 'egg'. She had been concentrating so hard on her playing that she had failed to notice one of these 'boat spiders' sitting on the ceiling above her. Consequently, when it had let itself drop and had dangled in front of her nose, she had panicked sufficiently to leap up, scream and brain herself on the roof.

With all the furore, we had, once again, completely failed to phone my father. Later, when all was quiet, Geoff looked up from his book.

'When did she reach the ceiling?' he leaned back and ran a hand through his hair. He had had it all cut off for interviews and was still finding the lack of length a bit sad. 'She didn't reach the ceiling when she moved in.'

I looked at him. 'Yeah, damn those children for growing, maybe we ought to stop feeding them.'

He smiled. 'Yes, yes, I know, but if she reaches the ceiling now and she's only 13, how long can she stay in that room?

I winced. 'Not long really. I suppose we could always swap her and Sam about?'

Geoff snorted. 'The way Sam's growing, he's going to be the taller of the two, so we won't have very long before he hits the ceiling as well.'

I nodded; there wasn't a good answer for this one.

Geoff picked up his mug of tea and stared into the depths. 'Maybe we ought to be thinking about a bigger boat.'

I groaned, thinking he was just messing about. 'Oh no, we've only just finished this one, if we go for a larger one we're going to have to buy another complete wreck and start all over again ...'

'Well, we've done it once; I suppose we could do it again.' He looked at me. 'What do you think?'

Oh poo, he was serious. 'Well, even if we have to spend some of the profit from Happy on a larger wreck, at least we would have enough left over to get you re-trained.'

Happy Go Lucky went on the market in April 2007. Due to her odd shape, the fact that she had three static bedrooms and that, compared to most holiday boats, she was bloody huge, ungainly and a royal pain in the arse to moor, we knew that the only people interested in buying something like this would be another family that wanted to live aboard. We had resigned ourselves to a fairly long wait; some boats take years to sell.

Exactly three weeks later we had a firm offer – much to our surprise, horror and more than a little panic. A lovely lady called Jane and her daughter were selling their house in Devon and moving up to Bath. Jane's boyfriend lived on a boat over in that direction and she was used to the vagaries that living aboard entailed. She already had a mooring sorted out and was just waiting for her house sale to complete. We weren't in any major rush, so agreed to take the boat off the market and just wait it out with her. She expected to move in at the beginning of July.

Having resigned myself to a long sale, this sudden movement took me by surprise. I knew we were selling Happy for all the right reasons, but I was going to be really sad to lose her. We had had some great times on *Happy Go Lucky*, and she had, over the last two years, gained a beautiful interior and a fair amount of personality. I always pictured her as a huge and slightly dippy dog, eager to please but not too bright. It was going to be really difficult to find another like her.

Once again the search for a new boat became all-encompassing. I spent so many hours at the Internet cafe in Ely that they gave up asking me if I wanted a drink and just produced a coffee as soon as I walked through the door.

With a little experience under our belts, everybody had ideas of what improvements would be needed on a new boat. High on Charlie and Sam's list was access to the Internet; both felt that only being able to use it at school or at Arwen's was nowhere near satisfying enough.

One Saturday morning, with Geoff and Steve, who within the last two days had become the proud father of a little girl called Ruby, doing something technical with a load of tubes and a water pump on the flood defences in an effort to get water to the boats, I decided to take an early morning trip to the cafe and continue my boat search. The kids were mooching around doing nothing much, so when I asked them if they wanted to come and play on the Internet for a couple of hours I was almost crushed in the rush to find shoes and get out of the boat.

An hour later, we were all settled, each with our own screen, and I blocked the bickering out as I tried to decipher the boat specs on various Dutch sites. I would come back to reality occasionally, just to check that the kids hadn't got bored and escaped, but they were both sitting there, dwarfed by headphones, with big grins, each on their own separate sites; Sam catching up with the world of Pokémon and Charlie immersed in strange talking cat videos on YouTube.

About an hour later, howls of laughter dragged me away from one particularly nice barge, moored just outside Rotterdam, and I turned to find out what had caused this tear-jerking hilarity.

Harry Potter Puppet Pals are an odd little YouTube puppet show that has the ability to reduce children to giggling lumps of yuck.

'Mum, Mum!' Sam grabbed me and pointed at the screen. 'Look at this, it's called "Wizard Swears". It's really funny.'

Charlie nodded, but couldn't speak, as she was still trying to get her breath back from laughing so hard.

I frowned. 'Wizard Swears?'

Sam sighed. 'They're not rude, just really funny.' He rolled his eyes, showing that I was obviously not on his wavelength and being very boring.

Luckily for my obviously over-delicate sensibilities, our booked time was up and we headed toward Starbucks for a naughty coffee.

I watched Sam and Charlie walking ahead of me up the hill, and thought how nice it was that they seemed to get on most of the time.

Sam reached over and thumped Charlie on the arm. I was just about to tell him off when I heard him say, 'Unicorn turd!' He winced and ducked slightly as if he expected

237

Charlie to give him a kick up the rear as she so often did, then relaxed as she turned toward him and yelled, 'Blast-ended skank!'

They grinned at each other.

'Dragon bogies!'

'Floppy-wanded Dementor botherer!'

'Cauldron bum!'

'Swish and flicker!'

'Voldemort's nipple!'

'Jiggery pokery!'

'Broom head!'

'Leprechaun taint!'

'Dobby's sock!'

I watched them, giggling and pushing each other, getting louder with each ridiculous insult. I had to smile at their antics but decided that no matter what new technology came along, we had managed perfectly well without the Internet for the last two years and we could do without it for the foreseeable future – cauldron bum, indeed!

That evening I was attempting to moan about it to Jude. The family had recently sold their narrow boat and had purchased a wide beam. I was completely envious; there seemed to be so much room – still less than a small, two-bedroom flat but, compared to a narrow boat, it was a veritable mansion. However, with all the new baby stuff cluttered around, I could see why they needed it because babies don't care where you live. When they turn up they seem to bring half of Mothercare with them.

Ruby was absolutely gorgeous. Even after the morning sickness had subsided, the rest of the pregnancy hadn't been particularly easy for Jude and I think the whole family were relieved to see the outcome so healthy and ... loud.

This had been my third attempt to see her but every time she had been asleep. On this occasion, I could see so much more of her, which appeared to be mainly the inside of her mouth as she screamed and screamed, defying all Steve and

Jude's attempts to calm her and we felt that visitors, however well-intentioned, were not what the family needed at that moment. So we left the presents and made a swift exit.

Little Charlie gave us a mournful wave as we left; I got the feeling that his little sister wasn't entirely living up to his expectations. I grinned and waved back at him, thinking that he needn't worry. It would only take about a year and then he'd be wishing for the immobile, noisy baby back.

Summer crept toward us and we waited, mainly mooching about enjoying Happy being fully finished. We kept in touch with Jane and things seemed to be moving along fine.

Our exit date was July 3 and we spent the two weeks prior to that packing everything up and squeezing it into storage. By June 29, we were just waiting for the money to transfer and, as we still hadn't found a new boat – although I had become slightly addicted to YouTube and knew all the Potter Puppet Pals sketches off by heart – we had planned to spend the summer with Geoff's mum again and would search for a new boat from there.

Jane had moved out of her house and had called us, laughing, to say that she had just sold her bed and her television; she was now truly homeless and was moving up to a friend's house to await completion.

July 5 and we knew we had a problem. Jane called in a panic and advised that her house sale had fallen through, right at the last moment, on the very day of completion. Evidently the person buying her house had lied to the mortgage lenders and the whole deal was off. I wasn't sure who to feel sorrier for, her or us. At least we still had beds and all the home comforts, she was left with nothing but an empty shell, and she was so upset.

During the time we had been waiting for the house sale, we had had many phone calls about Happy and being prudent (or cynical), I had kept a list of all those interested and we now went about calling them all and telling them that Happy was back on the market. We didn't really feel that there was much point, as by this time we were at the beginning of the summer holidays and, with only six weeks before the kids had to be at school again, it was unlikely we could sell Happy in so short a time. I have to admit I was relieved and when I sheepishly admitted to Geoff that I was happy that the sale had fallen through, he just laughed and refused to admit that he felt the same.

We had one gentleman who called us back and arranged to come and see her, and, as usual, we hoofed the kids out to 'play in the sunshine and take the stinky dog with you'. Kids and stinky dog gave us the usual hard stares and took themselves off to fly kites on the flood defences while we cleaned poor Happy yet again from top to bottom.

Gerald McKenzie turned up alone and, after a cursory glance at Happy, said she was exactly what he was looking for and would be in touch. The clean-up had taken three hours and the viewing took less than ten minutes; we didn't expect to hear from him again.

Watching him wander back along the flood defences, I snarled, 'What a waste of time.' Oh well, at least the boat was sparkling and beautiful – in fact it looked so fantastic with the morning sunshine coming through the freshly cleaned windows that I was loathe to let kids and stinky dog back in.

Two days later and we were due in dry dock to re-black Happy's hull. June had been a strange month. There were huge floods all over the country and with Happy in dry dock, there we were, living in a boat on dry land, while the rest of England seemed to be growing gills. The whole experience was rather surreal. Each night we would watch the reports of the floods, while coping with the unnerving sensation of our beloved boat not moving at all. The lack of sensation made all of us a little nauseous.

We had hired an industrial pressure washer and the first

morning we all assembled with brushes, sponges and other implements of destruction and prepared to do battle with the weed, mud and freshwater shelled things that had attached themselves to Happy's bum.

Within an hour, Sam had decided that he had 'helped' enough; he was soaking wet, muddy to the point of being unrecognisable and was completely fed up with the whole process. I wasn't too disappointed at him expressing a deep desire to go back into the boat, as he was, like most small boys given sudden access to an industrial pressure washer (an implement of mayhem way and above anything he had had access to before), far more inclined to try and wash off his sister than the boat. We never managed to decide whether it was by accident, or whether he lied to us about not being able to hold it and was doing it on purpose. I suspect that once he had hit her by accident, he had found the screams to be very gratifying and was intent on replicating the experience.

Charlie was not so happy about it, but did manage to exact a very gratifying revenge by waiting until he was spraying the boat, creeping up behind him and turning the washer on full: the water pressure far exceeded Sam's body weight and he shot backwards, landing in a murk-filled puddle, screaming and soaked.

Charlie, on the whole, was much more professional in her handling of the pressure washer – *after* she had amused herself once more by turning the washer off, waiting until Sam looked at it in confusion, and then turning it back on again, causing more screams from him and howls of delighted laughter from her.

'Ah, Mum,' she gasped, holding on to the boat with one hand and her stomach with the other, 'I've seen that done on films but I didn't think he would be so daft as to actually fall for it.'

She staggered off toward Sam, still giggling, her wellies squelching through the growing mud pool under the boat, obviously intent on finding out what else he was 'daft' enough to fall for. Sam, finally working out that he had been had, threw the nozzle down in disgust and stamped off toward the steps (well, he tried to stamp, but it's really difficult to stamp in three inches of slop), stating that he hated Charlie and was going inside.

So with Charlie now firmly in control of the pressure washer, something I suspect she had been aiming for all along, she settled down to work on the boat and was actually very good at it. It was just unfortunate that while washing off the windows she hadn't spotted that one of them was actually open, managing to fill her bedroom with muddy, stinking water.

With Happy down a hole, it was quite difficult getting on and off her, as our main gangplank wasn't designed to rest in an upwards position. So poor Herbert was back to walking a thin plank, a skill he had never mastered. We got around this by one of us holding him in the boat and the other waiting on what would be the bank when there was water in the dock. The one in the boat would put their hands either side of him to keep him on the plank until the other could grab him and hoist him up on to the grass.

This worked for the first day, as he had taken one look at all the pressurised water and screaming going on below him and decided that staying in his bed until the last possible moment would definitely be a preferable state of affairs.

The second day, we made a start on the actual blacking. Again Charlie enjoyed this, and proved to be very good with a bitumen-covered roller, although there were whole sets of clothes that had to be ceremonially burnt when she had finished, as we couldn't find a set of proper overalls small enough to fit her. We had decided that we didn't want to open big buckets of the special blacking paint that Geoff had purchased, so we had taken to pouring it into roller trays; this was working quite well and Happy looked beautiful, all black and shining.

We had finished the first coat and were all standing back to admire the effect when Sam, being 'helpful', hoisted Herbert on to the gangplank and then, that job done, turned back to his colouring and left him to it. With us standing on the ground, a good six foot beneath the plank, there was absolutely nothing we could do, other than watch anxiously, all lined up under the plank ready to snatch him from mid air.

Herbert took three steps forward and, feeling the fresh air on his coat, gave himself a luxurious shake and once again, promptly shook himself straight off the plank. We all rushed forward to try to catch him but somehow, in all the running and screaming, we got in each other's way and Herbert dropped straight through the middle of us and into one of the trays that was half filled with tar-based paint. It was a long drop for a small dog and we all held our breath waiting for him to start crying or show that he was hurt in some way.

No, in glorious Herbert style he had landed on his back in the bitumen. He rolled himself over, getting blacker and stickier with all the struggling, then climbed out of the tar bucket and promptly fell into a mud-filled corner.

We all watched, wincing with every new glob of yuck that Herbert covered himself in – the more muddy and tarry he got, the less any of us wanted to grab him. He staggered up the stone steps out of the bottom of the dock, relieved himself on the grass, then stood waiting for someone to pick him up and put him back on the boat. The silence stretched on. Herbert looked at us and we looked at him. Charlie summed the whole situation up quite well: 'I'm not touching him,' she muttered and wandered off down the dock to check out any missed areas around the rudder.

Finally Geoff brought out a large bowl filled with warm, soapy water and I gingerly caught our muddy, hairy, little mucky puppy. Oh God, he stank and was obviously pleased about it as all he wanted to do was snuggle up to me which he usually avoided at all costs. I swear that rotten animal has a really warped sense of humour. So with Herbert wriggling, by the time Geoff came back it was difficult to tell who was the muckier, me or the wretched dog. We spent a good half an hour with the Fairy Liquid, but it was all to no avail; the tar was stuck in lumps all over him. There was only one thing to do: out came the clippers.

Oh poor Herbert. He was pretty funny to look at before, but now he just looked diseased. The bitumen had worked its way down to skin level in some places and, mindful that he was an old dog, who, like all ancient granddad types, really liked being able to shuffle around in his shaggy old coat, (he was always very indignant when I inexpertly clipped him in the summer and with every passing year his indignation was turning to downright outrage), I only took off the bits that were really solid. By the time I had finished he had numerous two-inch circles of skin showing through hair that, because it had been washed numerous times, stood away from his back like six inches of dirty brown fluff; he resembled a moth-eaten ball of candyfloss with skinny legs and an evil expression – he was not a happy boy.

When he was dry, we got him back on the boat where he stuck his nose under his blanket, then ran round in circles until he was completely mummified with only a nose sticking out. Other than for meals and relieving himself, he didn't leave that blanket until we had Happy back afloat.

The rest of that week went pretty much without a hitch and, eventually, the dry dock was once more filled with water and Happy was afloat again. It seemed a shame that all our hard work couldn't be seen as it was under the water, but it was nice to know it wouldn't have to be done again for another three years.

Happy had been back in the water for all of 48 hours when we had a call from Gerald McKenzie making an offer, subject to a satisfactory survey. Once again we were thrown into disarray. Thinking that we wouldn't bother selling her for at least another year, we had moved all our possessions back on to the boat while she had been in dry dock, and had assured the kids that there would probably be no change until next year. Now here we were again, moving everything off.

Chapter Twenty-eight
Sold

GERALD'S SURVEY WAS BOOKED for the end of the last week in August, which put us in complete flap. School was due to start two weeks after the survey, and we had resigned ourselves to starting the sale process again at Easter the next year. With this offer, all plans were changed yet again and we rushed around, once more removing all our possessions from Happy, leaving only the absolute necessities aboard, and beginning a search for our new home again.

Once again, every boat we looked at was too expensive, too small or totally trashed; it was a horrible flashback to the first search. However, unlike the last time, we now actually knew what we were looking for and could spot real ringers from a mile away. After a couple of really unsuccessful viewings, it occurred to us that we had been very lucky with Happy as our first boat.

As the day of the survey approached, the more nervous we all became. What if Happy wasn't worth what we thought she was? What if the surveyor hated her? What if there was a major problem that we hadn't noticed? This would have put a hitch in all our plans – well, it would have done if we had had any solid plans.

The weekend before the survey was the IWA waterways festival at St Ives, and in the hope of finding a new boat, we arranged to meet Mum and Dad there and headed out for a day of sunshine and boat viewing. The rain and floods had certainly taken their toll on the grounds and we found that the whole festival site was one big swamp.

As it was nice and warm, we had all turned up in shorts and summer gear, desperate to enjoy a bit of sunshine. Watching the festival-goers staggering and squelching through the gates before us, we decided that just removing shoes would be the easiest option and we dragged ourselves through the morass, Glastonbury-style, alternately giggling and making 'yuck' sounds as the cold mud oozed through our toes and over our ankles.

After about an hour of laughing at people falling face-first into the mud (we did help them up and laugh at the same time), I was struck with the differences in attitudes from a year ago. Faced with this mess before we embarked on this lifestyle, I would have taken one look at the mud and turned about-face and headed home, terrified of getting muddy, or looking stupid, but now it was all just funny, as we slipped and slithered from boat to boat. Occasionally, we stopped to dangle our feet in the water and wash the worst of the mud off.

The children had a great time. Mum and Dad, however, were not so impressed. My father had broken his ankle six months previously and his leg, due to the bad break and his age, was not healing well. Consequently, he was trying to limp through this lot with one gammy leg and a cane. My mother summed it all up with a sigh.

'I used to enjoy days out with you,' she muttered, desperately trying to pick her way through the now so churned-up mud and water that it resembled chocolate milkshake, without getting her feet dirty, 'but now, you never do anything "normal". Do you actually enjoy this?' She indicated the site with a wave of her handbag.

I considered the question. 'Yes, actually. I don't actually see anything wrong with this, you can't control the weather, it's not damaging me in any way, and we really want to see the boats, so what's the problem?'

Mum sniffed. 'It's all so, so ...' she scrunched up her face, obviously reaching for the correct word. 'BASIC!'

Hmm, well if that's all she could come up with, I didn't really feel that was a bad thing,

'What's wrong with basic?' I asked, grinning at her and reaching up to wipe a splat of mud off my face. 'I like basic. You know where you are with "basic", and let's face it, you can work on basic, make it better and you can't do much without the basics, can you?'

Mum frowned at me. 'Basics are for workmen to deal with,' she sniffed again and, turning, strutted off toward the coffee tent. The effect would have been quite excellent, if she hadn't had to lurch from grass tussock to grass tussock in an attempt to keep clean.

It was a lovely day, but with renewed interest in boating, and problems with housing, the price of boats had soared. There was nothing we could afford, but, as before, it was nice to see what other people considered a good boat and we left with some good ideas, a couple of leaflets on water purification and bags of really excellent fudge.

Watching my mum and dad helping each other over the mud, I felt a twinge of guilt and when I caught up with them at the cars, I gave Mum a hand off with her wellies.

'Do you really hate this?' I asked her. 'Would you prefer that we were "normal" and lived in a house and all that sort of thing?'

Mum opened her mouth to reply but Dad cut across, 'Don't be ridiculous, we can't even imagine you being "normal".' He poked my mother in the arm. 'Anyway, she has great fun shocking people with your exploits, she loves the fact that her friends don't know whether to commiserate or cheer you on.'

Mum laughed. 'You are a bit of a conversation stopper.' She looked down and grimaced at the state of her white trousers. 'Mind you, you're welcome to this lifestyle, I think I like my house.'

The day before the survey, we moved Happy down to a local marina that boasted a crane to lift her for the survey and a resident surveyor. This was a huge worry for us. We had heard some horrific stories about 70-footers breaking in half when hauled out of the water by crane. It didn't help when we met the crane driver to sort out the schedule for the next morning. He looked to be all of about 15 years old; he had obviously encountered these doubtful looks before as he assured us he was well into his twenties. This didn't alleviate my fears at all. I would have preferred him to be a weathered 55-year-old, with a grumpy disposition and worn thumbs from years of crane driving.

Happy was due out of the water first thing in the morning, and by ten o'clock the surveyor had arrived, along with Gerald, and we were all standing around pretending to look unconcerned. The surveyor, I am sure, actually really was unconcerned. Geoff and I, well, we were close to completely bricking it.

The young crane driver fixed the straps around Happy and (very expertly, I have to admit) manoeuvred her out of the water, bringing her back to hover about six feet above dry land. This enabled the surveyor to take steel thickness readings across the hull and check out any pitting that was evident.

The whole survey took about four hours and, luckily for all concerned, the surveyor signed her off as worth the asking price and that was the end of that. Although I found myself a little disappointed that we had no reason to cancel the sale, I knew we needed to sell her and I still thought that our reasons were good, but that didn't stop me wishing for a lottery win or some sort of change in circumstances that would have meant we could have kept her.

After the cheerful surveyor had left and Happy was nestled happily back in her natural environment, we were all sitting in the kitchen, enjoying a cup of tea.

'I have a bit of a problem,' admitted Gerald, 'I have to get back to teaching in a couple of weeks and I need to move Happy down to Oxford. I'm not really sure what to do with her, this has all come a bit late and I haven't really the time to move her now, have I? How long do you think it would take?'

Geoff got out our well-thumbed *Maps of the Waterways* and we calculated that it would be, at the most, ten days to get her back to Braunston from where we had originally started out and then another two weeks to get her to Oxford.

While Gerald wandered off to get a road map out of his car, Geoff and I talked it over. The opportunity of a 'road' trip, the opportunity to take her along the Oxford Canal and another four weeks on Happy, all of this we could achieve if we offered to deliver her.

Geoff and I looked at each other; were we thinking the same thing? While not entirely unwilling to lose Happy and start yet another unknown and probably insane phase in our lives, an offer to deliver her to Oxford for Gerald would give us an excuse to stay on her for another month before we had to say goodbye. Plus we could charge for delivery. Gerald would be happy, we would be happy and it would give us more time to work out what the bloody hell we were going to do next.

When Gerald came back with his maps, we made the offer; we would deliver Happy to Oxford and would have her there by the end of September. He agreed and, after calling the bank, delivered into our bank account £10,000 as a down payment on the full and final amount which would be sorted out on delivery. He then shook us warmly by the hands and left, saying that he would keep in touch and looked forward to seeing us in Oxford.

We were a little shocked that someone we hardly knew would give us £10,000, and then just leave – there was nothing to stop us just unhooking Happy from the bank and running off with his money. I was in awe at the trust he showed.

The biggest problem with this trip was, obviously, the kids' education, and at a bit of a loss as to what to do, we did our usual thing and had a mass family meeting with chips and bubbly stuff. Sam always thought he was getting the banned lemonade at these meetings, but what he really got was organic elderflower cordial mixed with fizzy water. As I have said before, Sam, colours, additives and confined spaces absolutely do not mix – we have found this out over the years, usually at the cost of something breakable. He goes completely off the deep end and just screams and runs and doesn't stop for about an hour.

We outlined the plan to the kids, a feeling reminiscent of that first meeting when we started all this. The reaction this time couldn't have been more different. Sam was having some problems with bullies at school and while Charlie was getting on well at hers, she hadn't been there long enough to form firm friendships and felt she would be happy to start again at another; both were more than happy to move away and, like us, felt that a bit of an adventure would be fun. They really didn't care where we ended up and agreed to give home schooling a really good try.

There was now nothing left to do but tie up loose ends and get underway as soon as possible. We stayed at the marina overnight, having a great time watching their resident seal flop about on one end of the mooring. Charlie tried her best to get near it, but even her animal magnetism couldn't overcome the creature's cautious nature. The next morning, we thanked the marina and headed back toward our normal mooring to start preparations.

After a weekend of rushing about and squeezing more stuff into storage, we advised the marina that we would be leaving soon and set to clearing the grass of all our wood and burnable material that we had collected over the last year. Keeping only enough for the trip, we gave away a lot of kindling and coal, did a couple of trips to the dump and finally reached the bottom of the pile.

I couldn't believe it. Underneath all the bits of old wood, bags of coal and other detritus was the original pump-out tank.

'What the hell is that doing there?' I asked Geoff.

'Well, it's too heavy to lift,' he said. 'I tried to sell it on eBay, but nothing came of that.'

'Wow, a tank full of old poo,' I laughed. 'I can't imagine why it didn't sell.'

Geoff snorted. 'It is NOT full of old poo.' He gave it a kick and it made a hollow, booming sound. 'There is nothing in there; it's a perfectly good pump-out tank.'

We stood and looked at it for a while. 'So what are we going to do with it?' I asked, eventually.

Geoff sighed and walked away, leaving me staring after him in bewilderment. A couple of minutes later he returned, carrying his angle grinder and a jigsaw.

'What the hell?' I raised my eyebrows at him.

'Can't move it in one,' he said, 'I'll have to cut it up.'

'OH YUCK no!' I yelped, stepping backward. 'All the poo will come out, it's going to stink.'

'Marie, there is NO poo in there, I guarantee it,' and with that emphatic statement, he settled his safety goggles on to his face and grinned at me around the sudden screaming rotation of his angle grinder blade. I fled.

Half an hour of screeching, sawing and swearing later, I deemed it safe to take him out a cup of tea. Still unbelieving about all the poo, I took a deep breath before opening the hatch, determined to get the tea over to him and get back into the boat before I took another.

He was standing next to three roughly hewn sections of steel box. Squatting down, he was staring into the darkness of one of the sections. I knew he had an appalling sense of smell, but I couldn't believe that he was that close to it.

'How's it going,' I warned him of my approach and took a tentative breath at the same time. To my surprise, the only smells were river, hot Geoff and a slightly metallic odour, presumably from an angle grinder blade under duress.

'Fine – here look at this.' He dug around inside the tank

with the trowel he was holding.

'Oh God, don't be disgusting,' I scrunched my nose at him. 'What ARE you doing?'

'Look at this,' he repeated and brought the trowel back into the sunlight.

I approached cautiously. Compost, it just looked like compost – fine, dark, fibrous and soil like. Well, I suppose after two years that is what I should have expected; it looked as though it would grow great tomatoes.

'OK – you win, no poo.' I handed him his tea, still carefully avoiding the trowel. 'The trouble is, I know what it *was* and, whatever it is now, I shall always think of it as poo – so there.'

It appears that however many changes you make in your perspective of life or how many metamorphosis-type changes you put yourself through, one fact remains the same: shit is still shit. However, if you look away for long enough and just get on with your life, when you take a second look, it may have turned into something wonderful and it's only your memories that stop you from acknowledging it as such.

The rest of the weekend was spent selling useful gadgets and giving away things that were loved but had no monetary value or real use. Unfortunately, Herbert came into this category.

Poor Herb had become more and more senile and just plain old. He moved stiffly and had a huge amount of difficulty getting on and off the boat, his legs would give out at the most inopportune moments and in the days running up to leaving, we had fished him out of the river on four separate occasions. Obviously becoming worried by what was going on with his suddenly uncooperative limbs, he gave up and took to weeing in the boat; I was at my wits' end and took him to see the vet.

'There's nothing really wrong with him,' Mr Davis, Herb's vet, informed me, 'he's just old and well, well past his prime.' He took a long look at Herb, sitting on the examining table, and shook his head. 'He's quite a sweet old thing, isn't he?'

I sighed. 'We're just about to set off again,' I explained. 'This is a four-week trip; he's never going to manage getting in and out of the boat, he wees everywhere, he gets upset with all the rushing about, then he wees, then he gets upset about that and I don't know what to do with him.'

Herbert staggered to his feet and shook himself, just managing to stay upright. Just to make me even more miserable, he came over and climbed into my arms, stretching up his ugly, little gargoyle face to lick my nose. Oh, this was horrible.

'Well, it's not really fair to keep him in an active lifestyle when he is just watching it all go on around him.' The vet scratched Herbert behind his gammy ear. 'I don't want to suggest putting him down, but he's too old to re-home ...' he trailed off. 'Isn't there a family member with a more sedate life that could have him?'

I shook my head and buried my face in Herbert's stinky neck ruff. Swallowing the lump in my throat, I put him on the floor and picked up his lead. 'I think I'll wait for a bit and make a decision tonight.'

Mr Davis smiled and nodded. 'We're open tomorrow if you need us. Don't worry about making an appointment, just bring him in, and I'll make sure I see you.'

I thanked him and, picking Herbert up, tucked him under my arm. Next morning, I had a good whinge down the phone to Helen.

'I don't know what to do with him. I'm damned if I'll have him put down when there's nothing really wrong with him apart from being a little incontinent, nobody else will have him and, if we keep him, I know he's just going to be stressed and unhappy. Then there's the problem of what do I do with him after we sell the boat, we can't take him to Lillian's – she's so allergic she'll explode – and the only really nice and financially possible boats we've found have been in Holland or France so what happens if we have to go abroad for a couple of months?'

'Well, I can have him while you're at Lillian's,' Helen said. 'I'd like to say I'd have him for good, but Tara and Paddy would just eat him.' There was silence, then: 'Give me five minutes.' Helen laughed. 'I've had an idea, but I'll have to make a phone call, I'll come back to you in a minute.'

Approximately ten minutes later she was back on the phone. 'I have an answer to all your problems.' She laughed. 'Do you remember Linda?'

I struggled to bully my brain into some semblance of order. 'Yes, lives in Scotland, has two boys, loads of mad old dogs, is that the one?'

'Yes, that's her.' Helen paused. 'She's happy to take Herbert, she met him at my place and thought he was lovely.'

'Really?' I thought about it for a moment. I had never actually met Linda, one of Helen's friends from her greyhound rescue days, but had spoken to her on the phone more than once. She seemed lovely, dog mad and quite insane, but lovely. I made a snap decision.

'Yes, of all the places I can think of where Herb will live out his days in the lap of tolerant luxury, she would be just the person to provide it.' I had a horrible thought. 'How the hell am I going to get him to bloody Scotland?'

'I'll take him,' Helen paused. 'I'd like to come down and see you before you disappear again. Linda's coming to visit next weekend and she says she can pick him up then; he can stay with us for the week, what do you think?'

The relief washed over me like a huge, warm wave. 'That will be brilliant. Tell you what, I'll meet you at IKEA in Birmingham, at least that way we only do half the journey each.'

Six hours later, Helen and I had wandered around IKEA

while Herb waited in the car, had a good chat, numerous cups of coffee and I was giving Herbert a hug goodbye. 'I shall miss you, you stinky, useless piece of carpet.' Herbert really couldn't have cared less, he was well acquainted with Helen, having stayed with her on numerous occasions, and, knowing that she was good for the odd piece of doughnut, he struggled out of my arms and leapt into the back seat of her car, where he sat poised, waiting for the journey to start. I smiled.

'He hasn't been fed today, and he'll need another wee in about an hour.' Helen just looked at me.

'Marie,' she said, 'I've known Herb almost as long as you have, don't worry, he'll be fine.'

I nodded. 'I know, it's just ...' I watched Herb snuggle down into her travel rug and laughed. 'Obviously time to go.'

So dogless and slightly saddened, but confident that Herbert would be happy and well cared for in Linda's mad 'Old Dogs' Home', I headed back toward Cambridge. On Monday morning, I called Charlie's school to start making the preparations for home schooling, a subject about which I knew nothing.

The school couldn't have been more helpful. They provided all the books she would need, as well as a list of all the subjects and the parts of those subjects that she would have been studying throughout that half of the term.

Sam's school were also helpful, but had some real problems when we couldn't tell them where to send his records. I could see it from their point of view – it wasn't normal to drag your kids out of a perfectly good school, sell your perfectly good home and have no idea of what you were going to do next. There was really nothing I could say in our defence.

Chapter Twenty-nine
'Road' Trip

WE SPENT THE EVENING of September 3 saying goodbye to all our neighbours. They had been great over the last year and a bit, and I was genuinely sad to leave them. Narrow boat owners make (on the whole) perfect neighbours, although maybe we had just been incredibly lucky, especially with Charlie and Dion next door. They were incredibly quiet and considerate and, much more importantly, they put up with our kids' occasional screaming moments, talked to them, listened to them, and were generally just nice to be around.

Steve, on the other side, had been helpful and, even though he really was the original party man, he always loaded his noisy, chattering guests into his boat and then took them away for the evening. The next morning they would reappear, much subdued and slightly bleary, but his entertaining skills had never caused us any problems.

The rest of the crowd down the line were hardly ever seen until you needed a hand and then they would be with you at a moment's notice; this was especially true of Lewis, a taxi driver who was also retraining to become an electrician. When I first met him, I'd had him pegged as 'seriously grumpy' but that wasn't true at all, he just never felt the need to endlessly chatter.

It was hardest to take our leave of Dion and Charlie and Jude and Steve. Little Charlie was just about to start school; Ruby was now six months old, and had stopped screaming; Jude was now back at full health and they were starting to go through the process of moving to Australia. I couldn't believe how much I would miss them. Just those odd cups of coffee, not very often but just occasionally, it was great to know that you could go and have a good moan at someone who wasn't family.

Dion and Charlie were grumpy with us for going.

'You do realise we are going to have to put up with new neighbours now,' Charlie moaned. 'They might be horrible.'

'Don't worry, I'm sure it will be someone you can laugh at.'

Dion grinned – obviously I had handed him the perfect opening. 'Not as much as we laugh at you,' he said.

September 4 and we were up and about by six o'clock. It was shaping up to be a beautiful day and, looking at my steps gently warming in the sun – they were being left behind for Dion and Charlie to use – I experienced a horrible pang of sadness. By eight o'clock, we were packed, our mooring was clear and we were all standing on the banks saying a last goodbye to what had been our slightly strange but wonderful world.

As we pulled out, various neighbours leaned out of the windows and waved us off. There was lots of shouted advice and waving and ribald comments (no change there then). My last image was of Steve and Jude with Charlie and Ruby leaning out of their boat's windows and waving us off as we sailed on past; I almost cut the engine there and then.

Geoff had aimed to get to Denver Sluice at about midday. Having missed coming through it the first time, due to the major shopping trip with Helen, I was quite looking forward to it, even though Geoff was obviously worried. The trip to Denver was about as boring as life can get; I was amazed at the complete lack of landscape. The river is very wide, straight as an arrow and has bridges over it, and that's it, there really is nothing more to say. The land around is flat, boring and grows things – I kept looking out of the window to try and find a landmark but only the bridges stood out, dark against the completely featureless surroundings.

We had pulled into the moorings at Denver by 11.50 a.m and Geoff wandered down to the lock to see what time they wanted us there. He came back and reported that we would have to wait for the tide to drop, but we should go up to the main lock moorings at one o'clock.

We hung around, had lunch and chatted to the people behind us. They were also heading through the lock. Not having seen the Denver Sluice before, when we pulled up and waited for our turn to go through, I was amazed at the size of it; it was huge, dominating one complete side of the river.

We were held on the lock moorings until just after two o'clock; I know that tide and time wait for no man, but obviously man waits interminably for the tide. Finally, the lock-keeper judged that we could get through safely and let us in. As we came out the other side, I was disappointed at the view; huge, slimy mud banks littered either side of the river, but there was less than half a mile to Salters Lode and Geoff assured me that, once through, the scenery would change completely. I was a little worried when I distinctly heard him mutter, '*If* we get through.'

It seemed only a matter of minutes before I could see the top of the Salters Lode lock and Geoff urged me to slow down. The water beneath us was running quite fast and I was horrified when he pointed out the tiny little channel over to our left that we would have to use to gain access to the lock.

With the river running this fast and our great underpowered beastie trying to make that turn, I felt that the whole experience was one that I would rather have avoided (shopping with Helen seemed a much better option and I sincerely wished she was here right then).

I pulled Happy as far over to the right as the mud banks would allow and then began the left turn; power on as hard as we could, tiller hard over, trying to gauge how far the river would carry us past the turn while going at this speed.

I *so* nearly made it, but not quite, and we ended up with Happy's nose embedded in a mud bank, just at the mouth of the turn, but at least the flow of the river brought the back end around, so finally we were facing in the right direction. With the back end being pulled around by the water and the front end only lightly embedded in the mud, it didn't take much for Geoff to push us back into free water again; the lock-keeper hailed us as we approached.

'Aha, I thought there was someone coming, I could hear the screaming.' Oh, thanks a bunch, mate...

Once through the lock and into Well Creek, the scenery changed dramatically. Well Creek becomes very narrow and quite overgrown, and, being denied a good meal by the winds on the Ouse, the midges gathered here in this still, calm area attacked with enthusiasm. I took to standing at the back of the boat armed with fly spray and, with the terrors of the tidal Ouse behind us, we drifted happily down the narrow, green channel in the sunshine, leaving only a waft of insect repellent and coughing insects in our wake.

We bumbled along and Charlie, happier now that the scenery wasn't quite so alien and there were things of interest to look at, joined us. She sat in the sunshine with a book and one of the occasional glasses of real ale that she was allowed.

Over the last year and a half, we had completely forgotten how low the bridges were in this part of the waterway, and Geoff had to react pretty fast at one of them. We warned Charlie to get off the top of the boat as we watched it approach and she just lay flat on her back giggling, hoping to watch the underside of the bridge pass over her head. It may be that she was skinny enough to have achieved it, but it was doubtful, and Geoff grabbed her as the bow entered the bridge and bodily pulled her on to the back. She was still bleating and complaining when we heard a 'crunch' and turning around watched the chimney hit the underside of the bridge and get sheared clean away. Charlie turned a little pale and she and I crouched in the engine room as the bridge went past, far too close overhead.

Once through, she jumped back on to the roof and collected our mangled chimney from the top of the boat and brought it back to Geoff.

He looked at the sad, sheared and crumpled piece of metal, and said, 'Well, let's just hope it doesn't rain, otherwise the Morso is going to be full of water.'

As the evening progressed, I wandered off to make dinner and Geoff started looking for a suitable mooring. Once again our size prohibited us from a lot that were available, and we stared mournfully at other, longer moorings that were already packed with boats, their owners obviously having stopped at a sensible time.

Eventually, when we were about half an hour away from full dark, Geoff slowed down and turned us toward the bank.

'We'll just stop under that tree,' he pointed over to the left at a huge willow that was dipping a vast amount of its leaves into the water. 'It's not ideal, but at least we can keep the back end out. And it's warm enough not to need a fire.'

He pulled her over and I stood ready with a rope. The easiest way would be just to tie the rope to one of the thick branches. First there was a gentle thump, the bow lifted and tilted perceptibly over to the right, followed by a swishing, grinding noise as the whole left-hand side of Happy lifted about three inches up on a silt bank and there she stopped. Oh bugger.

It was our first night away from known territory for over a year and immediately, despite all our presumed experience, we were once again aground. I looked at Geoff as he stood there with his lips pursed and just laughed and laughed; it was all so ironic.

'Well,' I managed, between gulping air, 'here we are again.'

Geoff looked at me sniggering and giggling, still standing

there holding the rope, and took a look around at the 'mooring' and just joined in. Charlie, appearing to find out what all the howling laughter was about, just took one look at us, another at the mooring, shook her head and walked away.

When we could breathe again, Geoff hopped onto the bank and stretched the ropes across the water, attaching them to the spikes set in the ground and just left her there with her bum waving around in the waterway. We figured nobody would come past in the dark and, as we were planning to leave early in the morning, we quite frankly didn't care at all.

Next morning, we were still aground and with two years' worth of experience, we were old hands at this; there was no shouting or panicking, we just kept pushing, rocking and using the engines and eventually we came away into the middle. Yes, there was no shouting, pouting or whinging, it was efficient, but it seemed so dull. Where was the excitement? The adrenalin? Once back out into water, I frowned and turned to Geoff.

'It doesn't seem so hard any more, does it?'

Geoff raised his eyebrows. 'Would you want it to be?'

'I don't know, not really I suppose, but I think it proves that we are ready for something new.' I looked at him leaning nonchalantly, sun-browned and messy-looking against the top of the boat – he looked like every other long-standing boater we had met. 'Do you think I have a pathological problem and need excitement?'

He turned to me and grinned. 'You're a woman, yes of course I do.' I hit him.

We followed Well Creek into Outwell and, from there, on to the River Nene which, while wider and easier to navigate with our great lump of a boat, was again completely devoid of features. On one occasion, I dragged the kids out of the boat to have a look at one of the huge wind turbines that were dotted across the landscape, but other than that we reached March by ten o'clock and took the same mooring that we'd had on the way down, just facing the other way; it seemed rather significant.

The plan for that day was to leave the boat in March and take a family trip back into Cambridge to purchase all the kids' books and study guides for home schooling. I'm not sure that either Sam or Charlie had quite understood what was going on as they only seemed to hear 'train ride' and 'buy ... for Sam and Charlie' and were looking forward to the whole thing immensely. Geoff had taken the idea of home schooling very seriously and, as we walked into the train station at March, began explaining Victorian railway architecture to the kids. They stared at him in horror for about two minutes before both of them shook their heads and ran away down the platform, at which point, deprived of an audience, he tried to explain it to me. Lasting slightly longer than the children, I began to hunt around in my handbag for a bag of toffees I had seen in there that morning. Offering him the bag, I smiled and he just said, 'Am I boring you?'

'Hell yes.'

'OK.' He took a toffee and we lapsed into blessed silence. When he had finally finished the toffee, he started again.

'In 1847 ...' I pursed my lips and squinted at him; he just laughed.

Luckily, the train arrived and we all leapt aboard. The sun was still shining and the day's shopping was a real break. It was actually nice to have spare money to spend for once. We treated ourselves to pizza for lunch and raided the city's excellent selection of bookshops. The children were a little miffed when they finally realised that we weren't buying anything of interest, but soon rallied together and by six o'clock, we were staggering back through the streets of March, laden with books and bags. Back on the boat, we unpacked all our purchases and the kids spent the next hour looking, with growing horror, through all their study guides.

As I unpacked the groceries, Geoff held up a new can opener. 'Why did you buy this? We already have one.'

'I don't know,' I took it from him and put it in the drawer. 'I saw it in Lakeland and just bought it.'

I always bought them when I saw them now. We didn't have 'one', we actually had four and I had them hidden all over the boat 'for emergencies'. I didn't think he needed to know that, so I didn't tell him – he would have only given me the 'look'.

We stayed overnight in March and were back on the water by six o'clock the next morning. The children had taken to sleeping in until about nine so Geoff and I had three hours of sunshine, hot tea, early morning mists, local wildlife and a leisurely breakfast; it was complete bliss.

As we travelled through the villages, relaxed and just enjoying the ride, I wondered if the children were feeling the same way. I noticed that a lot of the schools had started their autumn term and, watching the students walking together in little chattering groups, resplendent in obviously new uniforms, I was pleased that Charlie and Sam weren't around to see it, as I was entirely unsure as to whether they would be smug or sad; they seemed to change their views from day to day.

Ashline Lock, just before Whittlesey, was our first unmanned lock for two years; it was quite nice to rediscover the old skills, although I didn't think we would be so happy to rediscover the old aches and pains that a day full of locks would bring.

With the weather being so glorious, there were still a lot of boats travelling. We didn't bother to stop in Whittlesey this time, and, with me in charge of Happy, we headed onward toward the dreaded Whittlesey Corner.

I wasn't worried about it; we had made it around last time, so we knew without a shadow of a doubt that we would make it around this time as well. As we approached the Corner, I was going too fast, again, and we didn't make it. I ran Happy soundly into the trees at the side of the turn and Geoff, giving me a look of absolute disgust, had to go back to the front with his pole. We finally made it round with only one deep scrape on the new blacking.

Stupid trees. I figure the only reason Geoff made it round and I didn't was obviously due to the trees having grown vastly in the last two years. That was my excuse anyway; Geoff was smug.

'Yes,' I muttered at him, 'I know, I know, slow down.'

Stanground Sluice, in bright sunshine and coming from the other direction, gave a completely different impression to the previous visit; still not a bat in sight, no lightning, no thunder and once through, we pulled into Peterborough calmly and efficiently.

Once again, I was oddly disappointed. Where were the terrors that I remembered so well? There was nothing here, it was just a nice mooring in a tree-lined park that gave us the opportunity to have a picnic and for the kids to play ball games and scream each other into lassitude. Sitting on the grass with an egg sandwich, I replayed the last visit in my mind. Finally I gave up and turned to Geoff.

'Why is this so different from last time?' I broke the crust of my sandwich off, finally caving in to the threats of a nearby swan. 'I know the sun is shining and we aren't under pressure, but I didn't think it would feel so different.'

Geoff looked around. 'I don't think it is different,' he said, 'we are.'

'What?' With the swan looming and hissing over me, I couldn't really grasp what he meant and, standing up, went and sat with him on the bench.

'Well,' he looked over at Happy, rocking gently on the end of her tethers, 'we were so unsure of what we were doing, didn't know where we were going, and now we know it just doesn't really matter because, Best Beloved, we are like cats.'

'Cats?'

'Yes.' Geoff stood up and adopted an oratory pose. 'I am the cat that walks by itself and all places are alike to me.' He grinned.

I stood up and hailed the kids.

'Come on, guys! Your father has started quoting Kipling, it's time to go.'

Geoff put on a very overdone 'hurt' look. 'You would have preferred Shakespeare?'

I turned to the swan, who was trying to sneak up on the picnic bag. 'Kill,' I commanded, pointing at Geoff.

We had hoped to make it all the way back to Fotheringhay, but dawdling for too long in Peterborough had put a stop to that, so we decided to stop just outside Nassington. Full of nonchalant experience, and lithe as cats, we pulled Happy into a reed bed and Geoff made a casual and athletic leap for the bank. Wool gathering, looking around trying to spot landmarks from the previous visit, I wasn't really watching what he was doing, and was only alerted that there might be a problem when the sound of furious splashing, accompanied by a string of expletives, wafted on the warm evening breeze toward me from over the side of the boat.

I peered over the side and spotted Geoff apparently walking on water – well, to be honest, he was more running, jumping and bounding on water. I watched him with wide eyes as he made a leap for the bank and collapsed panting in a heap in a mound of nettles (ouch).

'What on earth are you doing?' I enquired gently when I thought he may have enough breath to answer.

It turned out that he had jumped into what he thought was the bank beyond the reed bed, and it wasn't. There was still about four foot of water beneath him, but the reeds were so thick, they had bent and he had been able to use them as a semi-solid surface and run across them, although with every step he had sunk and had to take another, which was why he was moving so fast.

Finally regaining his breath, he wandered along the bank and held out his hand for me to throw him the rope, mooring pins and hammer that I had lined up on the roof. I threw the hammer toward him and it hit him on the foot. When he had finished hopping about, I (more carefully) threw a mooring pin toward him; too carefully, it disappeared into the river. The second pin was more successful and the rope he caught. Watching him hammer in the pin, it occurred to me that experience was really no match for poor aim and plain stupidity.

Later that evening, with the kids tucked up in bed, we spent another fruitless hour going through boat magazines in an effort to find another home. Geoff leaned back and tossed the magazine down the boat. I looked up, surprised at his vehemence.

'What do you *really* think about getting a barge?' He looked into his tea cup. 'I mean a proper barge; I really fancy getting something that would be able to go to sea.'

I squeaked slightly, 'What – really go to sea? Like sail to America or something?'

'No, not that far. Just off shore, so we could bring one back across the Channel,' Geoff grinned. 'You said there were some really great boats in France and Holland.'

I winced. 'Yes, there are, but I was assuming someone else would bring it back and it would be delivered ... Don't you have to have some major qualifications to take a boat to sea?'

Geoff got up and ferreting about in the bookcase brought out a booklet marked 'CEVNI'.

'What's that?' I took the booklet from him and studied it.

'CEVNI is the qualification you have to have for European Inland Waterways.' Geoff took the booklet back and began leafing through it. 'It's pretty much like the one we already have for the UK, just European.'

I looked again at the book. 'How long have you had that?'

He had the grace to look a little embarrassed. 'About three months.'

'And when exactly, were you going to broach the subject with me?' I grinned at his silence. 'Surely this "CEVNI" isn't the only thing you need to get a boat back across the Channel?'

'Well, no, you need to be able to operate a radio and there are some other courses we could take, "Day Skipper" and that sort of thing.'

'I think your walk on water attempt has addled your brain.' I stood up and collected the cups to go and make another cup of tea. 'I get really seasick, you know.'

Geoff, knowing that he was well on the way to winning this conversation, laughed. 'Don't worry, we'll pack a whole load of sick bags and nausea tablets for you – and think of the lovely view of the marine life you'll get when you're hanging over the side.'

'Shut up, Jesus!'

By ten o'clock the next morning we had moored in Fotheringhay; it was an incredibly hot and airless day. Pausing only for a quick history lesson on the site of Fotheringhay Castle, much to the chagrin of the children, we meandered along the footpath to Warmington for a shop visit, Geoff and I still discussing Mary Queen of Scots and her heartless beheading, Charlie and Sam running ahead of us, hitting each other with sticks.

Chapter Thirty
Either I Hate Insects or They Hate Me

TRAVELLING FOR THE NEXT couple of days, I was disappointed that the journey was less than exciting. In fact, the only memorable incident between Fotheringhay and Erthlingborough came once again at a mooring. Seeing a lovely, sheltered, wooded spot, we had pulled over and, as we had no intention of leaving the boat that evening, we had decided to just tie her front and back to trees. Geoff clambered into the undergrowth holding a rope, intending to just pass it around a branch and tie it back on the T stud on the top of the boat. In this way, we wouldn't have to get off the boat in the morning; we could just untie it at the top, pull it away from the tree and head on our merry way.

As I watched him trying to climb a large tree I became aware of an odd noise, a humming. The engine was off, and I looked inside the engine room to see if it was the electrics – no ... I stood on the back with my head cocked, trying desperately to place the sound. Geoff had managed to scale the tree to the first branch and was now hanging from it monkey-like, swinging backward and forward trying to pass the rope to Charlie who was standing on top of the boat, giggling and deliberately failing to catch it, so that she could watch Geoff swinging about upside down. Sam, sitting on the roof watching them, was shouting instructions.

I worked out that the sound was coming from the tree to my left and, grabbing a branch, I moved it aside in an effort to ascertain what on earth was making the irritating noise.

As I moved the branch, the noise increased and I peered

into the foliage wondering what on earth it was. Hanging from one of the branches was a moving mass from which the deepening hum emanated.

Oh crap, crap, crap. I put the branch back very carefully and shouted,

'Get back on the boat, Geoff. Now!'

'What?' he peered at me, red in the face from his upside-down position.

Not wanting to make any quick movements, I hissed at him,

'Get back on the boat, right now.'

'Why?'

'There is a swarm of bees in this tree and I think I have just pissed them off by rustling around in the branches.'

The noise increased and small furry bodies began to emerge from the tree, flying around my head. Charlie took one look and, grabbing Sam by the hand, she abandoned Geoff and the ropes. She hustled them both, screaming, down the roof and, throwing Sam safely into the boat, she followed him with an impressive and athletic dive through the front hatch which she then closed and bolted. Geoff, so slowly I could cheerfully have killed him, climbed down off his perch and back on to the boat. By this time I was standing rigid and immobile (no sudden movements) and had my own set of little yellow and brown stripy satellites; the humming had become a deep drone. More and more bees appeared and I was beginning to panic.

'For God's sake, will you get back on the bloody boat?'

Geoff looked surprised and finally took in all of my little friends hovering above my head and my wide-eyed and lock-jawed immobility.

He made a jump for the gunwales, dragging the rope with him.

'Finally,' I hissed, exasperated, 'thank you.' I turned the engine on and held my breath as Geoff pushed us away from the bank with the use of the barge pole. The sound of the engine starting brought on a new note from the tree and my nerve finally broke. Slamming Happy hard into forward I held on to the tiller with one hand and flapped the other about my head. This infuriated the bees further and, as more came to find out what was going on, we hightailed it up the river with a buzzing kite tail of enraged insects trailing behind us.

Still breathing heavily, we finally stopped a little further on, and moored on open ground without a tree in site.

Apart from killer bees, there was very little of note. Locks held no terrors for us, we had been this way before, so there was nothing new to see and I was still having real difficulty linking this gentle sun-filled, holiday-type travel with the incident-filled journey of two years ago.

We stopped at Erthlingborough again, but unlike last time, due to Sam's face being its normal size and not looking like a hamster that had swallowed a red nightlight, there was no rush and we pottered about, chatting to people about boats and enjoying the sunshine. We also had time to have a long wander around the huge car boot sale that is held there, where we watched the kids pander to their latest craze and spend all their money on Yu-Gi-Oh! cards, exclaiming with delight over each new bargain; all in all, a thoroughly relaxed and enjoyable day.

Just past Billing Aquadome, we came out of the lock at a poor angle. We needed to turn sharply right, which would have put us nose to nose with a boat coming the other way, but, instead, and trying to avoid the other boat, I kept Happy going in a straight line and found myself once again in the huge expanse of water that had so terrified me on the way up.

I pulled the boat deliberately out into the centre and cut the engine.

'What are you doing?' Geoff looked around and then frowned at me.

'This is where I was telling you about,' I indicated back

at the lock. 'Look we were coming from the other direction and I missed the lock and ended up here with that wind – I thought I was going to die.'

Geoff laughed and looked around. 'It doesn't look that scary to me,' he said.

'No it doesn't, does it?' I also looked around. 'Isn't that odd.' I put Happy in forward again and turned the same 180-degree turn that I had before. She came around like a perfect lady and we headed back towards the mooring.

In counselling terms 'empathy' is viewing a specific situation from another person's viewpoint, and this view will always be filtered through your own experience and perception. Obviously on the way up I was viewing this turn and many other situations through the perception of an inexperienced novice, floundering in an unknown situation that I had been forced into by circumstance. On the way back, alternatively, we were seeing it all through the eyes of a relaxed and experienced 'old hand'. It's true that your perception makes a world of difference to everything you do.

Our next stop was for a day in Northampton. Charlie got her hair very trendily cut and then moaned that there were no friends to see it. We stayed overnight, moving Happy down a quarter of a mile in the morning to enable a restock of supplies at Morrison's (I couldn't believe how many can openers they had there!) Pulling away from Northampton, we headed toward the lock at the Northampton Arm; I was looking forward to being back on the canal again, rather than this wide river. The moorings were non-existent at the lock, so, while waiting for Geoff to open the gates, I pulled Happy over to the right and just held on to a tree.

Standing there for a couple of minutes, my hand began to itch and I let go of the tree to scratch it against a branch. A couple of seconds later and my forearm began to itch, so I turned to scratch it with my other hand. ARRRRRGH! My whole arm was covered in red bugs. I let go of the tree with a scream and let Happy drift free, while performing a wild 'bug' war dance on the back of the boat, knocking them off me and into the water. Without much of a current, we hadn't moved far and I peered into the branches of the tree to see where they had come from.

The tree was crawling with them, under every leaf and up and down the branches – yuck! I have no major problem with bugs per se, as living on a boat you tend to become completely blasé about having to collect up to ten large spiders out of the shower before you get in; you need the spiders, they eat all the midges and mozzies. But en masse, like these little red things, they completely freak me out. So I wasted no time in applying some power and moving Happy over to the other side of the channel, as far away as possible.

As the lock gates opened and I prepared to enter, still shuddering and scratching occasionally, I noticed another boat coming alongside the tree and a woman reaching for the same branch.

'No!' I yelled across the water to her. 'Don't hold that, it's covered in bugs.'

The lady, obviously in her later years, put her hand up to her ear. 'What?'

'Don't hold that tree – it's covered in bugs.'

'What?'

'DON'T HOLD THAT TREE, IT'S ... oh never mind.'

She smiled and nodded, waving at me; it was obvious that she couldn't hear a word I was saying. I smiled back and carried on pulling Happy into the lock.

There was only a small rise in water needed and we were out pretty quickly. As Geoff got back on to the boat we could hear screams from behind us.

'What the hell's going on back there?' he asked, leaning on the tiller and trying to peer over the lock gates.

I shrugged, knowing that there was no way I could adequately explain the sense of horror and loathing that a

273

crawling mass of bugs engenders. I did try to warn them, I really, really did.

'No idea ... shall we go?'

After dragging ourselves up the Rothersthorpe Flight, we filled up with diesel and water at the top, noticing how much the diesel had gone up in price, before heading on to Gayton Junction. I remembered, with a wince, the amount of crockery we had lost last time I tackled this junction, so was very slow and sure as I approached the waterways' equivalent of a crossroads.

It was maniacal. There were so many boats zipping past, it resembled Spaghetti Junction at rush hour. Having spent the last two years on a relatively unused waterway, I was completely befuddled and just couldn't see a way of getting into the flow of traffic – it's not like we have traffic lights.

Eventually we moved into the flow by just using our size. We crept forward and just didn't stop. Ignoring those who were screaming and trying to stop, we just bullied our way in and put on the power, keeping our heads down as we tried to outrun our pursuers.

A couple of days later and we were once again facing the entrance to the Braunston Tunnel. I called the kids out of the boat as the tunnel entrance appeared; Charlie in particular had been looking forward to this as she hadn't been through it the first time. Sam, who is his father's child without a doubt, was grumpy at being pulled away from his maths book and, after a cursory glance over the roof of the boat, humphed and went back to do 'something actually enjoyable'. Charlie watched him stamp through the engine room with a pen stuck behind his ear. 'Weirdo,' she muttered.

Entering the tunnel, I was hit by the old fears; dark, cold, dripping ... Aha, here was an obstacle where the feelings were the same. Charlie alternated between worrying about the roof collapsing on us and rushing up and down the gunnels of the boat staring into the darkness for as long as she could stand it, then scuttling back to safety.

She had bought new and expensive skater trainers in Northampton and had sulked because I wouldn't allow her to wear them while just slobbing around on the boat, my justification being that as the kids all wore them half undone with the laces trailing about, they were actually more of an impediment on slick surfaces than an aid.

Consequently, she was wearing her old ones – just as dangerous – but having won on the issue of not wearing the new ones, I wasn't prepared to push it. We were about two-thirds of the way through the tunnel and Charlie had walked over the roof to sit in her favourite place: the very front tip at the bow where she could dangle her legs over the front and feel like she was hanging above the water. I never really liked her sitting there and allowed it only on open water where we weren't likely to scrape her legs off on any obstacles. She promised to be careful and, as we were travelling so slowly, I felt it would be all right.

She had been there about five minutes and was enjoying watching the opening on the other side of the tunnel approach when there was a sudden scream. I slowed down, knowing that as I could still hear her babbling incoherently she hadn't fallen in. There was a series of thumps and she came back over the roof.

'What's up?' Geoff asked her.

'My shoe,' Charlie pointed into the water. 'You have to stop, my shoe fell off and it's in the water.'

I cut the engine and we all peered over the side into the black water.

Geoff gave her a hug. 'It's gone,' he said, 'never mind.'

I couldn't resist adding smugly, 'Lucky you weren't wearing your new ones, eh?'

Charlie glared at me and spent the rest of the tunnel peering backwards to see if she could spot it.

We moored up at the other side of the tunnel, not willing to face more locks at that time of day. I took a good look around at the other boats, wondering if Mr Blobby might be here; now we would be able to show him how fast we could do a lock and I wouldn't worry about just pushing him into the river. But, of course, he wasn't there.

We spent a pleasant evening watching Charlie staring into the mouth of the tunnel behind us, hoping that her shoe would come floating toward her. By 11.30 the next morning, we were exactly back where we had started two years and four days previously.

Sam had been promised another trip to Gongoozler's Rest and had been asking for days, 'Are we nearly there yet?' So we decided on an early lunch and wandered down the tow path, in the sunshine, to indulge, for maybe the last time, in one of their memorable fry-ups.

The tiny restaurant was packed and we had to sit on the seat outside for ten or fifteen minutes waiting for a table. However, within three quarters of an hour we were all seated comfortably, each eyeing the huge breakfast that had been placed in front of us with something akin to excited panic. As we made a start, voices wafted through the open door of the boat from a couple enquiring if there were any tables free. They were shown to a table opposite ours and, as they sat down, the entire clientele became silent.

The couple were about 50 years old, a little shabby-looking in the way of most boaters. He was wearing a pair of well-loved jeans and she was resplendent with waist-length salt and pepper hair, a pair of faded green cords and deck shoes. Either it was a marriage made in heaven or a more recent love affair, but they had eyes for no one but each other, which was lucky really because if they had looked away from each other and around the place, it wouldn't have taken a huge amount of vigilance to notice the smothered sniggers emanating from the rest of the patrons.

Both were wearing acid yellow, hand-knitted jumpers in fantastic 1970s style with the yoke, cuffs and hem in bright blue, green and red Austrian-patterned wool. They were eye-searingly painful to look at, but you couldn't stop your eyes being dragged back, screaming, to stare at these jumpers, which, had it been night time, would surely have glowed in the dark. On a couple of occasions I caught Sam staring and, as he opened his mouth with a slight frown, I kicked him gently on the shin and shook my head at him, putting my finger up to my lips.

'Shhhh, no personal comments remember.'

Charlie had far more problems with that restriction and kept sniggering, even as she made frantic hand movements that were supposed to imply, 'I am trying to stop, I just caaaaan't.'

The only way we could stop her laughing aloud was for Geoff to give her a blow-by-blow account of how black pudding was made. This at least accomplished the desired effect of stopping her laughing, but also made her turn slightly green and pass the offending foodstuff quickly over to his plate. Geoff was happy – he had Charlie's, Sam's, mine and his own. I sometimes wonder if he needs to put quite so much detail into the explanation of black pudding, but it always has the desired effect. Looking at the huge pile of food on his plate, I actually found myself wondering if I was going to have to send Charlie back to the boat for the sack trolley.

We all lingered over tea and coffee, and I noticed Arthur and Martha of the screaming jumpers get up to leave. Silence fell once again as all eyes were fastened on the painful knitwear. We all watched them climb the steps and heave themselves out on to the tow path, where they wandered on, hand in hand, toward the local marina. I really hope that, at their later time of life, they were going a bit deaf, as the sound of hysterical laughter from about 12 people, even muffled inside a narrow boat, must surely have reached them as they went on their way.

Three hours later, re-filled with water, we had visited

Midland Chandlers and had installed a new chimney, Charlie was lolling around in the bath (I figured our bath was too shallow for her to drown through stomach cramps after such a huge meal) and we were on our way again.

I was excited to leave Braunston as we would be heading in a totally different direction; new things to see, new people to meet and new things to collide with – great!

Chapter Thirty-one
Pastures New

AS WE TRAVELLED, I noticed the winding hole that had been the limit of our training day with Dave. Ah, if only he could see us now: experienced, competent and still running into things and trying to sink our boat.

So, now in uncharted territory, we headed toward the first of the Napton Locks. There were a lot of boats moored along the side of the canal, some in horrendous condition, with broken windows and huge sheets of paint flaking into the river, yet still with obvious signs of live-aboard activity. I still can't work out whether these people live in this condition because they want to. If they do, that is fine – it's their choice – and if they choose to live that sort of alternative lifestyle, I may not agree with it, but they have the right to do it. However, if they have to live in these vessels because the choice is either that or the streets, due to the high cost of housing and all the other rubbish that goes along with life these days, then it is so far off acceptable it's unreal.

Looking at some of these living quarters, I remembered how I felt about Happy when we first looked at her. At least she had been clean, dry and warm – in fact, compared to some of these she was a veritable luxury cruise liner and I felt slightly ashamed at being so horrified.

With these thoughts in mind, I noted the approach of the top lock and took over driving from Geoff so that he, as usual, could do all the heavy stuff. This is another thing I had noted that we do differently from 75 per cent of all the other river users, especially the holiday-makers; it is usually the bloke who drives and the poor woman who is left leaping about trying to open the locks.

After long experience, we have worked out that I am certainly better at getting Happy through small spaces than Geoff is; it may be that I have perfect eyesight, whereas Geoff is slightly long-sighted, or it may be that I just have better depth perception. Whatever the reason, eight times out of ten, I can bring Happy into a tiny lock pound without touching the sides and bring her to a stop without hammering her into the lock gates at the end. Geoff tends to bring her in like a pinball.

Geoff, on the other hand, can open a lock much, much quicker than I can, as he is stronger and faster. Consequently, we approach locks like it's war, leaping about on dry land and keeping the boat rock steady, and we can be through in the fastest time possible – sometimes we even have time to laugh at other people, just a little, before we go and help.

I took a second look at the lock ahead of us. Even by single-boat canal standards, this one seemed awfully small and I slowed down further to make sure I was completely lined up. This was one of the eight times out of ten, and she went in straight as a die.

With about 10 foot of her 70-foot length inside the lock, she stopped. I waved at Geoff who was chatting to another boater at the far gate.

'I'm stuck!'

He wandered toward me, followed by the other boater (whose name was Marty, we later found out), both looking confused.

'Look,' I pointed at the front. 'I'm stuck. Have a look and see what she's caught on, can you?'

Geoff and Marty peered into the pound.

'I can't see anything,' Geoff stepped on to the roof and jumped up and down. 'Look, she's moving.'

'Well, she may be moving up and down,' I grumped, gunning the engine, 'but she's certainly not going forward.'

Geoff scratched his head and jumped back on to dry land. He wandered to the edge of the lock and looked over the back gates to see if anything had caught us there, no ... nothing evident.

'Try reversing her back out,' he suggested.

I shrugged and bunged Happy into reverse. There was a swashing, scraping noise and then she began to reverse.

Geoff watched and then laughed. 'It's the fenders,' he said, pointing down the side of the lock. 'This lock is so narrow, with the fenders down, we're stuck.'

Good grief, he was right. Happy was seven foot six and the lock was obviously just over eight foot wide; with the fenders down we had become stuck like a cork in a bottle. I remember Dave saying something about fenders and locks, but we had never been in a lock smaller than about nine foot wide so it had never been an issue.

Geoff jumped on to the boat and, as I pulled her back to free water, he ran around and lifted all the fenders to lie, dripping the slime and weed that they had picked up from their scrape along the lock walls, all the over the roof.

By this time, with all our faffing about, we had monopolised the lock for far too long and the queue either side had become extensive, with lots of owners peering at us, trying to work out what the hell we were doing. Looking back at the ever-increasing line behind us, I noticed that every one of them had their fenders already on the roof. Ah well, you learn by experience. With Marty's help, we bashed through the lock in double quick time and shot out the other side. With red faces, we desperately tried not to notice that the line was now so huge the moorings were full and newcomers were trying to hold their boats in mid-stream with little success. And there seemed to be a fair few bumps and curses. Whoops, sorry.

It soon became very, very apparent that we were one of

the biggest and the slowest things on the canal and it didn't take very long for me to become used to the look of wide-eyed terror on the faces of the oncoming pilots, as they emerged around tight corners and came face to face with us coming the other way.

As they came fully alongside, we still had another 30 foot trailing out behind and they would stare as we kept going and going, watching us as we disappeared behind them. Being so large and heavy, we were also very slow and much less manoeuvrable than the smaller holiday boats. It was this lack of manoeuvrability and our length that caused me the biggest headache on this leg of the journey.

British Waterways were busy doing some work under one of the bridges between locks and, with their workboat moored under the bridge, it made the canal excruciatingly narrow. Geoff was driving; we had two boats behind us and could see a line of three coming the other way. Geoff frowned for a moment and, taking in the scene of the workboat, the very narrow gap and all the traffic, completely out of character for him, he just gunned the engine and narrowed his eyes.

I was totally confused; this wasn't like Geoff at all. Taking a straight line, he whooshed through the gap and, with a nifty bit of steering, manoeuvred around the oncoming boats and out along the now empty canal. It was only past the boats that he slowed down and we looked behind us.

'I thought that was likely to happen,' Geoff muttered.

I looked over my shoulder and was horrified at the scene of chaos and disaster under the bridge. The narrow boats behind us had followed us through and the oncoming ones had also made a try for the gap; they had all collided abreast of the workmen. The bridge amplified sounds of screaming, shouting and swearing, and the squeal and crunch of tortured metal followed us in a guilt-inducing wave down the river for far longer than it had any right to.

'That's going to screw up some precious paint jobs,' Geoff grinned.

I looked at him. 'Did we do anything to cause that?' I asked, still staring back at the chaotic, noisy huddle stuck under the bridge.

'For once, no,' Geoff ticked off the reasons on his fingers. 'One, our bow was under the bridge by a long way before any of the others tried to come through, so it's our right of way; two, I just wanted to get Happy out of the way, which is why I shot through, can you imagine something this size snarled sideways in amongst that lot?'

I looked back and shuddered. 'Unfortunately, yes.' We looked at each other and burst out laughing, and we were still sniggering and giggling when a sharp bend crept up on us and we had to restore order enough to deal with yet another bloody lock; at least this was the last one of the day. I remember thinking our first day on the Oxford Canal had been memorable, if not entirely successful.

Unlike other places that we had visited, mooring on the Oxford was an absolute delight; with miles and miles of tow path, you just decided where you wanted to stop, pulled over, drove in some stakes and there you stayed. Fantastic.

The next morning, Geoff and I were up and about early, as had become our normal routine. I still loved these early mornings, which had become more delightful as autumn started to arrive. They gave us time to potter about, have a cup of tea on the back of the boat while wrapped up nice and warm and I think both of us really cherished these few quiet morning hours before chaos and destruction threw themselves whinging out of bed, demanding food and entertainment.

This morning started out exactly the same as all the previous ones on this trip with the addition of mist so thick we couldn't actually see Happy's nose from where we were standing on the back plate. We stood with our tea and toast, resplendent in woolly hats, gloves and big overcoats, gently yawning and leaning on each other, trying to discuss the day ahead but really just enjoying the peace and quiet.

Geoff put his tea down on the engine room sliding hatch and, frowning, stared hard into the thick swirling mist.

'What the hell is that?' he asked, pointing over the canal.

'What?' I leant round him and tried to see what he was pointing out to me.

'That!' He jabbed a finger into the mist, and, slowly, I could start to make out a hulking, dark figure standing silent and still in the mist.

We both froze, breath puffing in clouds, further obscuring the view, and stared at the mist-covered apparition. It was sort of cow shaped, or at least it would have been if it hadn't been sporting a small hump on its huge, black back and what appeared to be at least three foot of black horn sweeping out sideways away from its head, parodying the caricatured plaits on a cartoon Swiss milk maid – certainly not a Friesian or a Jersey then.

Staying quiet, wc waitcd as the animal turned its head and took a long sniff of the morning air; it then started to make its stately way down to the water's edge. Further dark shapes appeared out of the mist, all with the same hump and majestic horns, although none boasting quite the breadth of the first one.

'Water buffalo,' Geoff whispered.

Not knowing why we were whispering, I spoke up. 'Don't be ridiculous, what are water buffalo doing in bloody Warwickshire? They're native to India and I don't think they swim, well actually they do, but they wouldn't swim from India.'

At the sound of my raised voice, the animals looked up and then, as one, turned and wandered back into the mist.

'I don't know,' he shrugged, 'but they were definitely

water buffalo.'

We stood and watched the alien animals disappear into the mist, both confused by what we had seen. In the thick mist and being still slightly dopey in the early morning, it was a very surreal experience. It wasn't until three months later that I actually found out there is a farm in Napton that has a herd of over 80 of the things. I'm not sure whether I was relieved or a little disappointed; I had sort of hoped that the mist hid an inter-dimensional rift or something. Sigh, no such luck.

By 11 o'clock the mist had thinned sufficiently for us to be on our way. Chaos and Disorder had woken up and life was back to normal. It was a very short run to Napton's top lock, and I must have been still either partially asleep, or still thinking about water buffalo, because as we exited the lock, I was going too fast, couldn't make the sharp right-hand bend back onto the canal and ploughed Happy's nose straight into a wall. Oh yes, definitely back to normal.

Unfortunately, this one little accident set the tone of the travel conditions for the next couple of days. Being used to piloting on a wide, deep river, I had, I have to admit, had some problems with the narrow waterways. This stretch of the Oxford Canal was particularly problematic, as it had some seriously nasty curves in it. Your average 35-footer would find it merely inconvenient but we, or more specifically 'I', found it a right royal pain in the proverbial.

Not only did I have to remember to sound the horn at every opportunity, to let everybody within a mile radius know that a big blob was coming through, but I became more and more angry that bloody holiday-makers didn't do the same. Crowds of them sitting on top of their boat would come into view without returning our horn sounds, but as we had heard nothing, we had assumed that there was no one about and had powered on forward toward an upcoming bridge. After assuming wrongly twice, we went through exactly the same list of events:

- Notice bridge coming up around a corner
- Sound horn loud and long
- Listen
- Hear nothing
- Increase speed and head for the centre of the bridge to minimise bank effect
- Notice smaller holiday, hooligan-filled narrow boat closing from the other direction
- Notice that they are not slowing down and haven't even noticed us (all boats look the same length head-on)
- Watch them helplessly realise that we are twice their length, half as manoeuvrable and stuck with nowhere to go under a bloody bridge.
- Watch them throw beer cans in the air and rush around trying to stop their craft
- Listen to a fair amount of verbal abuse along the lines of 'bloody river rats' and 'that thing's too big'
- Have a shouted conversation regarding horns
- Listen to their replies, which basically could be summed up as 'the rules of the river don't apply to us'
- Stick two fingers up at them and carry on past, while smirking and watching them trying to get their boat out of the mud at the side of the bridge.

Getting yourself spaced as evenly as possible between the bridge pillars to minimise bank effect is a good thing to do, especially if the bridge is very small. I always managed to achieve this and I think only on one occasion managed to really screw it up, causing our back end to rub across the bridge pilings.

On open water, however, I really couldn't get my head around bank effect at all. I will quote from Wikipedia:

'Bank Effect' refers to the tendency of the stern of a ship to swing toward the near bank when operating in a river or constricted waterway. The asymmetric flow around a ship induced by the vicinity of banks causes pressure differences (Bernoulli's principle) between port and starboard sides. As a result, a lateral force will act on the ship, mostly directed towards the closest bank, as well as a yawing moment pushing her bow towards the centre of the waterway. The squat increases due to the decreased blockage. This phenomenon depends on many parameters, such as bank shape, water depth, ship-bank distance, ship properties, ship speed and propeller action. A reliable estimation of bank effects is important for determining the limiting conditions in which a ship can safely navigate a waterway. This phenomenon has several different names, including bank suction, stern suction, and ship-bank interaction.

Hmm, very technical. What this actually means in real terms is that if, like me, you have a tendency to bring the back end a little too close to the bank when attempting to get around a tight corner, bank effect takes hold, pulls your rear end aground and pushes your nose out into the middle of the waterway, so slapping you diagonally across the canal, where you then stick until your wonderful husband wanders up with a pole and pushes you straight again. This isn't much of a problem until there is someone coming the other way who doesn't expect a 70-foot barricade stuck across their path of progression. There then follows a panicked race: can we get our boat out of the foliage before the oncoming boat hits us? And can he slow down to avoid hitting us until we can get our boat out of the foliage?

By the time I had hit the bank for the third time in as many hours, we gave up and compromised. Geoff would drive through the really curvy bits as he didn't seem to be affected by bank effect and I would bring it into every lock as I wasn't affected by Geoff's lock 'pinballism'. We were both happy, but not as happy as the other river users that I was no longer at the tiller.

Early the next morning we had a phone call from Amelia, who, having taken a job as a lettings agent about three months earlier in Didcot, had moved to Oxfordshire. With our rapidly dwindling amount of clean clothes in mind and our lack of anything resembling wheeled transport, I asked her if she would mind meeting us in Cropredy and giving me a lift to the nearest launderette – not exactly a fun-filled day out, but it was getting to be an emergency.

She agreed with a laugh, mentioning that it was parents who were supposed to be saddled with their migrant offspring's washing, not the other way round, and couldn't I just be normal for once. Seeing the irony, I laughed, and offered her and Huw a bed for the night and a cooked dinner in return for their help.

Thinking that we would really have to buy some food if I was to make good on my offer to feed them, we stopped at the Fenny Compton wharf and enjoyed a rather long walk into the village for a visit to their little shop. We had nearly arrived at our destination when Charlie gave a short shriek of outrage and shot off into the road. Confused and relieved that there were no cars, we watched her wander over to a small, fluffy lump in the road and pick it up.

'Oh God,' I nudged Geoff. 'What the hell has she got this time?'

'I have no idea,' he replied, 'but you can guarantee that if Charlie has found it, it will be broken, need feeding and will probably cost us a great deal of money in vets' bills – and then it will spitefully die and leave her bereft, something else we are going to have to deal with.'

Curious silence fell as we watched her walking back across the road, with something fluffy held between her cupped hands.

'Look, it's a dove.' She held up a bemused-looking bird to show us and grinned – oh dear.

'That is not a dove,' Geoff poked it with a forefinger. 'It's a bloody stinky pigeon – is it hurt? What are you going to do with it?'

Charlie thought for a moment. 'I dunno. Keep it warm, feed it, I'll call him Grubs.'

Great, just what we needed – *another* occupant – and with her hands full Charlie couldn't help carry the shopping back to the boat.

Stopping for the night just past Fenny Compton Tunnel (a poorly named, thin, little brick-walled cutting which was now open to the sky and very overgrown), we studied Grubs closely and found that there wasn't anything physically wrong with him, but mentally he was, without a doubt, the most ridiculous animal in the world. He stuck to Charlie closely, and seemed to suffer terminal apathy. He ate well, he slept, but, above all, he *stank*. He was the smelliest thing I had ever encountered and would have even given Herbert a run for his money.

The next day we travelled toward Cropredy and the promise of clean underwear. Amelia and Huw turned up as we moored. Grubs took one look at Huw's huge mop of tight, curly, blond hair, flew up, settled himself into it and stayed there. Even when Huw went outside and jumped up and down in an effort to dislodge him, he held on tight and stayed there against all efforts to remove him, rubbing his beak through the curls and cooing in deep satisfaction.

Despite Huw's new hat (which would insist on pooing down his neck), we had a pleasant evening and all finally retired at about midnight having finally removed Grubs from Huw's head after the wretched thing had fallen asleep.

The next morning, Amelia brought in a cup of tea for Geoff and me to enjoy in bed. 'What's that smell?' she enquired, wrinkling up her nose.

I yawned. 'It's probably your stepfather.' I nudged Geoff

and a muffled 'Oh, thanks!' came from under the covers.

'No,' she sniffed again. 'It smells like cat. Phew, it's horrible.'

I took a sniff; hmm it was a bit horrible. 'Either it's the pump-out tank which needs seriously emptying or it's that wretched bird of Charlie's.'

Amelia laughed. 'Charlie warned Huw that she was letting Grubs out of her bedroom, and he went outside for a smoke – funnily enough, he's wearing one of Geoff's hats.'

We laughed together. Funny, now that Amelia had mentioned the smell, I found it really pungent. Sighing, I got out of bed and, picking up a torch en route, I opened the toilet and looked down the hole.

'Erm, Geoff, I think we have a problem.'

It had been a little while since we had last pumped out, and there was absolutely nowhere with a pump-out machine until we reached Banbury. Geoff looked down the hole and worked out that we had about a day and a half's gap left and that the smell was due to the seals around the toilet base beginning to give way again.

These seals gave way on a regular basis and we always carried spares, but it was a horribly smelly job to replace them. Which was why, knowing full well that Amelia and I were going to be out of the boat for the best part of the day, I suggested that they be changed sooner rather than later. And with that instruction imparted, Milly and I gathered up every dirty piece of clothing we could find and fled.

It was the first time I had been in a car with Amelia since she had passed her driving test and I was understandably nervous. It was only after the fourth or fifth gasp at a corner that Amelia turned to me and, slapping at my white knuckles with a pen, made me let go of the handle on the dashboard.

'I do this for a living, you know,' she said and, pinning me to the seat with a hard look every time I flinched, we carried on into Daventry.

Strangely enough we had a lovely day. With there being

nothing we could do other than sit and talk while watching the washing go round and round, that's exactly what we did, and by the time we got back to the boat with the clean and lovely smelling washing, we were both relaxed and quite cheerful. It made me even happier to note on entering Happy that, not only had Geoff fixed the seal on the toilet tank, he had also set Huw and the kids to cleaning the boat up. Happy shined like a new pin.

Amelia and Huw left that evening, both having to go to work on the Monday morning. They informed us that they had filled in an application for a flat, rather than living in a shared house as they were currently doing, and so by the time we reached our final destination, they would probably have a place of their own.

I was a little unsure how I felt about this news. What right did she have to grow up like this, I thought, as I watched them walk away, hand in hand, down the tow path toward their car. I smiled; at least Huw was the type of guy who would actually laugh and put up with a stinky pigeon on his head for an entire evening and if that isn't a good way to judge a future son-in-law's character, I really don't know what is.

The next morning, we left Cropredy and headed on toward Daventry, and after a pleasant but totally uneventful day we moored up next to some big fields, where we figured the children could go and run riot with a boomerang that Charlie had purchased a couple of weeks previously but hadn't had the opportunity to test.

Home schooling was not going well. I had a nasty suspicion that schools don't actually instil a wish to learn into children; they just feed them the information they need to pass the exams. Any time we told Charlie to think for herself, she would throw herself into her bedroom and sulk, or just shout that she couldn't do it. I was beginning to have long and wistful reminiscences about them going to school. Sam, on the other hand, would be quite happy with maths or

IT, and would spend hours messing about with these two subjects. But if I suggested geography or history or comprehension, he would often join Charlie in a shared and noisy tantrum; ah well, at least they were doing something together.

I don't blame the children, but I do blame Geoff and myself – obviously, we were not cut out to be teachers, as more often than not we would just let them get away with it for an evening's peace and tranquillity, and when we did insist that the work was actually completed, all too often it would end in tears, either the children's or mine.

So on this rather gorgeous September evening, instead of getting on with the vagaries of the digestive system or writing stories, Geoff took the kids off to play boomerang in a local field. I entertained the vague hope that he would find interesting flora and fauna that maybe they could incorporate into a fascinating 'biology lesson'. 'Don't be ridiculous,' I chided myself; if Geoff found some interesting fauna, he'd eat it or just give it to Charlie to domesticate.

As I stood leaning on the tiller with my eyes closed, revelling in the late afternoon sunshine, I heard a little thump and looked down. Twelve pairs of black, shiny eyes looked back at me and, as one, their owners opened their tiny beaks and went 'peep'. It was very late in the year for such tiny ducklings to be about, but here they all were. I looked about for their mum and spotted her skulking behind another boat.

The ducklings were the cutest thing I had ever seen, all black and fluffy, with tiny little serious faces. I went into the kitchen and fetched some wholemeal loaf, then stood at the back of the boat, leaning on the tiller and smiling at the ducklings' antics as they bobbed and weaved, mobbing each other to get to a particularly good bit of bread floating on the water.

They went through all the bread in a matter of minutes. Mum and three of the more enterprising ducklings had climbed out of the water and were shouting at the boat from the tow path. Laughing at the ducklings energetically jumping up and down and peeping loudly, I cordially wandered over and emptied the last of the crumbs into a pile on the tow path. Mum and the three babies fell on the offerings and their squabbles made me laugh again.

Out of the corner of my eye, I spotted a huge, overfed tabby cat lurking in the bushes that bordered the canal and before I could find something to swat it with, or draw breath to shout, it had made a huge leap, grabbed one of the ducklings and hightailed it up the tow path. As I saw it move, I made a leap of my own toward the ducks, in the mad hope of frightening it off. It didn't work, and as I'd jumped, I managed to catch one foot on the T stud at the back and landed face first on the tow path, just late enough to frighten mum and the other two ducklings into complete hysterics and watch the cat scarper.

As I got slowly to my feet, I noticed that my hand was bleeding, as was my nose from where I had mashed it into the ground. I had twisted my ankle, and was covered from head to toe in dust and feathers. I stood up and began to dust myself off and, naturally, it was at this point that Geoff and the kids wandered back into view.

Charlie stopped, took in my completely beaten-up appearance and asked, 'What on earth have you been doing?'

I glared at her, and, climbing back on board, I slammed open the doors to the engine room.

'Feeding the bloody ducks.'

Chapter Thirty-two
This is Not the Time for Things to Go Wrong!

THAT EVENING, COVERED IN Germolene and with a swollen nose, I settled down to watch a DVD. It was only nine o'clock and I really fancied watching something pointless. We had been staring gormlessly at the telly for about an hour, when, getting up to make a cup of tea, I noticed that the lights were very dim.

'What's up with the lights?' I asked Geoff.

He looked up from the book he was reading. 'Oh, I thought it was getting hard to see.' He wandered down to the engine room and came back to report that our batteries had run out of charge. I shrugged. Ah well, it happened sometimes; without a full day's run to charge the batteries, we often got only half an evening out of them. There was really no point sitting around in the dark, so we had an early night. The next day was again only a short run, which brought us to the outskirts of Banbury. We moored in time to go down to the big shopping centre which is just off the canal and treated ourselves to dinner in a restaurant, then staggered back to the boat about eight o'clock. The main thing on our minds was a new car; our little Daewoo Matiz wasn't big enough to swing a cat (although I could think of one that I would really, really like to have tested that cliché with), let alone big enough to pack all our worldly goods into when we finally handed over Happy to Gerald in a couple of days' time.

As we headed back to Happy, we were all in a slightly pensive mood. Nearing the end of our 'road' trip, we were actually going to have to move off her and find something else to do. We hadn't found another boat, we hadn't made any firm plans, the future was a blank and at some point we were actually going to have to sit down and make a plan to fill it with something.

Ah well, push those worries aside, tomorrow is another day as they say. We opened the hatch and, reaching into the boat, I flicked the light switch; nothing except a vague glow. Damn, no electricity again. Ah well, another early night.

The next morning brought two major problems. We still had no electricity so couldn't have a cup of tea, and the smell from the bathroom had become pungent again. We really needed to get to a pump-out today. Avoiding looking down the toilet, I left Geoff in charge of the sleeping kids and, with his head in the electrics, I walked back down the tow path, intent on using Starbucks' loo and collecting the takeaway beverages so necessary to get us functioning in the early morning.

On my return, I opened the front door, carefully juggling a tea and a double mocha with peppermint shot and whipped cream (a girl could get used to that first thing in the morning) and was confronted by Geoff, waving a bit of wire at me.

'Look at that,' he grinned. 'I found it.'

'It's a bit of wire,' I tried to edge round him. Come on, matey, my coffee's getting cold.

'Yes, but it's an important bit of wire, this is the wire from the alternator – no wonder we haven't been getting any electricity.'

I finally managed to sit down and grab a sip of my lukewarm calorie fest. 'That's lovely, can you fix it?'

Geoff pondered for a moment, and, grabbing a greasy bag, unearthed a chocolate croissant. 'Oh yeth,' he spluttered around a mouthful, 'it might take a couple of hours though.'

Great, ah well, nothing for it. I waited until the children

were awake and then dragged them out for a cooked breakfast. On the way back, we spent an hour on an extremely entertaining kids' playground. It had some horrific adult torture implements disguised as educational play equipment and by the time they had finished whizzing me about and bumping me up and down, I vowed never to have mocha for breakfast ever again. Luckily Geoff rang me to say that everything was fixed and the kettle was on, and, with that good news, we headed back to the boat.

The smell from the bathroom and, strangely enough, also from our bedroom, was now utterly disgusting, and the first job of the morning was to pump out. Being used to pumping out being free in Cambridgeshire, I was horrified at the £15 we were required to pay – well, we would have been required to pay, if the guy's pump-out machine hadn't broken only five minutes into the exercise. It was a pain, but at least we figured it would have reduced the mass in the tank, which would give us another couple of days in which to find another one.

On the other side of Banbury we discovered the delights of lift bridges, all of them down. There is a knack to lift bridges: you have to pull the boat over to the side of the canal, let the bridge opener off the boat, wait until the bridge is up, and go carefully underneath between very narrow walls. Glancing upwards at the inland waterways equivalent of the sword of Damocles hanging over your head, you hold your breath and, when it doesn't fall, you breathe a huge sigh of relief and then pull in again to let your partner get back on; how people do it single-handed I'll never know.

After seven of these wretched things, we had had enough and decided to moor up for the night. It was quite early and, as we were fairly close to one of the garages listed in the local paper, we decided to go and see if we could find a new car.

The address of the garage was a little vague to say the least. It was listed as Adderbury, but after taking the hour and a half walk to that village, we couldn't find it anywhere. The walk from the canal to Adderbury is horrendous; there is absolutely no provision made for walkers along that stretch, the cars come past at 60 or 70 miles an hour as you stagger, tripping over lumps and ditches, the three miles into the village. By the time we got there, we were tired, hot and fed up, and knowing that we would have to face the same walk back just made it worse. When we worked out that the garage that we were looking for wasn't in the village, well, I can't remember being that irritated for a long time.

Finally making it back to the canal, the kids and I made a grateful break for the boat. Geoff hesitated.

'What's up,' I called back to him.

'You carry on,' he said, 'I'm just going to walk a bit in the other direction and see if the garage is that way instead.'

'OK,' I called, thinking 'weirdo'. 'I'll have the kettle on for when you get back.'

Geoff was back within 20 minutes. 'We went the wrong way,' he laughed. 'It's just over the bridge.'

The kids did not find him funny.

I was quite happy to be out of the boat the next morning the smell from the bathroom had become almost intolerable. You had two choices: either sleep with the windows closed and suffocate due to the smell, or sleep with the windows open and freeze to death. The smell drove all of us out of the boat by nine and we straggled down the road to the garage.

After much discussion, we had decided that we were looking for a big car with four doors and a large boot. There was still a huge amount of stuff that we would have to unload from the boat. This garage was advertising a Toyota people carrier which would be ideal.

What we ended up with that day was a two-door, sporty Ford 4x4, with a less than ideally sized boot but very pretty. I blame Geoff for giving in too easily. The Toyota was horrible, faded to an almost pink colour and sported chintz curtains. Charlie and I, even bleating together, shouldn't really have been able to break one of his plans *that* easily. But the Ford was nice and the garage was very helpful. When we explained our circumstances (and gave them a cheque for the full amount) they were more than happy to come and pick us up from wherever we had made it to and bring us back to pick up Mab, as she was christened by the kids, after her MOT.

We were on our way again and, at Aynho Wharf, we paid for a full pump out and bought some supplies. As we pulled away, it started to rain – the first rain for two weeks – and I went to drag out the waterproofs to find that, once again, against all reason and experience, we had put them into storage.

We had arranged to meet Gerald at Lower Heyford the next day. I have to admit I wasn't exactly pleased to see him, not that there was anything wrong with him, he was a nice guy, but he was buying our boat and, quite frankly, I was entirely unsure as to whether I wanted to sell her. Not that we had a lot of choice – it was his money that had just bought our new car, and we were planning to get a new one, so I kept telling myself it would be OK, but that didn't stop me feeling a little sad.

I was surprised at the intensity of my feelings. I have lived in many houses during my working career, usually moving every two years, and have never worried about leaving a house, never having found one that really felt like home.

After all the work and the various traumas over the past two years, Happy felt like 'home'. We had been through a lot with her, had completely changed her and modernised her and I loved everything about her. Not only about her, per se, but also about the lifestyle that she embodied and the changes that living aboard had wrought. Geoff, knowing how I felt, kept up a continual chatter about the prospective new boat, what we were hoping to get, what we were hoping to do and, little by little, it became another adventure to look forward to.

I didn't mention it, but I still harboured secret regrets about the loss of Happy and day-dreamed about winning the lottery and having our own fleet. But sitting on the roof, feeling the rain running down the back of my neck, it did occur to me that maybe it would be nice if the next boat had a wheelhouse.

The next day, Gerald turned up on his push-bike, which we loaded on to the roof. Trying to absent myself from all the technical explanations that were sure to be going on, the kids and I settled into a pile of DVDs and swore to keep as far away from the back of the boat as possible. I did stick my head out once or twice while delivering mugs of tea, but didn't get involved. Seeing someone that wasn't Geoff handling my boat was just too much and I felt sick and sad every time I saw it.

I had to admit Gerald handled her length very well and, by the end of the afternoon, he was sure that he could complete the final leg of her journey to her new moorings by himself, or at least with the aid of his family.

As we pulled into our mooring for the evening at Gibraltar, we watched him cycle away into the gloom and the headache that had been lurking at the edges of my consciousness finally evolved into a full-blown migraine, complete with disco lights and sound effects. I don't have them very often but when I do, oh boy do I know it. The kids rushed around putting out lights and helping me toward the bedroom. Charlie, knowing which drugs to look for, rushed into the bathroom and then emerged white-faced, saying that all she could find was an empty packet.

This was very bad. Without some serious painkillers, I was liable to be laid up for three full days and that was three full days that we really couldn't afford to lose. Geoff gave strict instructions to Charlie to watch her brother – and her mother – and then shot out of the door.

He was gone for about half an hour, but when he returned he had a supermarket bag holding lots of much-needed drugs.

Later, when the drugs had kicked in and the lights in my head had switched off, I asked him where he had got them from. He shrugged.

'I went a couple of boats down and spoke to one of the owners, told them what the problem was and he immediately grabbed his keys and drove me to the local supermarket, waited around for me to get what you needed and then drove me back here.'

'Oh, what a sweetie.' I stood up and, ferreting around under the sink, found the rather good bottle of wine that I knew was under there. I wandered down the line of boats until I found the one Geoff had described, gave him the wine and thanked him profusely.

He blushed and muttered, 'We look after each other.' I nodded and thanked him again. I was going to miss this so much it brought my headache back.

Waking up the next morning, I was completely confused; we had completed a full pump out the previous day – how on earth could the boat still smell so bad? Maybe it wasn't the pump-out tank at all, maybe that duck-eating cat had actually snuck in and sprayed all over the bedroom. I sighed, hmm, not really likely.

Hunting for a lost slipper, I got down on hands and knees to look under the bed, aha, there it was. I reached under and grabbed it, overbalanced and put my hand down on the carpet. It was completely soaked.

What the hell? I got up and, grabbing a torch, peered beneath the bed. It was horribly apparent what had happened. The pump-out tank had actually overflowed, but because Happy was lower at the back than the front, all the liquid had slid under the wall and along the top of the tank, running down the sides to soak the carpet in urine and other 'stuff'. Oh YUCK.

After washing my hands for a full five minutes, I finally got my OCD tendencies under control and went to tell Geoff.

'What are we going to do?' I addressed his bottom, which was all that was sticking out from under the bed. 'We can't sell her smelling like this.'

Geoff climbed back to his feet. 'Let's clean the carpet and see how she smells after that,' he instructed.

For three hours, I squashed myself, a bucket and a scrubbing brush under that stupid bed; the carpet was still wet when we went to sleep that night, but at least it smelt more of lemons than pee.

Leaving the carpet to dry, we carried on toward Thrupp, our ultimate destination. We took far longer than normal at our final lock, Shipston Weir, spending time studying the walls and watching the water that was leaking through the badly fitted lock gates hitting the sill and exploding back upwards in a beautiful, diamond-effect light show, courtesy of the low sun. We finally left the lock and I spent some time staring back at it as it very slowly disappeared into the distance. I wondered if I would ever go through a lock again or whether I was destined to become a 'Gongoozler'. I shook my head; if I couldn't see the lock from a boat, I vowed never to go near a lock again.

Just past Thrupp, we moored up outside 'The Jolly Boatman'. We had four days in which to move out, and it wasn't really enough time. One day to pick up the car, one day to move as much stuff as possible into storage, one day to do the final packing, one day to clean and do the final, final packing, and there was a horrible possibility that, in amongst all the moving and cleaning, we would have to lay a new carpet in the bedroom, which now smelt like a cat had died in a vat of lemons.

Amelia and Huw, two days away from moving into their own pad, came down to help and, surprisingly enough, they really did help. They took it upon themselves to keep the kids occupied while we ran around inventing new swear words and stuffing items into boxes; it was the best thing they could have done. They also went out for takeaway food and delivered all our rubbish to the tip – the thanks they got were heartfelt and genuine.

The new car arrived the next morning and, after packing it to the roof with belongings that we felt wouldn't be needed for the next month, Geoff and Huw took off for the day to dump it at storage, leaving Amelia and I to pack some more boxes.

Watching me pack up my kitchen, Amelia suddenly remembered all the items that she was short of in her own flat, and we ended up packing half of the boxes in her car. Saucepans, cutlery, cooking utensils, mugs ... it wasn't as though I didn't need those items, it was just that she needed them more, and for once I could do the proper 'mum' thing and help out a little.

That evening, we went out for a meal and although the food was very good, the mood was quite sombre. Amelia was having problems dealing with our complete lack of anything resembling a plan and became quite vocal about the remote possibility of having 'normal' parents; I assured her it wasn't likely to happen and asked her, 'If we were to move back into a house now, and become "normal" as you so call it, what difference would that make to you?'

She looked at me over a cup of tea. 'None, really, but at least my parents would be the same as everyone else's.'

'And that is important because ...?' I prompted.

She sighed. 'Actually,' she looked down, 'I quite like telling people about how mad you are, and if I do anything that seems a little insane I can blame it on family influence.'

'Gee thanks – do you do insane things a lot?'

Huw butted in, 'Only when she's bored.'

I laughed. 'Being bored and doing insane things is a family trait,' I informed him. 'You'd better watch out, it will only get worse as she gets older.'

The evening finished with everybody in a much happier frame of mind. We had become resigned to not knowing exactly what we were going to do next and Amelia had decided that she was quite happy to be the boring one for the next couple of years, although, after that, anything might happen. I had informed her that any time she felt like breaking away from normality, not only would I finance it if I could, I would physically cheer her on.

The next morning started very early, a little hung over, and spitefully bright, as if pointing out exactly what we were going to be missing with the loss of Happy.

A smaller narrow boat pulled in front of us and, after a quick chat, graciously agreed to take all my beloved plants, including Charlie's odd collection of strange and bizarre cacti. Although lovely people, they didn't make me feel any better by expressing shock and horror that Happy was being sold.

Sitting down to dinner that evening, I took one mouthful and suddenly couldn't eat any more; Geoff raised his eyebrows at me.

'I'm sorry,' I sniffed. 'It's just really hit me – in two days' time, we are going to be rolling in money and will once again be completely homeless.'

Geoff took a mouthful of his own tea. 'I know,' he said, 'but we'll buy a new boat, and it will all be all right.'

'The kids think they want a house, you know.'

'I know,' he sighed. 'I just don't think I want to go back to "normality". It would be so boring.'

'We can't just keep travelling around looking for a new boat. The whole home schooling thing isn't working out well and I'm really aware that we aren't working very hard at it.' I took a deep breath and continued, 'We don't even know where we are going when we leave the boat. I mean, what direction are we even going to be heading in?'

Geoff put his cup down on the shelf. 'Tell you what,' he shuffled over until he was sitting next to me. 'Let's head

303

over to Suffolk. We can land ourselves on my sister for a little while, at least we'll be able to use the Internet, and it will give us a base to work from.'

'Well, any plan is better than none at all.' I took another deep, shuddering breath. 'I don't want to sell her; I can't remember now why we felt we needed to.'

Geoff assumed a superior expression. 'It's because those wretched kids keep growing, especially that Charlie and ...' he shook his head, 'I really need to retrain so that I can get a job.'

'Oh yeah, that little thing. Tell you what, I can sort out one of those problems, we'll just stop feeding Charlie.'

With at least a sort of mini plan in mind, I felt somewhat better; at least I knew where we were going when we finally got into our car and drove away.

Our final day of boat ownership arrived and we woke in the morning, aiming to be sad all day, but as the lemon scent had now worn off the carpet, the smell of cat was now overriding every sense, even the emotional ones. Geoff had bought a new piece of carpet and underlay the previous day and his first job of the morning was to get rid of the smell. He dragged the old carpet and underlay out of the boat and almost immediately the smell began to clear. It was such a relief, I was sorry we hadn't done it three days previously.

By four o'clock, everything was done. Gerald had called by and picked up the keys, and Amelia and Huw, with lots of kisses and goodbyes, had wedged themselves into their car, overflowing with household items that either they wanted or we didn't have space for in our car, and had convinced them that they needed.

Happy was depersonalised, empty and echoing. We did a final walk-through, checking under beds and in cupboards. The new carpet looked great and smelled of, well, new carpet; we had cleaned and polished and scrubbed and the whole boat looked crisp, clean and professional.

Under Sam's bed, I found his ready-packed rucksack

containing his beloved beddybear, one hand-held games console, some games and a handful of Beano comics. I showed the contents to Geoff.

'There would have been ructions if he had left this behind,' I laughed shakily. He smiled and, taking the rucksack from me, continued walking up the boat.

Charlie and Sam were sitting quietly (for once) together on the sofa. Charlie had her rucksack and Geoff gave the one he was holding to Sam with a shake of his head.

'Come on,' Geoff indicated the door. 'Time to go.'

The kids nodded and climbed out through the doors and on to the tow path.

'Have you got everything?' he looked enquiringly at me as I leaned against the kitchen unit.

I sighed. 'I think so. Come on, let's get out of here.'

Out on the bank, he stood for a moment in the twilight. 'Are you sure, you lot, that everything is out, because once I lock this padlock we can't get back in.' After a moment's silence, we all nodded. Geoff hesitated for a few moments just waiting for the normal 'Argh, I forgot ...' and then turned and decisively locked the padlock into place.

Without a word, we all hoisted our backpacks and headed down the tow path toward the car. Just before the bridge, Geoff and I turned to look back at Happy, floating in the darkness.

I looked up at him. 'We had fun?'

He nodded. 'Yes, we did. Are you upset?'

'No, not really.'

He nodded again. 'Come on then, onward and upward. Let's get this monkey show on the road.'

As he left, I stood for a moment and thought about what I had just said. It had been the truth, I wasn't really upset, and I *was* looking forward to doing something else. I peered through the deepening dark for a final glimpse of Happy. Without her cheerful, yellow lights throwing squares and circles of reflected illumination on to the tow path and into the water, she looked dead and cold.

I turned decisively away. Geoff was right, onward and upward, a new boat would be great. I thought about it for a moment, then shouted up the tow path to Geoff who was standing under the bridge watching me.

'Geoff?'

'Yes?'

'I've made a decision.'

He stepped out from under the bridge with a quizzical and wary look. 'What would that be then?'

'Do you know where the passports are and how fast we can arrange tickets to Holland?'

He frowned. 'Yes, and pretty fast. Why?'

I squared my shoulders and took a deep breath; a new challenge, new things to learn, new things to run into. I grinned at him and, heaving my rucksack out of the dirt, threw it over my shoulder.

'Let's go to sea.'

About the Author...

© Inkwell Photographic

Marie Browne

Marie Browne is a gently harassed mother of three who, for the past fifteen years, has been desperately trying to escape the Customer Service industry.

Apart from her husband and kids, the best things in her life are real ale; barbecues; ugly mad dogs that nobody else wants and cream-covered designer coffees. She also has an obsession with shoes but her husband is threatening to get her help for that.

No Legs To Dance On
A Thalidomide survivor's story

"A magnificently frank and breezy book – often very funny"
Libby Purves, BBC Radio 4

While the battle for the compensation of Thalidomide victims was raging in the 1970s, former Labour MP Jack Ashley asked in a parliamentary debate how Louise, then 11 years old, could look forward to "laughing and loving with no hand to hold and no legs to dance on".

Louise was born without arms and legs. Her wealthy father David Mason, led a high profile campaign against the drug company for proper compensation for the victims. Despite growing up in an institution, Louise grew up to have a full and happy life and two children.

This is the story of how she has laughed and loved

ISBN 9781906373573 - £9.99

Diary of a Diet
- The Little Book of Big

The book that eats the Size Zero debate for breakfast and coughs it back up with a side of comedy carbs, features the ordered ramblings of outsized and outspoken newspaper columnist Hannah Jones. Her diary will find resonance with all women, whatever their shape or size, who've felt pressure to weigh out their self-esteem along with their chips. It's a sharp, witty and heartfelt study on living life in the fat - oops, sorry! - fast lane to self-acceptance.

Diary of a Diet is about Hannah Jones' ongoing struggle to commit to get fit, stick to a sensible eating plan or think, once and for all, that she's simply fabulous just the way she is right now.

ISBN 9781906125042 - £6.99

The Dark Threads

"Essential reading..." Dorothy Rowe, author and psychologist

The true story of how a bright teenager was transformed into a zombie thanks to a cocktail of drugs and electric shock treatment for an illness she never had.

Jean lost years of her life in the sixties and early seventies when doctors misdiagnosed her mental state as chronic schizophrenia.

Sucked into the psychiatric system, she lost her job, her boyfriend and all self-esteem until she managed to break free.

Told with humour and insight, using extracts from her medical case notes, Jean's memoir raises disturbing questions.

ISBN 9781906373597 - £7.99

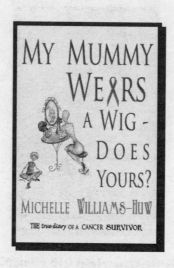

A true and heart-warming account of a journey through breast cancer.

A diagnosis of breast cancer made Michelle Williams-Huw, mother of two small boys, re-evaluate her life as she battled her demons to come to terms with the illness. *My Mummy Wears A Wig* is poignant, sad, revelatory and deliciously funny. Readers will be riveted by her honesty and enchanted as, having hit bottom, she falls in love with life (and her husband) all over again.

ISBN 9781906125110 - £7.99

A Seaman's Book Of Sea Stories

A superb collection of nautical tales selected by Desmond Fforde. All profits benefit The Prostate Cancer Charity.

Meet Hornblower, Cochrane and Uffa Fox, among others, and be transported from Cape Horn via the Skagerrak to Dunkirk and the Far East.

As an island people, the British have always been conscious of the importance of the sea and proud of its 'hearts of oak': the men and the ships which have shaped Britain's history.

Set between 1800 and 1945, some of these stories are true, some fiction, but together they capture the essence of the unpredictable interaction between sea and man which makes for such fascinating reading.

Available November 2009

ISBN 9781906373986 - £7.99

For more information about Accent Press
titles please visit

www.accentpress.co.uk